BUYOUT

BUYOUT

THE INSIDER'S GUIDE TO BUYING YOUR OWN COMPANY

RICK RICKERTSEN

WITH Robert E. Gunther

Foreword by Michael Lewis,
author of *Liar's Poker* and
The New New Thing

AMACOM
American Management Association

New York • Atlanta • Boston • Chicago • Kansas City • San Francisco • Washington, D.C.
Brussels • Mexico City • Tokyo • Toronto

This publication is designed to provide accurate and authoritative
information in regard to the subject matter covered. It is sold with the
understanding that the publisher is not engaged in rendering legal,
accounting, or other professional service. If legal advice or other expert
assistance is required, the services of a competent professional person
should be sought.

www.buyoutbook.com

Library of Congress Cataloging-in-Publication Data
Rickertsen, Rick.
        Buyout : the insider's guide to buying your own
company / Rick Rickertsen with Robert E. Gunther.
            p.   cm.
        Includes index.
        ISBN 0-8144-0626-2
        1. Management buyouts.   I. Gunther, Robert E., 1960–
        II. Title.

    HD2746.5.R54 2001
    658.1'6—dc21   00-045094

Printing number

10   9   8   7

For
Iris
and
Ocke

CONTENTS

FOREWORD

I t's a pleasure to introduce this richly informative and admirable book, which offers not merely a glimpse but a clear, wide-open view of the high peaks of finance.

Buyout is really two books in one. The first part is an instruction manual for well-to-do people who have decided they would like to become really, really rich. The author, Rick Rickertsen, wouldn't put it quite that way, I'm sure. Like many of the most successful people in business, he believes that business professionals are more likely to get rich if they don't spend all their time thinking about getting rich. If asked, he would probably say that he's written an instruction manual for corporate executives who have grown tired of the upper tiers of wage slavery and have summoned the nerve to seize control of their companies and their destinies. The money is merely symptomatic, a pleasant side effect, of that admirable willingness to take risk. And perhaps he's right.

Still, as everyone who has watched the Internet boom knows, the best way to get rich is to have equity in a successful company, and this book helps them to do it. Happily, as the author points out, history is currently conspiring with all potential readers. Many industries are following the example of the Internet boom and finding ways to give equity to their employees, or risk losing them to Internet companies. As Rickertsen puts it, "All companies will have to become Internet companies if they want to compete for talented managers." And, of course, the best way for a manager to get a big piece of equity is to buy the company from the current absentee owners.

The trouble is, How exactly do you buy out a company? Although low finance has been denuded of much of its mystique and complexity, high finance remains opaque. What, pray tell, is an 83(b) election? How do you write a confidentiality agreement? Why does anyone work for a commercial bank, anyway? Only insiders know how this stuff works. Enter *Buyout,* and its author, who, as a leading buyout expert, is himself an insider. In clear, simple language he brings the complexity of high finance to its knees and leaves it begging for mercy. He explains its inner workings so that even a journalist can understand them.

In the process, it would seem, he undermines his own interests. After all, one of the advantages long enjoyed by capitalists in their dealings with entrepreneurs is that the entrepreneurs don't fully understand what capitalists do or how they think. This book corrects that deficit. It teaches people who seek capital how best to deal with the people who control the capital. This raises an obvious question: Why would a buyout expert write a book to help ordinary corporate numbnuts get the best possible deal from buyout experts? At first glance the book appears an act of self-destruction; it's as if the U.S. government sent a crack team of American physicists to China to help the Chinese fine-tune their long-range nuclear missiles. There are, I think, several reasons.

I know the author well, and so I also know that he is at least partly motivated by warm feelings for people who take risk in life. He is one of those rare people who actually feels good when others do well for themselves, especially if they have stuck their neck out in the process. Put another way: He likes to see people stick their necks out so that he can feel good for them when they are rewarded for it.

Altruism, however, is never a satisfactory explanation for the behavior of a successful businessperson, even one as nice as Rick Rickertsen. My guess is that he has a narrower motive, too. The business world is changing. Increasingly, it favors people who actually do things at the expense of those who lend them the money to do it with. Sooner or later, the author may have figured, someone was going to explain everything to the guy across the bargaining table, and so it may as well be him, lest he appear to be just another greedy capitalist.

Yet there is still a third motive at work here, and it is perhaps the most powerful: the simple desire to make sense of one's experience. Anyone who has lost millions of dollars of other people's money by sinking them in a company run by a man who wears pinkie rings and hangs stuffed marlins on his wall needs the loan of an ear. He has had a wonderfully traumatic experience; he needs an audience to share it with.

As I said, *Buyout* is really two books in one, and it is. The second book is a vivid description of the world through the eyes of a capitalist. This worldview may prove more useful to capitalists than to those who seek to use them, but it will please both, and anyone else who likes a good story, well told.

MICHAEL LEWIS

INTRODUCTION:
SEIZE YOUR DESTINY

T he company was being sold. The managers of Techway, Inc.,*
an information technology services division of a large defense
contractor, were told their parent firm was jettisoning the
unit. It no longer fit the firm's core business. The division the managers had worked so hard to build was now on the auction block.
Over the previous two years, they had turned around a period of
declining revenues and mounting losses, made the unit profitable,
and thus created significant shareholder value for the parent company. And now, their reward for all their efforts was to be put up
for sale and most likely be absorbed into a larger rival.

When they had recovered from the shock, the managers had a
thought: They would buy the firm. This is a desire many managers
have—to own their own company or to buy another firm and run
it—but only a few ever act upon it. The Techway managers decided
they would try to seize their destiny. Techway's leaders had already
improved the firm, but they knew they could do much more to
create value if they had the chance and were free from the restrictions of their corporate parent. They could make an independent
Techway into a powerhouse. And they could run it themselves!
Freedom at last!

But could they actually pull it off? Techway had annual revenues of more than $300 million and 1,200 employees. Techway's
managers wondered if they had the money to do such a deal. While
they all earned comfortable salaries, none of them was independently wealthy by any means. How could they buy a $300 million
firm? How would they value the company? Could they finance it
with a bank or did they need an equity partner? How should they
structure their own piece of the deal? What kind of agreement
should they seek with the seller? Would the parent company go for

*Techway is a real technology services company whose name has been changed
to respect the confidentiality of parties involved in the transaction.

it? Would they succeed or end up out on the street? Who would help them? Whom should they call first?

This book provides answers to these questions. We'll look at how the managers of Techway addressed each stage of the buyout process: finding partners to invest, putting together a management term sheet with investors, creating a strategic plan, negotiating the deal with the seller, finding funding from banks, handling the "ground war" of legal and accounting details through due diligence, running the company, and making a profitable exit.

You'll also hear stories of managers who have completed successful buyouts. You'll find out how Dan Gillis went from being president of a $165 million unit of a German software company to an owner of a thriving U.S. software firm. He and his management team put together a deal in a matter of months. They went public just seven months later, and there was a smile on his face as Gillis banged the gavel at the closing bell of the New York Stock Exchange. No wonder. The managers had turned a $1 million investment into a $40 million share of a rapidly growing software company.

You'll hear how Stu Johnson, who had served in many senior positions at Bell Atlantic, Contel, Burroughs, and other major corporations, left the corporate life to build the company that would be his legacy. He drew together the most talented team of managers he had worked with during his career into a new information technology services provider targeting the middle market. "If you have truly been successful in your career, if you truly believe your resume, if you believe you have done all the things you are telling people you have done, go and do it," Johnson said. "There are not enough of you out there."

You'll find out how Roger Ballou, former senior executive of Alamo Rent-A-Car and American Express Travel Services Group, put together a group of travel services firms to create a new company that would change the face of the vacation industry. It was a company that he not only led but also owned. "I felt like the dog that finally caught a car," he said.

The Power of Equity

Why is Bill Gates so rich? He is, of course, a very talented business leader. That is why Microsoft has been so successful. But Gates became the richest man in the world because he had *equity* in the company. Henry Kravis understands this. That is why KKR realizes such high returns. They're in the business of investing large amounts of capital to buy equity in growing companies. But what really drives KKR's outstanding returns? The key is picking great managers to run these companies.

It may be too late for you to become a twenty-three-year-old Harvard dropout launching a small software start-up, but there is still hope. You can become a big equity holder by buying the business you are sitting on now, or you can go out into the marketplace to find a new company to acquire. In an environment in which investment capital is abundant, high-quality management talent is the scarcest commodity. There are billions of dollars in capital and hundreds of private equity firms, every one of which is looking for a stable of twenty or thirty managers who can head their companies. This means skilled managers have much more leverage in leading the buyouts of companies than they have had at any time in business history. This is the managers' time, and you should be seizing the moment!

As a management buyout investor for more than fifteen years, I have consistently been amazed by how little senior executives understand their huge opportunity to create equity value for themselves by purchasing their own company or operating unit. A top manager with a shot at being a CEO might be making $300,000 per year. But as a buyout leader he could create $30 million of equity value away from the parent, running his own company.

For all their skill at leading teams of people and companies, most senior executives don't understand how to buy a company. Why? There are many reasons, among them:

• *Complexity and risk.* The act of acquiring a company is a complex and difficult task. It requires substantial expertise in a broad range of fields such as finance, negotiating skills, team leadership, valuation techniques, and strong people skills. Buying companies is not for everyone, but for the bold it can be a businessperson's greatest triumph, not only leading to great financial rewards but also to a unique feeling of independent success that few ever achieve.

• *Lack of expertise.* Not many senior managers have experienced the acquisition process. From the outside it looks highly daunting. And it is a challenge, but once you have an understanding of the mechanics and the leverage points, the black box will open and the mergers and acquisitions world will no longer look so intimidating.

• *Lack of industry guides.* Few reference sources on the buyout world exist, and many investment bankers and buyout professionals would probably prefer to keep the art to themselves rather than open the world up to managers. It's a little bit like the folks who believe you are either born to sing or not to sing; some have the gift and some don't. But I strongly believe that we can all learn to sing and that all managers can learn how to run their own buyouts. I believe that empowering every manager with the inside knowledge of running a buyout will only lead to many more buyouts being pursued and completed successfully. This result will only produce accelerated growth for the buyout world. After all, the managers still need the money and the guidance, and that's why buyout professionals are here.

This book aims to debunk the myth that only "buyout artists" can run deals and strives to provide managers with the tools to lead deals rather than stand by and be led by others. Good managers should be in the driver's seat, but they are often stuck in the passenger's seat. It's time to get behind the wheel.

Anatomy of the Buyout (and the Book)

What is a management buyout? Management buyouts (MBOs) are acquisitions of an operating company or a corporate unit in which the current or future senior management of the business participates as a significant equity partner in the acquisition. They used to be called leveraged buyouts, but this term fell out of favor with the last dance of the Predator's Ball. It is no longer used in the industry, or in polite company, although the concept of leverage is alive and well, under other aliases.

What are the stages of the buyout process? The following

stages, illustrated in Figure I-1, characterize the general buyout process and the structure for this book:

• *Find or create an opportunity.* You need to first find or create a company where you can best leverage your background and management skill set. Many times, it is the company of which you are a part. As we'll see in Chapter 1, Dan Gillis knew what he could do with Software AG Americas (SAGA) if he could break it loose. Other times, it is a company outside your own. In Chapter 2, we examine how Roger Ballou used his experience in the travel industry to draw together a series of acquisitions into a new company. We explore strategies for identifying acquisitions beyond your current company in Chapter 4.

• *Develop a business plan.* You need to develop a credible strategy for the company to demonstrate opportunities for growth and increased profits to potential partners and other investors. Much of the value added from the deal comes from your ability to manage the business more effectively as an independent unit. How will you improve the business? What are the growth prospects? We discuss the key elements of successful business plans in Chapter 5.

• *Find a willing seller and strike an agreement.* This may sound self-evident, but thousands of hours and tens of millions of dollars have been squandered working diligently on transactions where there really isn't a willing seller. Many companies or individuals who have their companies on the block are only willing to sell under impossible circumstances. In this case, they only *appear* to be sellers. They will waste your time. Sometimes an unwilling seller could become willing under certain circumstances. Would your firm or unit be willing to sell? If not, under what circumstances might it consider selling? If it is a lost cause, you might consider whether there are other businesses in your industry that you could purchase as an outsider. Once you have a willing seller, you need to strike a deal, working through price and terms to create a term sheet and purchase agreement. The sell-side deal, including developing a letter of intent with the seller, is considered in Chapter 6.

• *Find an equity partner and come to terms.* Once the deal is identified and the team is in place, the next stage is usually for the management and equity partners to work out an agreement for

Figure I-1. The key stages of the MBO.

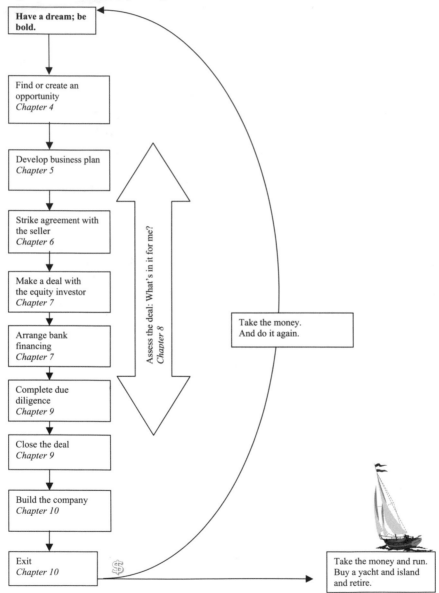

partnering to pursue the project. This agreement sketches out in general terms the relative investments of each of the parties, how equity will be divided, and how management equity will vest. This effort determines what management will get out of the deal. From a manager's perspective, make no mistake about it: This is the Holy Grail of the buyout. The deal you negotiate here sets the foundation for all that is to come in the future. You must get it right. This is *the* deal from the manager's perspective, and too often managers end up at the mercy of the buyout shop because they don't understand the process and the financier's motivations. This book will make sure you maximize your leverage on this piece of the deal, which is a central theme of this book. The agreement with the equity partner is discussed in Chapter 7.

• *Line up bank financing.* You've done some preliminary work on lining up financing at this point, but you need to make sure it is there when you are ready to close. In addition to the equity investment of the buyout firm, you need to line up bank financing. In fast-paced deals, timing can be a significant issue. Bank financing is also considered in Chapter 7.

• *Figure out what the deal means to you.* One of the overriding questions throughout the process is: What's in it for me? Managers need to translate the deals with equity partners and the seller, and performance projections for the firm, into their own personal bottom line. Is there enough potential for return to justify the risk? This assessment begins in a crude form at the start of the dream—with a few penciled calculations on a cocktail napkin. As each piece of the puzzle moves from hypothetical numbers to actual numbers, this assessment is updated. It serves as a touchstone for decisions about issues such as what to offer the seller, what kind of deal to negotiate with the equity partner, how to divide the equity among the management team, and whether the deal has enough of an upside to attract good equity dollars. You also need to determine how to share this equity with the top management team and give other managers a stake in the company. This assessment of what's in it for you, and discussion of a model for making these calculations, are examined in Chapter 8.

• *Sweat the details in due diligence.* You have a willing seller, a stunning strategy, a crackerjack management team, a good deal, and money ready and waiting. But is everything what it appears to be? Was the seller a little too willing? Are there hidden problems? One of the advantages of buying your own unit is that you generally know where the bodies are buried. Still, the diligence process always produces some surprises, both negative and positive. Usually you can find some means of managing or circumventing the negative ones, but sometimes they can kill the deal. The more front-end homework you do, the fewer surprises you will have at this stage. You will need to manage a small army of experts, including lawyers, accountants, and other professionals to guide you through the details of the deal. This is where one-page agreements become phone-book-size legal documents. What looks good from 10,000 feet can turn ugly when you get down to the ground level. This stage raises questions that can cause the deal to break down if they are not handled effectively. The due diligence process and pitfalls are discussed in Chapter 9.

• *Run with it*. When the paperwork is signed, the work is just beginning. This is the point where you have an opportunity to put your strategy into action. There is no corporate parent to blame if things go wrong, but also no one to hold you back from achieving what you know you can. With a motivated management team and skin in the game, this is the point where you determine whether you can turn your entrepreneurial ideas into a great business. Good partners stand back and let good managers work. Post-MBO operations are explored in Chapter 10.

• *Plan your exit*. The profits of the company and equity gains are merely ephemeral until you find a way to cash out. Most managers are not planning a speedy exit from running the company, but most managers and all investors want to get at least some of their equity cashed out within three or four years. One of the ways to do this is to go public. Most managers only hear glamour and big bucks when they hear "initial public offering," but it also means you now have to answer to a larger group of investors and may face increasing pressure for short-term earnings, so the pros and cons of the initial public offering should be considered carefully. Perhaps a strategic sale is the best way to go. It depends on the business, but one item is critical: You have to know your exit strategy *before* you do the deal. In Chapter 10, we examine four possible exit strategies.

• *Buy your yacht.* It may be that sailing is not to your fancy, but you'll have to find something to do with all that capital. Of course, you could always decide to turn it around and invest it in your next management buyout, earning an ever-increasing stake in the American Dream.

The stages of a buyout do not always appear in this order (although the yacht typically doesn't sail until the end) but usually show up at some point along the way. And the pace of a deal can range from being fast and furious, as was the case with SAGA, or completely glacial, taking more than a year to complete. You match the process to the demands of the deal. Most often many deal paths are processed simultaneously, so multitasking is an important skill in managing a deal. Each of these issues is examined in more detail in later chapters.

You Can Buy a Company

I have worked on hundreds of deals in the past fifteen years and been involved in closing deals totaling well over a billion dollars in purchase price. I've led successful deals that have generated excellent rates of return for our investors and have helmed my fair share of deals that have cratered—burning through millions of dollars in the process. I've had numerous companies go public and have had the pleasure of chairing a New York Stock Exchange company and standing on the exchange floor the day it went public. It's been an invigorating and interesting journey. But there are two things I really love about my job.

The first has been the ability to work closely with my partner to build a successful investment firm and to work with the exceptional people that comprise Thayer Capital. They are an incredible group, and the single best thing about my job is the chance to work with the younger professionals at the firm and to see them grow as individuals and investors. Here, I could not be more lucky.

The second thing I love about my job is the opportunity to work with managers who lead the companies in which we invest. I have been blessed with the opportunity to work with an exceptional group of managers, and it is these business leaders who have made us successful investors. We provide guidance to them and a deal framework, but they are the ones in the trenches every day, fighting the fight and building these companies. They create the successes and we proudly ride along. And through our work and the tool of the management buyout they become owners of companies where they were employees before. They go from hired hands reporting to some board far, far away to significant owners running their own companies.

To me, this is thrilling and it's why I love my job. Through my knowledge and capital, I am able to help managers evolve from strong executives with little or no equity value to entrepreneurs commanding their own ship, with lots of equity. There is no greater feeling, as far as I am concerned, than that derived from showing managers who never, ever thought about doing a buyout that it is actually possible. Not just for Henry Kravis or Ted Forstmann, but for them! This is fun, and it is for these managers and every future MBO leader that I have written this book.

I wrote this book to empower you to lead deals, to seize your destiny, to take charge, and to knowledgeably make things happen at the pinnacle of American business: the leadership of the MBO. If you haven't thought about putting together a deal, I hope the stories here will inspire you. If you have thought it would be impossible to pull off an MBO, I hope the detailed information in this book will show you that with determination it can be done. And there are lots of resources out there waiting to help in the process (and share in its success). So what are you waiting for? If you are a talented manager with guts and ideas, you can do the same. This book and its Web site (www.buyoutbook.com) will show you how.

ACKNOWLEDGMENTS

I have been blessed in business to work with and learn from a uniquely high-quality group of mentors. First, to my partner of the last six years, thank you. Fred Malek grew up poor, pulled himself into West Point, excelled as a Green Beret serving his country in Vietnam, led Marriott Hotels to record performance for nine years, bought and ran Northwest Airlines, and founded Thayer Capital, our $1.2 billion investment firm. And those have just been his day jobs. He served President Nixon in the Office of Management and Budget and as head of personnel in the White House, ran a Republican convention and economic summit for President Bush, and then ran President Bush's 1992 campaign. He's the most disciplined and hardworking man I've met and he has set a standard of professional excellence to which I aspire. He's the "gold standard," and he's been a tremendous mentor.

Second, I thank the Thayer team for their support. No leader can succeed without a great team. And our team is the finest. My thanks to Jeff Goettman, Sisi Gallagher, Doug Gilbert, Rob Michalik, Daniel Raskas, Chris Temple, Doug McCormick, Jon Isaacson, Barry Johnson, Paulette Brown, Bettina Helsing, Ann Williams, and Jennifer Walaitis. You are the best, and the reason I come to work each day. Before I joined Thayer, I had the opportunity to learn from some other excellent investors and mentors. Here I thank Bill Barnum and Kip Hagopian of Brentwood Associates, and the world's funniest investor, Mike Fourticq of Hancock Park Associates, who taught me to still have a laugh no matter how much money you're making or losing.

As I make clear in the book, a buyout investor is only as good as the managers who run the companies. My deepest thanks go out to all the exceptional managers I've had the privilege to work with and learn from: Dan Gillis, Harry McCreery, Phil Norton, Paul Stern, Mickey Flood, Tony McKinnon, Stu Johnson, Graham Perkins, Roger Ballou, Bill Hoover, Chris Franco, Jim Paterak, Joe Kelly, Tony McKinnon, and Ron Christman, to name a few. This book is for you, the great managers, and for all the other managers who follow behind you with the courage to go out on their own and lead a management buyout.

Without Robert Gunther's hard work, partnership, and caring, this project would never have gotten off the ground. Thank you, Robert, and thanks to my good friend Professor Terry LaPier for pushing me on and introducing me to Robert. And my thanks to my old friend Michael Lewis, the finest writer I know, whose inspiration taught me in 1985 that mere mortals really can get books published and to whose prose I someday aspire.

My sincere appreciation to Al Zuckerman of The Writer's House for his diligence in finding a publisher and to Ray O'Connell and the staff at AMACOM for their enthusiasm for the project and improvements to the draft.

And last in the lineup but first in my heart, I thank Maria and Alexandra for putting up with me, and thank you for the patience you had while I wrecked our weekends and evenings working on this project.

BUYOUT

CHAPTER 1

The American Management Dream

"Behold the turtle. He makes progress only when he sticks his neck out."
—James Bryant Conant

On April 1, 1997, a smiling Dan Gillis, president of the American division of Software AG, stood on the front stage of a large ballroom at the Hyatt Dulles in Reston, Virginia. Hundreds of Software AG employees packed into the conference room, while others listened in on global conference calls from sites across the United States, Japan, and Israel. Employees arrived early. It was standing room only, a first for an employee meeting of the U.S. division of the German software maker since Gillis was named president in May 1996. In a memo to employees the week before, he had told them only that the meeting was for "an update of our progress" in the first quarter along with a few "special announcements." But there was an air of nervousness and uncertainty in the room. They knew it was much more than a simple update. But was it good news or bad?

There had been a lot of speculation. Employees of the U.S. division were aware that their German parent was losing money and wasn't producing new products. Morale was low and turnover

1

had risen to 40 percent. Too many financial types were working late hours. There were endless closed-door meetings and hosts of lawyers and other "suits" swirling in and out. Rumors raced through the hallways of the Virginia headquarters that the company was on the block. At one point, it looked like SAP might buy the German firm. Maybe Oracle would buy it. Then the word spread that Gillis was firing his entire executive staff. Worst of all, there was a rumor that Computer Associates would be the acquirer, a frightening prospect that would have meant the loss of probably 60 to 80 percent of their jobs. Most people were sure the news could only be bad.

So now, as the lanky president stood at the front of the room and joked that he hadn't brought them together to discuss the dress code, there was a sense of nervous expectation. After a few opening remarks, Gillis put up a slide stating: "Software AG has now become an independent software company." There was a half-second of stunned silence. After all, it was April Fool's Day. Could this be a joke? Then the entire room filled with applause. "As of yesterday, we signed all the papers and became an *independent* software company," Gillis said, pausing between each of his last words to savor the victory and allow the concept to sink in.

As Gillis described the deal and answered questions, he kept driving one point home: The company was now the master of its own destiny. "The key point is our success now is totally dependent on us," he told them. "I think in the past, we tended to look for excuses, and we could point to our parent company as an excuse. It is no longer an excuse. There is a tremendous upside here, but there is also a tremendous responsibility. We control our own future now. And that feels really good to me. How about to you?" Robust applause and wide grins, with just a hint of nervousness, reflecting the trepidation of cutting loose from the mother ship.

But for a company that had always waited to see what headquarters in Germany would say before proceeding, it was a hard message to absorb. Toward the end of the Q&A session, a question came in over the loudspeakers from an employee in Seattle. Gillis had told employees that the buyout would allow the U.S. company to pursue its own software development and acquisitions. The caller asked, "Are we constrained in any way from acquiring or selling technologies that may fit our market but not Germany's?" In answer, Gillis pointed to the overhead and read, "Independent software company. Thank you." After the exhilarating applause died down, he continued, "We are in no way constrained in our strategy. No way. We can set our own strategic direction and it is our own. *Nothing* can stop us from implementing it. That's got to sink in, doesn't it? I think that's the power of this. That's really what's happening."

He paused. "What do you think—is this a great announcement or what?"

As he listened to the applause, even Gillis didn't know at that point how great an announcement it really was. None of us knew.

Banging the Gavel on the NYSE

The announcement was the culmination of months of nonstop labor by Gillis and CFO Harry McCreery to make their dream of ownership a reality. They had maneuvered a multinational minefield of complex and vexing issues to hit a target the size of a pin. They had worked with our private equity firm to put together financing for the deal and hammered out an agreement with their German parent in an incredibly tight time frame driven by the parent company's German banks. Gillis and McCreery had managed to cut the company loose and saddle it up.

"[Many] folks were very doubtful that we could do this at the beginning," Gillis told the employees. "The Germans were doubtful. We were doubtful sometimes. There were so many complex pieces that all had to come together."

They had a challenging road ahead, but it would lead them to one of the most successful management buyouts (MBOs) ever. Net income more than doubled from 1996 to 1997, and revenue increased 16 percent to $181 million. Gillis and his team put in place a bold new strategy to rapidly grow through strategic acquisitions and by developing highly complex middleware, which links legacy mainframes to distributed computing networks and the Internet. Turnover among the employees plummeted as more than eighty employees received stock options for the first time, and morale shot through the roof in the glow of their independence. Customers and suppliers could feel it, too.

Just a little over seven months after completing the deal on March 31, their initial public offering (IPO) reached $10 per share at the close of trading, which meant that the $1 million stake invested by the manage ment team already was worth more than $40 million. Gillis and McCreery, who seven months earlier had been division managers, were now on CNN, wealthy beyond their dreams and captaining their own ship. Gillis was seen by millions on TV doing something that even the most powerful corporate chieftains can only dream about: He was grinning above the floor of the New York Stock Exchange (NYSE), banging away with the gavel to close trading. How did they possibly get there?

The American Management Dream

It began with the dream of a "peddler" and a "beanie." In McCreery's view, the world of Software AG was divided into "techies," "beanies" (i.e., the financial bean counters), and "peddlers" (i.e., marketing types). Gillis was the outsider. He came to the company in January 1995 after another firm acquired Falcon Microsystems, where he served as executive vice president. Gillis became senior vice president of sales at Software AG and was named president in May 1996. McCreery chided Gillis by calling him "a peddler." Gillis wasn't slick but was a hard-driving and straight-shooting Rhode Islander—a creative leader with the vision to dream the big dream and the persuasiveness and persistence to make it happen. His simply adorned office is dotted with photos of family, along with pictures of himself with visiting luminaries such as Steve Forbes, George Bush, and Colin Powell. Beneath an exterior as polished and soft-spoken as a private school headmaster is an unexpected passion. It showed itself in the MBO and in his one indulgence that followed his newfound wealth: a sleek, black Mercedes 500 sedan with plates reading AGS (his NYSE ticker symbol). He is justifiably a little proud of this achievement.

Gillis grew up in Providence, Rhode Island, the middle of five children, son of a railroad bridge foreman. He attended private schools and earned a BA in management from the University of Rhode Island before hitting the streets as a salesman for Kodak. He had a distinguished two-decade career in the computer industry, working at IBM, Exxon Office Systems, and Wang. In his last job prior to Software AG, Gillis had helped grow Falcon's revenue from $13 million to more than $180 million before the firm was sold.

McCreery was the insider, who had worked at the company for a decade and understood what made it tick on both sides of the Atlantic. He is a beanie, the complex-deal strategy guy who can run the numbers through their paces and make them dance. He has the studied cynicism and appearance of a tough Chicago cop. (He later commented on the buyout, "I just did what needed to be done, same as I always have, just with a more rewarding result.") This gruff attitude is tempered with an easygoing rapport and pervasive sense of humor. Above all, he is a contrarian. In a sea of high-powered European machines in the Software AG Americas (SAGA) parking lot, his is the lone GMC pickup.

As a kid, McCreery wound transformers in his father's shop in Chicago. He served as a gunner and mechanic in Vietnam, and when he returned, he ran a service station before earning his accounting degree at Walton College and earning his CPA. After cutting his teeth on the books at A.B. Dick, he served in senior executive positions with high-tech companies such as Syquest Technology, Automated Microbiology, and MAC Associates. He had led turnarounds and worked on half a dozen start-ups. He thought he had put that life behind him when he started with Software AG—until this deal came along.

About the only thing Gillis and McCreery had in common was that they both had served in Vietnam, where they had demonstrated their stamina and ability to hang tough under fire. And they were back in the foxhole again. They appeared to be an unlikely combination—in their professional backgrounds, appearance, and personalities. But they proved to be the perfect duo, because their differences gave them the complementary aptitudes and attitudes needed for success.

Gillis and McCreery had built SAGA into a successful firm—doubling profits between 1995 and 1996. But their German parent was in deep financial trouble, so it looked as if their reward for their successes might be a German bankruptcy or an acquisition that would dismantle the firm. It looked like a dark time. On the other hand, they thought, this might be the moment they were waiting for. It could be the opportunity to do more than run the company. This might be a chance to own it.

The Opportunity Presents Itself

About five months after becoming president in 1996, Gillis was standing on the other side of a table in Darmstadt, Germany, in Software AG's austere boardroom, staring down Dr. Peter Schnell. Schnell was the brilliant and mercurial technologist who had founded Software AG twenty-five years earlier. Schnell had built it from a start-up to a leader in mainframe database technology, driving revenue above $500 million by 1989 and becoming one of the wealthiest men in Germany. At one point in the 1980s, he was the king of German technology, with a company as large as Microsoft and bigger than SAP—and an ego to match.

Schnell, however, made the mistake of dismissing client/server systems and relational databases as inefficient computing platforms, and so failed to develop new products for these fast-growing segments of the market. From 1989, as global software continued to explode, his company's revenues flatlined. High overhead and unfocused, dictatorial management created inefficient operations that were bleeding red ink. These years of missteps helped bring the company to the brink of bankruptcy.

Gillis was in Germany for a monthly meeting of the executive committee. As he leaned across the boardroom table, he told Schnell that the company was going to lose DM 57 million. Schnell, who refused to admit there was a problem, went ballistic. He ran up and down the table, yelling at Gillis. "The partners and managers knew I was right, but nobody would tell this guy," Gillis said. Schnell was in denial and the company was cratering. Iceberg? What iceberg?

It was now October. Gillis knew they had a limited window of opportunity in which to act. He knew that their cash-strapped and hemorrhaging German parent would probably need to sell off assets to pay off debt coming due in April 1997. He knew that there was a good chance the company would go on the block, and that he wanted to be the buyer. If anyone was going to own this company, it would be them. But how do you acquire the $160 million division of a large German software company that is lurching toward death? It's no small order.

Back home after the October meeting, Gillis called McCreery and controller Gary Hayes together. "Look guys," he said. "This is not going to continue this way. One of two things is going to happen. The Germans will probably bring in new management that will demand we make more money, so we might as well start making more money and get ahead of the curve. And number two is, if we make some money, maybe we can buy this place. Nobody is going to be interested in it in the condition it's in now, so we've got to shape it up as fast as we can."

McCreery had frequently contemplated the possibility of buying the company, but it had always looked pretty unlikely. The German leadership would have to be pushed to the wall to part with its U.S. division. The U.S. software market was the fastest-growing and most sophisticated in the world. They wouldn't let it go unless there was no choice. Now there was no choice, but the deal was still a long shot. "It was finally clear they were going to hit the wall and there would be a five-day window of opportunity," McCreery said. "If you could key it up and the stars aligned, it could work—so it wasn't crazy, but it was pretty far-fetched at the time. The Germans just don't sell stuff."

Management also needed to find a financing partner who would wait in the wings for the time to be right, then pull the deal together almost overnight. "This [was] buying a rather old company from a German parent," said McCreery. "And you had to find a buyer who was politically correct to the Germans, which rules out 95 percent of the people capable of financing a deal that size. We knew the Germans would want a simple deal, quick, get it over with, no gaming and no arguing. You really had to bring the buyer and seller together and you had one shot. It had to be a match made in heaven."

Gillis held his tongue at the executive meetings in Darmstadt, but he kept working on his plans. After the October meeting, he asked a board member to approach Schnell privately about selling the U.S. firm. He thought it was an astute and politically correct way to approach Schnell, but the word came back quickly: "No way." The German board, finally aware of the magnitude of the problems, had already decided to take the rare and dramatic step

of replacing the founder. Schnell had been forced out and a successor was quickly named, but he had not yet taken the reins. Gillis
would have to bide his time a bit longer. "They were in a position
where they had to raise capital," Gillis said. "They had to sell an
asset. They had all the physical assets tied up with the bank. So the
only thing they could sell was something of value, which was us."

The $200 Million Phone Call

A lot of great investing hinges on being in the right place at the
right time. In October 1996, the gods of buyout investing were
clearly smiling down on me. I received a call from Phil Norton, the
CEO of e Plus, a local computer finance and services company.
McCreery leased computers from e Plus and had contacted him to
see if he could put him in touch with equity firms that might be
able to back the Software AG deal. I had joined the e Plus board
just four months earlier at the recommendation of my partner Fred
Malek. I had known Software AG from my days as a high-technol-
ogy investment banker at Morgan Stanley, so I was interested when
Norton pitched me on the opportunity. The company had a strong,
if tarnished, legacy and a good reputation for technology.

Two days later, on October 7, 1996, over lunch in the bustling
Market Street Bar & Grill in Reston Town Centre, I met with
McCreery and controller Gary Hayes along with Norton and e Plus
executive vice president Bruce Bowen. I found out that the U.S.
division had an outstanding customer base of 1,500 companies,
including Sprint, Morgan Stanley, Delta Airlines, the Federal Avia-
tion Administration, and Georgetown University. The U.S. unit was
growing but had not been allowed to pursue acquisitions and was
forced to send any cash it generated back to Europe to bail out its
bleeding parent. It appeared the German company might be forced
to sell the business and the expected asking price of $85 million
was in the right range. I was impressed with the managers and that
they were willing to put $1 million of their own skin in the game. It
almost sounded too good to be true. Something had to go wrong
soon. There are hiccups in every deal.

Both sides survived this first mutual interview. In November,
after his dance around the table with Schnell, Gillis and McCreery
met me one evening in the noisy lobby of the Reston Hyatt. There,
on the wicker couches under the sweeping glass skylights, we

began to discuss the terms of the management agreement. Gillis and McCreery had done their homework and knew the rough terms of management deals. We agreed management would receive options to acquire 15 percent of the stock at the investor's buy-in price. Of that, 12 percent would be granted at closing and the rest contingent upon meeting performance goals. Both sides knew that a 15 percent management interest was at the high end of the normal range at the time, but they had created the deal opportunity and had a strong strategy moving forward. I looked Gillis in the eye and we shook hands. We were ready to go.

The options would vest over a three-year period and we wouldn't touch the current management compensation system. Management would make an investment of up to $1 million for additional equity. For all of us, this was the most important deal of our careers, yet the agreement had just four points and fit onto a single sheet of paper.

Keeping management compensation sacrosanct ended up being our ace in the hole. Another buyout firm that was talking with Gillis and McCreery about the deal had a different approach. The investor asked Gillis what he made. Gillis responded that his total compensation with bonuses was more than $600,000. The investor suggested that it was too high and might have to be adjusted. Obviously not the right answer. During that one fatal phone call, the investor had demonstrated his penny-pinching style. This was incredibly shortsighted. If he was willing to be tight-fisted even before the deal was struck, Gillis thought, it was painful to imagine what he might do when he became the majority owner of the company.

In this case, our rival lost the deal. Given that our investment of under $30 million had grown to more than $200 million at the time of the IPO and much more afterward, that call had cost that would-be investor well over $200 million—a little pricey no matter what your calling plan. These deals are all based on trust, on all sides, and it doesn't take much to spook a potential partner. This incident helped to highlight our emphasis on supporting the managers we back. It is penny-wise and pound-foolish to sink so much into a company and then quibble with the very people who have the power to make the investment pay off.

In my meetings with Gillis and McCreery, we had put together the structure of the buy-side of the deal. The management agreement was set and the overall strategy for financing was in place. Now, all we needed was a willing seller.

Becoming the White Knight

Gillis knew it would take a little while for the new CEO to come to the full realization of the company's predicament. As expected, when CEO Erwin Koenigs appeared at his first meeting in Darmstadt, he was upbeat. "In December, he still felt pretty good," Gillis recalled. "He was going to save the world."

But then the full weight of the company's problems hit him. His "welcome to the company gift" was finding out that he was losing $3 million a month and had $70 million of bank debt coming due in 120 days. Rough day. Shortly after Koenigs had this epiphany, Gillis received a troubling call from his German boss that the company may go bankrupt if other banks decided to call their loans. It was only eleventh-hour negotiations by the aggressive and intelligent Koenigs that kept bankruptcy at bay. Even so, they only earned a reprieve to show a profit, raise cash, or face default by March 31. There followed a brief period of euphoria when it looked as if SAP would buy out its German compatriot, but the SAP board ultimately turned down the deal. There would be no white knight to ride in to save them. The clock was ticking.

Koenigs was direct. He started the January meeting with the words, "Gentlemen, we have a problem." Bank loans were coming due very soon. He began to lay out the situation and said they would need to do something dramatic. The situation was utterly grim. Koenigs was telling his top management team that this venerable, thirty-year-old global software giant was going under. They were toast.

Most executives at the meeting were probably tuning him out and trying to remember where they could dig out the latest version of their resumes. They hoped Microsoft was hiring. But, oddly, deep down inside, one man in the room was smiling. It was the U.S. country manager, Dan Gillis. This was the moment Gillis was waiting for—his whole life. At the break, he walked up to Koenigs and asked him, "Do you have a backup plan?"

"No," Koenigs replied.

Then Gillis uttered the most important phrase of his career: "I have one for you."

"What's that?"

"I'll buy the U.S. company from you."

Koenigs got it immediately. It would be a triple bank shot, and Gillis had just teed it up for him. He would sell all or a piece of the U.S. business, pay off the banks, save the company, and preserve German jobs. The deal would put the money into the coffers of the German firm in time to meet its March 31 bank loans. But that was less than three months away. Could that get done? Koenigs was planning a trip over to the United States in two weeks, and Gillis suggested they meet then to discuss the deal.

On January 30, 1997, Koenigs flew into Washington for a meeting with the managers of the company's U.S. division. When Koenigs arrived at the Reston Hyatt, he was having second thoughts about the deal. He wasn't keen on the idea of getting into bed with some hotshot U.S. financiers. He was afraid that after selling the company, the U.S. buyer might flip the acquisition for a tidy profit. McCreery had already spent the evening and entire day preceding Koenigs's visit arguing the merits of the deal with German CFO Volker Dawedeit. After prodigious efforts—and even more prodigious alcohol and food consumption—Dawedeit agreed that there really was no other way to save the company. This was their only marketable asset. They couldn't sell stock in the parent because the equity was tied up in Schnell's nonprofit trusts. Koenigs still had to be convinced. The discussions with Koenigs stretched from 5:30 P.M. until well after 10 P.M. Finally, he agreed. An excited Gillis phoned me at 11 P.M. to tell me it was show time. We were set to meet with Koenigs at 8:30 A.M. the next day.

No Second Chances

I was nearly asleep—ready to dream about once-in-a-lifetime deals like Software AG—when Gillis called. He said he thought we could make a deal, but we had just one day to do it, and it had to be tomorrow while Koenigs was in town. As I hung up the phone and looked at the dark ceiling, I was highly skeptical. Could a deal that came together so rapidly hold together? This was a key German asset. Would they really sell it? And what about Koenigs? I'd never met the guy and in ten hours I was supposed to sit across the table from him and do an $85 million deal.

Gillis and McCreery had briefed me fully on the terms of the structure, but chemistry with Erwin Koenigs would be crucial. My father is German, so I hoped I might understand Koenigs a bit. And I was prepared to bring out my two-word German arsenal if needed: "Wie gehts?" If he followed up in German, I'd be dead. More seriously, if the chemistry was wrong or he got the sense we'd damage his position in the U.S. market, the deal would be history. There was no warming-up period or informal meetings over cocktails. We had just one shot to make this work. If Koenigs as much as didn't like my necktie, the deal could be over in minutes. I slept poorly as I churned over the day ahead. It might have been less stressful if I were lukewarm about the deal. But I knew if we could buy this company with this management team, it could be a screaming homer.

We met early the next day in a conference room at Software AG's Reston headquarters. The meeting began well and only got better. Koenigs was a disciplined guy but very direct and struck me more like a decisive Silicon Valley CEO than a German bureaucrat. He was a man of action who needed to get something done, and his CFO, Volker Dawedeit, was a mountainous guy with a wonderful sense of humor. It is our style to be highly flexible as partners and we pride ourselves on not acting like snooty New York bankers. Koenigs and Dawedeit responded well and the chemistry was good. We got down to terms quickly and, amazingly, hammered out the deal. But Koenigs was blunt and any misstep on our side could scuttle the deal. We had to nail it. Within a week, we had exchanged a few pages of general guidelines over international fax. These documents would ultimately become more than 300 pages of dense purchase documents once the lawyers were through with them. It was a long way to the closing dinner.

Every day, Gillis called Koenigs to make sure he was still on board. The deal of his lifetime had been put together so quickly that he wanted to make sure there wouldn't be a change of plans. One day in March when he called, Koenigs asked him expectantly: "When are we going to close this deal?" Gillis breathed a sigh of relief. Koenigs needed this deal as badly as he did. "It was then I knew the deal was going to go through," he said.

Decisions in Darmstadt

In early March, I went with Gillis to Germany to present the plans to the German parent company board of directors (called the "Vorstand") and labor board. The labor board, which comprises employees, plays a central role in German company corporate governance. The board's reaction could make or break the deal. About fifty labor representatives gathered around a conference table for the presentation.

The fact that I could manage to fire off a few rough words in German at the meeting didn't hurt. We knew things were going pretty well when one of the board members, smiling, recognized my last name as German and asked if I had relatives in the shipbuilding industry. I didn't, of course, but at least they were warming. The key selling point was that the deal would allow the company to make its bank payments and protect the more than 1,400 German jobs. They also felt comfortable with the fact that we were backing the incumbent American management team they had come to know and that we wouldn't dramatically alter the strategy after we controlled the asset.

Although we were hoping for a favorable outcome, I wasn't prepared for the reaction we received. At the close of the presentation, the representatives began pounding their fists on the table. I didn't know whether this meant "Throw this bum from D.C. off the balcony" or "Let's close." But they were all smiling, so I assumed, as I later found out, that this was a sign of approval. It was music to our ears.

Suspicions of Affairs

The work was relentless. Gillis and McCreery were in a race to see who could get to the office first. Gillis finally conceded the competition when he found out McCreery was coming in at 3 A.M. The two financial people in McCreery's office were working night and day hammering out the details of the plan. The work was so intense and so secretive that the wife of one of the men later told Harry she suspected her husband of fourteen years might be having an affair. After all, he was working eighteen-hour days, wouldn't tell her what was going on, and came home every night with a smile on his face.

And perhaps she wasn't too far off the mark. For the core group of people who worked on the deal, most of whom had spent their careers chained to large corporations, this dalliance with a dream was risky business. It was a step away from the button-down corporate existence, giving up the tired German parent for the excitement and romance of a start-up. With this kind of heart-pumping passion, was there any need for sleep?

Independence Day

Sometimes there was a bit too much excitement. Two weeks before closing, our lead lender, who was providing $15 million in financing, pulled out. We couldn't believe it and immediately went into crunch mode. The software business was a tough sell to the bankers in the first place. There are few hard assets and the technology is difficult to understand. Now, with the deal deadline staring us in the face, we had no financing. Every deal has a visceral panic time and we had just hit ours. Sweat was beading on our foreheads. Miraculously, McCreery pulled out all the stops and found another bank to step in and back the deal. That got him the "deal MVP" honors, hands-down. "At the last minute, it was put together with baling wire," he said.

The closing on the night of March 31 was almost anticlimactic, with a bevy of lawyers brooding over the fine points of painstakingly detailed documents in the Washington offices of Thayer counsel Arnold and Porter. Anticlimactic for everyone except McCreery, who, wrestling with details until the end, finally breathed a sigh of relief. He did a victory dance in the office. Free at last.

While Gillis and McCreery prepared painstakingly for this deal, they also got some breaks along the way. "It was a lot of luck," McCreery said. "We chose the right partners. They threw the founder out at just the last minute. A month later and we might not have gotten the deal done."

In the year that followed the April 1 employee meeting, morale rose, turnover dropped by more than half, productivity increased, and the firm undertook an ambitious program of research and development. Within six months, it had made its first acquisition. Gillis brought in expert marketers from Iomega and hired a chief technology officer along with more than 100 employees. The company, which became known as SAGA Software, began developing its own products that would transform it from a software distributor to a creator. It established a strategy to lead in middleware, the software that links the Internet to legacy mainframes.

Even with its East Coast location, the company was becoming downright hip. Gillis started out one employee meeting by donning sunglasses and moonwalking across the stage. No Dorothy, we are definitely not in Darmstadt anymore.

The Road and the Claw

The roller-coaster ride was just beginning. Because the new company was performing so well, the next step was to start a grueling two-week roadshow leading up to the IPO. The IPO was a little earlier than we had originally anticipated, but the company and the market were right. Many people in finance like to endlessly debate the merits of timing an IPO, but for me the rule is simple: You get it done when the market window is open. You have to feed the ducks when they're quacking.

The warm-up act on the way to the roadshow was weeks of presentations to bankers, not to mention eighteen- to twenty-hour days preparing Securities and Exchange Commission filings. Just before the road show started, Gillis ran his presentation by the bankers at BancAmerica Robertson Stephens in San Francisco. His presentation, designed by a committee of investment bankers, landed with a dramatic thud. It drifted all over the place. It had no punch. There was silence. Then, one of the older sales representatives looked up and said, "I don't get it." Gillis and McCreery looked at each other and couldn't believe it. I was in the back of the room, bleary-eyed, watching our dream of an IPO evaporate. If the bankers didn't get it, how could they sell it to investors? Crunch time again. The bankers gave them suggestions and discussed pricing during a five-hour, five-wine-bottle dinner, which eased a little of the pain of the day's performance.

Gillis and McCreery had started that first day on the road at 5 A.M. and didn't make it back to the elevator of their San Francisco hotel until 11:30 P.M. And they still didn't even have a final presentation. McCreery pushed the button for the elevator and looked over at Gillis. They were absolutely whipped, yet they knew there were more than twenty days like this ahead of them.

"How did you like your first day?" McCreery asked.

The two men looked at each other and burst out laughing. The elevator doors opened and shut. Another elevator opened and shut. Still they couldn't get on. They were on the floor laughing. "We've got three more weeks of this," McCreery thought. "I'll never make it."

Gillis and McCreery tore the presentation apart the next day on the plane from San Francisco to New York. They threw out all the investment banker's advice and honed the pitch the way they wanted it. If this thing was going to flop, at least it would do so on *their* terms. The new presentation was a dramatic improvement and played to rave reviews in meetings with analysts and individual investors. They gave sixty-eight one-on-one presentations and about a dozen investor breakfasts and dinners in some twenty U.S. and European cities.

They flew from Kansas City to Minneapolis to San Diego to London to Edinburgh, typically touching down in three cities per day. When the roadshow started, they planned to be austere. They needed clear heads, they reasoned, so they decided they would be teetotalers until it was over. No beer or wine for the whole roadshow! Discipline! By the end of their first day, they got on their third flight and demanded two beers, followed by two more.

One evening, they had a dinner meeting scheduled with an investor in a San Diego restaurant. There was a noisy retirement party in the background. The investment banker had arranged for a massive tray of seafood. Gillis and McCreery picked at it as they waited for the investor, who had gotten lost. Finally, a diminutive woman entered the room and sat down at the table covered with crustaceans. They offered her something to eat. "I can't eat seafood," she said. "It makes me sick." There were crabs and lobsters everywhere. Gillis and McCreery burst out laughing. Needless to say, she didn't buy the stock.

But that wasn't the last they saw of that seafood. The next

morning at 6 A.M., the two men were ready to start another day of pitches in San Diego before heading out to Los Angeles and San Francisco. At their first meeting, Gillis opened the book and a crab claw fell out onto the table.

At one point, after a series of twenty-hour days, Gillis ran out of steam. In the middle of an afternoon presentation, he just couldn't speak anymore.

"I'm out of gas," Gillis whispered to McCreery. "I don't think I've got it in me to finish."

"You're not going to die on me, are you?" McCreery asked.

Through an act of will, Gillis took a breath and made it through the presentation. Such is the glamour of leading an IPO.

Looking Back

More than two years after closing the original management buyout, Gillis, McCreery, and I met again in the Market Street Bar & Grill to look back. Back on that auspicious day in late 1996 when I had first met McCreery at this same spot to discuss the deal, they were crazy dreamers who actually had the chutzpah to think they could pull off this wild deal. Now they are leaders of one of the most successful management buyouts ever—and multimillionaires. And through that one deal, I realized one of my largest business dreams and became chairman of the board of a wonderful software company publicly traded on the Big Board. A lot has changed.

Across my desk, I see hundreds of potential deals that are just as crazy. Many fall by the wayside because managers don't have the vision, know-how, or guts to make them happen. Gillis and McCreery would be the first to tell you that this roller coaster is not for the faint of heart. But it is one hell of a ride.

"Everybody tells you what you can't do and you have to totally ignore it," Gillis said. "They say you can't buy it from the Germans. You can't take it public. You can't grow it. You can't make it profitable. You can't do your own products. Don't listen. You just have to do your own thing. Then, once you do it, everyone says, 'I knew you guys could do it.' You get all this outside noise, but you just have to ignore it and keep going."

Was it a good deal for the German parent? Absolutely. Software AG Germany, snatched out of the jaws of death, survived and grew nicely under Koenigs's and Dawedeit's leadership. In 1999, following the U.S. example, Software AG did its own IPO—the largest European software IPO ever. It is now itself a public company with a quarter billion dollars in the bank. It also still retains a stake in the U.S. firm and receives a large and growing royalty stream on product sales. "Tell me that was a mistake," said McCreery. "You freed us. We send through a lot more money because we are free. You're a healthy, viable company and it turned around the day you did the deal."

I asked Gillis and McCreery: How has this changed your life? "Dramatically," said Gillis. And McCreery chimed in wryly, "What life?"

"Oh, it's changed dramatically for me and for Harry," said Gillis. "We're both financially much more secure than we ever were before. It has been fun to do a deal like this. It was exciting, and I think it's just starting. There have been ups and downs trying to make it work, but I think we've got a good management team and we believe we can make it happen. We're gaining momentum."

Bringing Their Dream to the World

What was the high point of the experience? Both men agreed it was when they took their new company to the NYSE with the IPO on November 18, 1997. The night before, we all drank brandy and smoked cigars at the Windows on the World restaurant at the top of the New York World Trade Center. The next day, we were there for the opening bell and stayed at the exchange through the day—watching the stock, which had a value of $1.47 when we bought the company six months earlier, climb to $10.25 at the close.

At the end of the day, McCreery woke up Gillis from the sofa where he had crashed just off the NYSE platform. The president of the NYSE led Gillis, McCreery, and me, along with other employees and family, onto the crowded platform overlooking the exchange. The trading floor below seethed like an anthill. Gillis slid the Lucite cover off the red bell button. It looked like the kind of button the president would push to launch a war. At fifteen seconds to 4 P.M., Gillis hit the button that starts the powerful, capitalistic chime of the closing bell and held it down with his left hand as he pounded the large, weathered wooden gavel with his right. It resounded against a pitted wooden chopping block where hundreds of leaders of industry have brought their dreams to the world. CNN and the world looked on. On the third blow of the gavel, the bell stopped ringing and the trading floor erupted into applause.

"That day was really a high point for me," said Gillis. "My family was there. The management team was there. We were all there. We'd just worked our asses off to get there."

"I just wish we could remember it," said McCreery.

"We'd done the deal," Gillis explained, "went through the banking, did the roadshow, and all of a sudden, you know, the culmination is you end up in New York at the NYSE and you're absolutely exhausted. You're really running on nothing."

"Yeah," said McCreery. "But it doesn't get any better than that. It doesn't get any better than that."

CHAPTER 2

No Guts, No Glory

"The trouble with the rat race is that even if you win, you're still a rat."

—LILY TOMLIN

What does it take to lead a successful management buyout? It takes strong management and leadership skills in the industry you are considering. That's the price of admission. But it also requires guts and vision—the ability to see opportunities that others can't see. Some of these opportunities are right in front of you, as Dan Gillis and Harry McCreery found at Software AG. Others arrive in the form of existing companies that can be purchased from the outside. Others are built from a series of acquisitions, as illustrated by the story of Roger Ballou below. We'll explore the details of leading a revolution from within or searching for external opportunities in Chapter 4. In this chapter, however, we step back to consider the tangible and intangible skills and qualities that managers need to lead a successful buyout. Do you have what it takes to succeed? Any competent manager can probably follow the steps outlined in this book, but what often separates successful from unsuccessful buyouts is not *what* managers do, but *how* they do it, the qualities and approaches they bring to the table.

First of all, it starts with the ability to dream. It requires the capacity to look beyond the organizational blinders and the earth-is-flat-and-you'll-fall-off-the-sides fears. It takes, first and foremost, guts to step off dry land and venture out in search of unknown worlds. For the buyout to start, there must first be a dream.

The Dream

During quiet moments as he rose through the ranks of American Express, the dream had been there. Roger Ballou thought there was great potential for rolling up premium tour operators in the travel industry. But Amex leadership always felt it was off the core strategy of the firm. So Ballou put the dream behind him as he became president of the company's Travel Services Group and then left to become chief operating officer of Alamo Rent-A-Car.

"You are sitting inside a company and say: 'I bet I could make a business out of this,'" said Ballou. "You hear guys talk that way at the water cooler or over drinks at night. Why don't they do it? By and large, it is a combination of fear and lack of knowledge. The fear is real. You have a mortgage; you've got a family. Stopping that cash flow and stepping out is hard. And you don't know where to start. I had this idea ten years ago, but didn't have a clue as to whom to talk to to pursue it."

Ballou, wearing a sports jacket without a tie, had the relaxed confidence of a retired senior executive as he reflected on his experience over lunch at the historic Willard Hotel in Washington, D.C. Now, leading his own series of buyouts, Ballou is working harder than ever, although it is a very different type of work than in his past life. Some might see his simple and functional office today as a step down from the posh elegance of his past management suites, but Ballou has proved he has the confidence not to hide behind an office, suit, or a title. He is articulate and poised. This new and simpler context for his work only makes his natural qualities of leadership more defined.

The confidence was always there. In 1995, before leaving for Alamo, Ballou had taken a hard look at buying out American Express's retail travel business. He knew that by spinning off the unit, he could squeeze out expenses from overhead and strip down corporatewide benefits that were far above the standard in the travel industry. "I knew exactly what I could do to add millions to the operation. It was very clear and crisp," said Ballou.

But he never pursued it. "At that time, I felt the scale of the acquisition was too big to step up and try to do," he said. "I had no idea if investors would think I was a whacko. I knew what the implications inside would be: I would be history very shortly. But that wasn't what deterred me as much as not knowing what to do."

Ballou has an undergraduate degree from Wharton and an MBA from Dartmouth's Tuck School. He has held senior positions at some of the largest and most successful firms in the world. But not even nearly two decades in the travel industry prepared him to leave the solid terra firma of his past career to pursue this dream. "It would be like saying, 'I think I am going to go sailing this weekend,' and stepping off the dock into a sailboat and heading into the sea if you've never sailed before. I wouldn't do that because I wouldn't know how to do it. I think stepping out onto the sailboat by yourself is a pretty good analogy for taking the risk of trying to find a management buyout firm and then seeing if you can work out a deal." As he looked out to the expansive white breakers, he again turned away.

Setting Sail

Ballou was vacationing in Nantucket when the wind finally picked up. He was thinking about leaving Alamo and, as he considered high-level job offers from several major corporations, he happened to mention the travel tour roll-up dream he couldn't shake to an old friend. It was my partner, Fred Malek, a travel industry veteran who had served as president of Marriott Hotels for nine years and then as president and vice chairman of Northwest Airlines. In late summer of 1997, Malek called Ballou on vacation and Ballou flew down to Washington to discuss his idea for consolidating tour operators for high-income travelers.

"Two weeks later, we had a letter of understanding," Ballou said. "I was still on holiday. The pace of decision making was way ahead of what I thought it would be. I thought it would take two or three months. Instead it took two or three weeks." They hammered out a management agreement and Thayer and Ballou committed $75 million to back the idea. Then Ballou went to work.

At this point, he had no company. All he had was his experience and a pad of paper. He camped out in borrowed offices at Thayer where he and his small staff were elbow-to-elbow, alone with their dream. It was not quite the life he had been accustomed to. "When you are one of the top-ten guys at a firm like American Express, you have a really good life," he said, explaining why it is difficult for many experienced executives to leave. "You can get tickets to anything you want. You are invited to A-list functions. You use the corporate planes. You have stock. You have a lot of comp, a lot of perks, and lot of power. It is relatively rare for guys at that level to want to go out on their own."

As he laid the groundwork for the business that would become Global Vacation Group (GVG), he had traded in the perks for a chance to change the industry. In March 1998, Ballou's group acquired Allied Tours. They finally had their own company, so they celebrated by signing a lease for offices. "You miss some of the resources—having the extra financial analyst [or the] extra human resources person," Ballou said. "These are the luxuries you get in the big company. Here, you have to prioritize, whereas in a place like American Express you can multiprocess. Here, if you want five things done at once, you have to find a guy who can do five things at once."

They proved up to the task. By the end of May, Ballou's GVG had purchased Haddon Holidays, Classic Custom Vacations, MTI Vacations, and Globetrotters, Inc. The team, in partnership with our firm, closed five acquisitions totaling more than $100 million in just three months. This was a monumental task. By the end of 1998, the company was one of the largest providers of value-added vacation products and services for higher-income travelers. It had 700 employees and had offered products to more than three-quarters of a million leisure travelers.

When GVG finished its initial public offering (IPO) on the New York Stock Exchange on July 31, 1998, shares that had been acquired at $5.25 were worth $14. In a matter of months, the company was worth $150 million and Ballou's stake had grown to $6.3 million.

Ballou, however, wasn't measuring his success strictly by the numbers as much as by the shock waves he could begin to see in the industry. "What was exciting to me and the management group I put together was the ability to change the industry," he said. "We will have fundamentally led the change in the industry, and it will probably occur five years faster than it might have otherwise."

He even managed to stir things up a bit at his old employer. Although American Express had thought Ballou's idea was off the core strategy when he had proposed it internally, within six months of the start of GVG, Amex was doing the same thing. Imitation is the sincerest form of flattery.

Today, the destiny of GVG itself is still uncertain. It could become one of the few large companies that dominate this part of the industry. Or it could be swallowed up along the way. "We will either be a big fish or get eaten by a big fish," Ballou said. Either way, he will have achieved his objectives of permanently altering the competitive landscape, building value for customers, and dramatically increasing shareholder value—including his own.

Knowledge Is Power

Part of the reason it is so hard for managers to leap into a buyout is that they don't fully appreciate their considerable leverage. What Roger Ballou couldn't see when he was a corporate insider and what my partner Fred Malek recognized was the value of Ballou's management skills on the open market. Most executives know what they are worth to the corporation and are pretty comfortable making sure they receive it. What they don't realize is that outside the corporate world, their ideas and management acumen may be valued at a much higher level. Excellent managers must learn that their value in a buyout environment is enormous and that they *can* capitalize on this value. Management talent is the limiting factor in today's buyout world. It's simple economics: The demand for strong management talent considerably outstrips supply, so management prices should go way up. But managers limit themselves because of uncertainty or lack of knowledge of the buyout process. This is why I have written this book: to provide great managers with the tools and insights to dream big and to pursue their greatest business goal.

The availability of capital in the buyout world has exploded.

Money for deals is ubiquitous. As shown in Figure 2-1, private equity funds have grown dramatically year after year. With $60 billion in these funds, that is the equivalent of more than $200 billion in buying power out there just looking for the right deal. The number of buyout funds with more than $1 billion in capital shot from just five in 1989 to thirty-nine in 1999, and funds with $500 million to $1 billion more than tripled from twelve to thirty-eight. Hundreds of domestic and foreign banks are standing by to finance both debt and equity. Capital has always been a commodity, but never has it been more plentiful than it is today.

Has management availability and expertise been growing at this rate? Very unlikely. This means the ratio of capital to expertise is increasing dramatically. In addition to this huge equity pool, interest rates are relatively low and bank debt is readily available. Expertise is more valuable than ever. What all this equity is seeking is good deals and management talent. *Senior managers have never had greater leverage, but they don't use it because, for all their experience at running operations, most don't understand the deal process.*

Managers have been stunned when they recognized the value of their skills on the open market. For example, a group of TRW managers, along with investors led by Bain Capital, Inc. and the Thomas H. Lee Company in Boston, spun off TRW's information systems and services division. They bought the company, renamed Experian, in a transaction valued at more than $1 billion on September 19, 1996 and sold it less than *two months* later for $1.7

Figure 2-1. Money is no object.

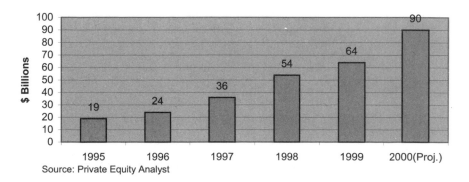

Equity Raised by Private Equity Funds

Source: Private Equity Analyst

billion to The Great Universal Stores PLC. The investors and management made more than $600 million in less than two months. A huge short-term home run like this is the exception, but deals such as this and the Software AG transaction are being done every day. This is the manager's time and now is the time to dream big and pursue the goal of owning and running your own company.

The Qualities of Victors

Besides the guts to step off dry land like Ballou did and sail into the unknown, what does it take to succeed in a buyout? Professional skills in the target industry are a requirement, although some of the most important parts of the deal do not show up on your resume. They are not the specific actions you take or documents you sign, but the intangible qualities and tangible skills you and your partners bring to the table. They have to do with trust and relationships. Before the lawyers get involved, deals are built on a handshake. Your partners have to trust you, and you have to trust your partners. More often than not, it is not the details of some bank agreement that cause a deal to crash and burn or never get started. These qualities of victors are essential to successful deals: credibility, compatibility, comfort, core skills, commitment, composure, and chance. These are recurring themes throughout the book.

Credibility
Building and maintaining credibility is critical, particularly for management. This will be the most important transaction of your career. The deal financiers are likely working on five to ten deals at once, and if yours fails, they are off to the next one. Normally, managers are putting up the least money, so their *capital* is their *credibility*. Selling the deal to potential partners and selling your strategies to investors when you go to an IPO are all based on the credibility of management. It can take you weeks, months, or years to establish this credibility and nanoseconds to destroy it.

The best way to establish credibility is to be prepared and be direct. Don't go to meetings with a financing source or seller with a half-baked idea. Be prepared with a full plan and for any questions that arise. Do your homework before contacting a financing partner or seller. Get their brochure, review materials, and understand the professional backgrounds of the managers and the types of investments they've done in the past. Understand their criteria for investment. If you call KKR with a $5 million deal (well below their radar), it's a ding to your credibility.

Set reasonable expectations. A glowing strategy that shows the company's revenues tripling every year may look sexy on paper but is simply not credible. All buyout investors know one thing for certain: The plan you give them won't happen exactly as laid out. On rare occasions the plan will be exceeded, but in 75 percent of the cases the plan will be missed. A well-thought-out strategy for more modest growth may be much better received than the proverbial hockey stick deal.

Take on a deal that fits your team. If your team has only had experience running a $25 million company, don't propose buying a $500 million firm. If you say you'll return a call today, do it today. If you say you'll provide a business plan in a week, don't do it in three. These small breaches chip away at your credibility. Finally, always be truthful. I asked one group of managers if they had their target company signed up under a letter of intent. They said yes. Was it binding on the seller? Again, they said yes. When I received the letter of intent a few days later, I found that it wasn't a binding letter. The team's credibility took a big step down into a hole that's hard to crawl out of.

Much of this probably seems like basic common sense, but you would be surprised at how many management ideas come across my desk that are simply not credible. You'd be surprised at how many deals are rejected for what may appear to be tiny, superficial details. But with a relationship built upon trust, these small signs are all investors have to base their decisions upon. My desk and the desks of most investors are stacked high with potential deals. Today's economic environment is frothy and everyone wants to be an entrepreneur. Investors are looking hard for reasons to kill a deal and remove the clutter. Don't give them any additional reasons to kill it by whiffing on the small things.

Compatibility

The second intangible is compatibility or goal alignment. The goals of management need to be compatible with those of your partners,

or you will be at cross-purposes. Differences in goals can either undermine the deal or undermine the company afterward. Make sure
the structure of the deal aligns your goals with those of your partners. Quite simply, if they make money, you should make money
and vice versa. Your capital should go in on the same basis as theirs.
Your strike price options should be at their buy-in price. It sounds
simple, but there are many nuances in hammering out deals, and
sometimes the alignment slips. For example, one executive realized
after the deal was struck that his options in the company didn't vest
until after his two-year contract expired. If his partners turned on
him, they could have technically fired him before his stake in the
firm was in place. Luckily in this case, there wasn't the remotest
possibility this would happen, but it certainly came as a shock when
he realized it.

One area of alignment slippage is in fees taken by equity sponsors or finders. Often the equity sponsor takes out large closing
and management fees on a transaction that management does not
participate in. Some of the fees compensate them for their work on
the deal, just as you get a paycheck, but others can be egregious.
Make sure *all* fees are fully disclosed, up front.

Comfort

Credibility and compatibility contribute to comfort level, but there
also needs to be a certain chemistry to make the deal work. Buying
a company is a lot like a marriage. You have to live with these people through better and worse, in the trenches on a daily basis. There
are millions of dollars at stake, so you've got to be comfortable with
your equity sponsors (and all the members of the team). You must
trust them, understand their criteria for tracking the performance
of the company and their expectations, and know who will sit on
your board. You cannot spend enough time with these people in
advance of selecting your partner. You must visit with several potential partners (no less than three and ideally at least five) to get a
good sampling and find the correct fit. Every one of them will have
a different approach to the deal, a different relationship with management, and a different culture. You need to be sure there is a
good fit with respect to personality, demeanor, investment philosophy, personal style, and long- and near-term goals. Do not get in
bed with a partner you have doubts about or don't trust. Although

it sounds simple, I generally believe managers do not give enough consideration to this key issue.

With each partner, determine as clearly as possible who will be your contact and work with you on the deal. Will the partner on the project stay attentive? Is it an important deal for your partner's firm? It had better be, because it is likely the most important deal you'll ever do. Finally, do reference checks on your potential partners. They'll do plenty of reference checking on you and shouldn't mind at all giving you their references. In particular, you want to talk with managers of other companies in their portfolios and ask to talk to a manager of one of their underperforming deals (we all have them). Ask to talk to a manager they fired in the last two years. How they handle adversity will tell you a lot about the firm.

Core Skills
Managers who make the leap to independence need to recognize the balance of skills required to make the independent firm successful. It is a given that leaders of management buyouts (MBOs) need strong management skills, the ability to run and lead a firm, and a clear strategy for building the business. This is what most strong MBO leaders bring to the table. But there is also a whole set of skills that are less likely to be in the corporate manager's toolkit. Leaders of these post-MBO companies need a strong and diverse set of capabilities including:

- Entrepreneurship and an ability to think outside of the box
- Deal-making skills and an ability to evaluate the fit of acquisitions and potential acquirers
- Corporate governance skills, such as how to form and manage a board
- Investor management and relationship skills, such as how to pitch to and interface with institutional investors

It is rare to find these diverse qualities in a single person. Some leaders have an entrepreneurial background from prior careers or internal ventures as well as corporate skills. Except for the CEO and CFO of a public company, most managers do not have much experience in investor relations. Usually, leaders of MBOs look outside themselves to develop a team with the savvy and experience to make the enterprise successful. Sometimes through acquisitions, they draw in entrepreneurs who are used to dealing with risk. By the time of the IPO, they draw upon staff with investor relations and Securities and Exchange Commission experience. Often the buyout firm's representatives can be helpful in building these skills through their own experiences or by putting you in touch with other managers in their portfolio who have more battle scars on these fronts.

In the early stages, the corporate and entrepreneurial balance is crucial. "Each of them comes to the game with serious deficiencies as well as serious strengths," said Ballou. "It is striking that they are almost mirror images of each other. The entrepreneur brings a risk orientation, the ability to bootstrap, and creativity, but tends to lack financial management skills, investor relations experience, analytical tools, and process management disciplines. [Those] coming from big firms generally have problems with day-to-day operational management, because most of them have moved to a level where they are out of the day-to-day. They are used to having a lot of safety nets. They are better at process management. You have to create a matrix of necessary skills."

Commitment
Before you get started, do a gut check. Do you really want to do a buyout? The process is difficult, time-consuming, expensive, and frustrating. You've got to be prepared to go down many blind alleys, or work on one project for a year and have it crater at the eleventh hour. You may have to be prepared to put your career on the line for an uncertain result. But if you are confident in your management abilities, you probably know you can put together another deal or find another job if this venture falls flat. If you want to lead your own company and maximize your ability to create net worth, it's a great way to go.

In many cases, those who are purely economically motivated may not be your best bets for partners. If they are only in it for the money, they are not focused on franchise building and shareholder returns. One executive was looking at buying a firm from two owners who described what they were seeking as "screw you" money. They wanted to take away enough that if they didn't want to keep leading the firm, they could thumb their noses and get out. The buyer walked away, clearly wanting more of a commitment to the success of the firm. This buyer didn't want partners who were going to make decisions solely on a short-term financial basis.

Composure
Deals are a roller coaster. There will be times when you are sure your deal has met an untimely demise. Some hidden problems, such as an environmental liability on a property that makes Chernobyl look like a dairy farm, will rise up and threaten to destroy the deal. Despite your best efforts, even the most successful deals die several times in the process. Even if you don't make a serious error that sends you into "deal hell," as described in Chapter 3, you will face times when you've given up hope of ever seeing the deal completed. The patient on the stretcher goes into cardiac arrest and, just when you start to wrap up the body, the eyes pop open again.

For Software AG, the bank financing evaporated just before closing, sending us scurrying around to find replacement funding. Sometimes these deaths can mean the end of the deal, but much more often they merely raise your blood pressure temporarily until they are resolved. If you can remain calm and keep moving forward, most of the time the deal starts breathing again on its own. But this deal death highlights a quality that every manager in a deal needs: a strong stomach for risk, a certain boldness, and the courage to take a daring leap in pursuit of a great reward. You are in for the ride of your life.

Chance
Everything about a deal has to do with timing. Usually the window to complete a transaction is very narrow. Either the opportunity passes or other players come in and take advantage of it. There is a lot of luck involved, but as Louis Pasteur once said, "Chance favors only the mind that is prepared." SAGA had a five-day window to do a deal and the managers nailed it, but only because they had spent months teeing it up. And it could have just as easily gone the other way. By understanding how these deals are structured and doing some advance work before the actual opportunity presents itself, you can ensure you'll be prepared to move quickly when the opportunity arrives.

Beyond Their Dreams

There is never a perfect time to do the deal. You have worked hard to get where you are. You have responsibilities to think about. Carefully weigh the risks and rewards. But if you find yourself waking up in the night and working over the details in your mind, if you can see the possibilities and have faith in your own ability to make it happen, if you know you could do more if you only had the chance, then maybe it is time to put aside your fear and put to the test whether this dream is real or just idle bravado.

This path is not for everyone. You may be comfortable and successful and have no desire to leave dry land to sail toward the edge of the earth. We have all seen the shipwrecks, and if you still are unconvinced, Chapter 3, "Avoiding Deal Hell," offers a few cautionary tales about the pitfalls of deal-making. It does take courage to put together a deal. But now you also have heard the stories of Dan Gillis, Harry McCreery, and Roger Ballou. They not only survived the journey but discovered rich lands beyond their dreams. They had the guts to find the glory.

The wind is rising. The sails are billowing. Will you answer the call?

CHAPTER 3

Avoiding Deal Hell

"A man who carries a cat by the tail learns something
he can learn in no other way."
—MARK TWAIN

B efore we race onto the entrance ramp of the expressway of deal making in the following chapters, let us take a brief moment to talk about safety. Not to scare you, but buyouts are high-risk enterprises. It is easy to dismiss the risks when you are cruising down the freeway, but not if you've been to a few accident scenes, as I have been. The reason for looking at a few deals that have crashed and burned is not to dissuade you from getting behind the wheel. Far from it. It is to make you more careful and to offer an investor's insights, as we examine in more detail at the end of this chapter, that can help you avoid the common potholes and hairpin turns that can send a deal to the scrap yard. What follows here is the cautionary tale of one such deal accident. The saddest fact for me, however, is that I was the driver.

In the past fifteen years, I've worked on hundreds of deals and spoken at length with many veterans of the buyout business about the dogs they've financed. We all have them, and virtually every buyout professional I know feels the same way I do: You never learn as much about buyouts and people's characters as you do in a deal that goes bad. On the good ones, you learn a bit about investing and more about cigars. On the bad ones, you visit the abyss and learn what risk capital really means. That's a visit to deal hell, a place I hope you never see.

I've been there. There are no surefire ways to stay out of this hot place, but you can better your odds if you either make your own mistakes or learn from those of others. I've tried both and, believe me, the latter method is always preferable. As Benjamin Franklin once said: "Experience keeps a dear school, yet fools will learn in no other."

If you believe you are invincible and would never stumble in this way, by all means head on to the next chapter. But for the rest of us, put up your clay feet and listen to a few dispatches from deal hell. Before examining how to do wildly successful deals in the following chapters, let's buckle up, climb into the simulator, and take a ride through the ashes of a deal gone awry.

Ceramic City

In 1989, I was an aggressive twenty-nine-year-old senior associate at a small Los Angeles buyout fund called Hancock Park Associates. My goal was to become partner and I knew how to do it: Find and close a good deal on my own. That was when I received a call about a deal from a southern California business broker. It seemed like the chance I was waiting for. The deals from this particular broker were usually too "doggy" (a technical financial term that means "poor quality") or too small for our firm, yet this one sounded intriguing.

Ceramic City* didn't sound like a flashy deal. Still, this ceramic retailer with twenty stores spread throughout New England had a lot in its favor. What made it interesting is that the Massachusetts-based chain was growing at more than 15 percent per year, new stores were performing well, and ceramic tiles were the fastest-growing and most profitable segment of the tile market. The New England economy had been in severe recession for two years and, in my bulletproof Harvard Business School judgment, had nowhere to go but up. The company had a hands-off owner living in Florida, which usually means opportunity. Management was reputed to be

*The name of this company has been changed for confidentiality.

good, growing revenue to about $20 million and earnings to $1.8 million. Furthermore, they were interested in putting their own equity into the deal, getting the old owner out of the way and controlling their own destiny. Bring it on, I thought. This is my ticket to partnership.

I flew to the East Coast to meet with the CEO and COO. The CEO, we'll call him Jim (to protect the innocent and not-so-innocent), had stock options that would net him $1 million in a sale, but he was willing to reinvest over half of his after-tax proceeds in a new deal. That he was willing to put up his own money was a good sign and virtually ensured he would be aligned with our interests as investors. The COO currently had no ownership at all and was also anxious to invest. These guys were best friends, which meant a compatible management team. Their investment and options brought their ownership to about 35 percent. Our firm agreed to invest $1.5 million and borrow $7 million to buy the company.

We seemed destined for success, and I finally thought partnership at the buyout firm was within my grasp. I started counting my winnings and visualizing a Balboa vacation home. But this deal made in heaven was destined to become a living hell.

The Pinkie Ring

The CEO wore a pinkie ring. Not a little unobtrusive gold band, but what looked like a lineman's oversize Super Bowl ring with a gaudy, chiseled diamond in the middle surrounded by smaller diamonds. The ring gnawed at me. Guys on the south side of Chicago wore pinkie rings—and they also packed heat. Although it made me uncomfortable, I didn't think there was a problem with the CEO. For all I knew, a ceramics trade show was a sea of pinkie rings. Besides, I thought it was probably just a sign that I was shallow and superficial as a human being to judge a man by his ring. I needed to rise above it.

After all, the CEO knew the business very well. He knew the brand, origin, and gross margin to the penny of every single piece of ceramic tile in the world, so he couldn't be all that bad. He seemed fairly normal in other dimensions of dress and demeanor. I got over it and closed the deal.

But the pinkie ring should have been red flag number one.

Then there were the late-night calls. When we were in the heat of the negotiations, he would call me late at night at home. He was nervous about the deal and the closing. He said the owner was driving him crazy and he wanted to get on to new opportunities. The calls came in at 10:30 P.M. in Los Angeles, which meant it was 1:30 A.M. his time. Maybe he was just a light sleeper or had pre-game jitters. I didn't see it as a sign that we were headed into trouble.

I missed red flag number two.

We closed the deal in September 1989. Everyone was happy. Our firm received a $150,000 fee and I got a check for $10,000, which was a big bump for me at the time. The CEO got his $1 million and was elated. One month later, we pulled off a $2.5 million acquisition of a local carpet and tile distributor. Horizontal integration! We were growing, doing deals, and we were off to the races.

Two months after the deal I had another red flag tossed in my face. I visited the company's new headquarters in Stoughton, Massachusetts. During the meeting, the CEO mentioned that he had gotten engaged. Terrific, I said. Congratulations! I knew he had been married before but didn't know of any current relationships. "Do you remember meeting my fiancée, Betty?" he asked. "You know, Betty, our purchasing manager." I congratulated him, but I got an instant pit in my stomach. He was dating the purchasing manager and I didn't even know it! These types of relationships among senior managers almost always lead to trouble.

That was red flag number three.

The CEO convinced us that he needed a new building to handle the growth after the acquisition. The new corporate headquarters seemed to be a fine vintage Massachusetts light industrial. The signage was dignified. The reception area was small and unobtrusive. Then I stepped into the CEO's new office. The CEO of AT&T should have it so good. It was about 2,000 square feet with a big mahogany desk and conference table for ten. That was just the start. A huge stuffed marlin hung on the wall behind the CEO's desk. Below the big-deal fish was a picture of his new forty-foot boat. There were fresh-cut flowers on the side table. And he had a wet bar. A wet bar, folks! Chivas, anyone? He offered me coffee from his personal Coffee-mate, but what I really needed just then was a martini.

Red flag numbers four through seven slapped me in the face.

At that very moment, I should have called him onto the lush carpet and ordered him to scale back and start thinking about his investors, but I restrained myself. To put it another way, I wimped out. I avoided the conflict. "Some office, Jim," I said as I sipped my coffee. The CEO explained that it was a great place for entertaining suppliers and an efficient space for meetings. This was the tile business. What did I know as a little Harvard Business School punk? Besides, we had seen a few months of financials and everything was pretty much on target. What did I care if he indulged himself just a little? The deal was on track. Relax, I said. You're paranoid. A pinkie ring is a sign of a winner in this industry.

In early December, I received November financials, which were slightly behind plan but up for the year. My boss congratulated me again on the deal. I figured I was as good as a partner by year-end. I visualized my new business card.

Then I got hit with a burning red flag even I couldn't ignore, no matter how hot I was about this deal. The second week in December, my secretary came in to tell me that Ceramic City's CFO was on the line. That's odd, I thought. I usually only spoke to the CEO, but figured he might be calling to ask some advice from a high-powered Harvard MBA on the nuances of finance. I was happy to oblige. I straightened out my new Hermes tie.

"Rick, it's Chris Williams at Ceramic City."

"Chris . . . good to hear from you. How are you?"

"Not very well, actually."

This was not a good sign, but I suspected he must have some personal problem he wanted to discuss with a budding master of the universe. Certainly, nothing could be going wrong with this deal—my deal, my ticket to partnership.

"Chris, you don't sound well . . ."

"I feel really bad about this," he said.

"Go ahead, Chris, just tell me what's up."

"Well, my conscience has gotten to me and I have to tell somebody what happened. I figured you're the right person."

The word *conscience* in this context is never a good sign. My forehead was warming. He had my attention.

"Listen, Chris, I can take it. What's the bottom line?" I asked. It was worse than I had ever expected.

"Well, when we prepared the financials on which you bought the company in September, we falsified the inventory records," he said haltingly. If "conscience" is a bad word, "falsified" is even worse. They had falsified records, which meant they had overstated profits. Through our discussion, I prayed that this was a small item, but I learned that their doctoring reduced profits by about 50 percent. My body temperature rose fifteen degrees and my undershirt dampened instantaneously.

In this brief conversation I had gone from being a deal god to a deal idiot. We had been hugely defrauded and would quickly break all bank covenants. We were likely to lose all our money, including a personal stake equal to two-thirds of my net worth. This would have a significant negative impact on our firm. Partnership? Perhaps at the local dry cleaner.

Here's what happened: The September deal had closed based on a June 30 audit by two (supposedly) high-quality auditors. In the middle of the audit, the CEO and purchasing agent (now his wife!) found out that the physical inventories of one of their largest tile items were vastly overstated. They had sold much more tile than the financials reflected, which meant they were much less profitable. When the CEO realized this, he had two choices. He could disclose the shortfall, restate earnings, and likely scrap or restructure the deal. He would then have no deal or would get much less than the $1 million he was to receive from the sale under the current terms. Say good-bye to the forty-foot boat, the marlin, and wet bar. Or he could do what he did: cover it up. He and his fiancée chose the latter course, rationalizing that they could make up the difference later. But the New England economy became progressively worse, along with any hope of covering up the deception. Greenspan I was not.

How did the CEO get not one but two auditors to sign off on inventory in the warehouse that didn't exist? He used a shell game. Believe it or not, the auditors had actually caught the problem. They had noted an inventory line item for Gumamella Italian ceramic tile that seemed way overstated to them, based on recent sales. They wanted to take a look. The call from the auditor sent the conspirators into a tizzy. But Jim settled in under his stuffed marlin and figured out exactly what to do. Have the auditors come see the tile, he said. It was all in the warehouse.

The auditors came down to see the merchandise. They went to a huge warehouse and saw box after box of ceramic tile labeled "Gumamella." When they added it up, it came to the right total. Bingo! They signed off on the report. What they didn't know was that the night before they arrived, the CEO, the purchasing manager, and the warehouse manager had changed the labels on all the boxes of random tile to say "Gumamella." They also changed the receiving documents to create a tidy paper trail. The CEO knew no auditor could possibly have any idea exactly what Gumamella, Mexican, or Spanish tile actually looked like.

After my humbling call from the CFO, I notified our banks and two days later took the red-eye to Boston to confront the CEO. He fiddled nervously with his pinkie ring as he denied everything. I had a signed affidavit from the warehouse manager stating exactly what happened the night they relabeled the boxes. Even with the proof of his guilt as plain as the stuffed marlin on his wall, he still denied it. I fired him on the spot. I put the COO in charge and began spending a lot of time in New England. After six months of swimming upstream against the deteriorating economy and increasing competition from big players like Home Depot, we declared bankruptcy. We lost all of our money and the bank took a 50 percent write-down on its loan. The only people that made out well were the bankruptcy lawyers.

The happy postscript to this story is that I didn't leave the investment business to become a telemarketer. I ended up making partner at Hancock despite this crash-and-burn experience. It was partly because of the hard work on picking up the pieces of Ceramic City and partly because I was helpful in another deal that went very well (a pool supply retailer named Leslie's Poolmart). So deal death didn't lead to career death, just a long winter in Stoughton, Massachusetts, which is about as close to death as one can come.

One of the most surprising postscripts to this story is that Jim landed on his feet. We had sued everyone and recovered some money from the accountants and some from the seller and got most of Jim's net worth. We didn't pursue criminal charges against Jim because our lawyers advised us it wasn't worth the trouble, especially since there was nothing else to get from him. So Jim moved to Texas with his former purchasing manager. Last I heard, he had become the CEO of another tile retailer, backed by a Texas venture capital firm. They never called us for a reference on their new CEO, so I can only wish them the best of luck. They will need it. Always do your reference checks. No matter how good people look on the surface, you don't know what kind of dark, slippery rock they may have crawled out from under—or what kind of tile is under that reassuring Gumamella label.

Lessons from Deal Hell

Not all deals fail as spectacularly as Ceramic City, but they do fail. Often it is from much more innocent causes, yet with just as devastating a result. As this story illustrates, there are risks involved in deals for both buyers and sellers.

The history of buyouts has some legendary corporate flameouts. The $1 billion purchase of Phar-Mor went belly-up within six months, entering Chapter 11 in 1992 after an embezzlement scheme by company executives. (The company emerged again in 1995.) It was Ceramic City with a few additional zeros at the end. That disaster was right up there with the 1989 "burning bed," the billion-dollar-disaster leveraged buyout of Sealy Mattress.

The more you know about what can go wrong with deals from an investor's perspective, the better chance you have to avoid the myriad potential deal pitfalls. Among the lessons I learned from Ceramic City are the following:

• *Watch for conflicts.* The problem with the Ceramic City CEO was that he was infinitely more focused on the sale than on making the business a success. Although he had equity in the deal, he also was making $1 million on the sale itself. He had been telling his fiancée and neighbors about it for weeks, and his focus on that pot of money caused him to put aside his judgment and risk his career. On the other side of the deal, if a potential equity partner has the incentive and the history to squeeze out management after the deal, watch your back. In the best deal, the interests of all parties should be aligned in making the deal and the business a success.

• *Consider the downside case.* It is very easy in the heat of the deal to look at the rosy best-case scenario. It is also important to take a long, hard look at the ugly worst-case scenario. Ceramic City was tied to the local economic cycle, and New England economy had been in a prolonged and terrible slump, particularly in real estate. We knew this when we bought the company, but we did lots of analysis on the economic trends and figured we were smart enough to bet that the economy couldn't get any worse. It could. Much worse. The economy sank further and stayed in a slump for three more years. Be careful that any deal you do can stand up to an economic slowdown. We also should have seen that the retail business had low barriers to entry, and Home Depot had no trouble moving in and driving down margins.

• *Be fanatical about your due diligence.* We did five reference checks on the CEO of Ceramic City, but they were all from his own reference list. Instead, you should ask each reference for the names of other references who are not on the list or who would say the worst things about the person. Believe me, I can script in advance what the references on a person's list will say: nothing but positives. That's why they're on the list! It's the people who know the protagonist who are not on the list that matter. Make those calls! I am not sure if this would have saved us from the Ceramic City fiasco, but it might have. We also did two separate audits and that still wasn't enough. Audits are not the gospel truth. Auditors don't have X-ray vision, and they cannot see into the dark hearts of managers or even beneath the labels of boxes. They attempt to tease out GAAP numbers as best an auditor can prepare them as an outsider. If sellers or partners want to screw you, they can. Furthermore, do more than your own reference checks. You should always ask your law firm to do a simple background and credit check on the CEO and CFO. It costs less than $2,000 per person and may be the best money you ever spend. Had the venture capitalists (VCs) in Texas run a simple background check, they would have turned up the litigation in the records and, I suspect, saved themselves lots of headaches.

• *Listen to your gut.* Because even the best due diligence may not turn up hidden problems with the deal, you also have to trust your own instincts. I had plenty of warning signs but was so horny to close the deal that I brushed aside all those red flags. Sometimes it's the small details, for better or worse, that turn you away from the deal. I will never do another deal with a guy with a pinkie ring. I know other investors who shun CEOs who sport tattoos or wear boots, shiny suits, or bolo ties, or are more than thirty pounds overweight. My personal favorite is the Silicon Valley venture capitalist who won't back any CEO whose last name is a vegetable. One can only imagine that at some point in this VC's past his deals with Bob Broccoli or Cal Carrot must have gone to seed.

• *Don't let sour deals sour relationships.* Deals come and go, but your reputation persists. In mopping up Ceramic City, we worked hard to take care of the lenders who had invested in the deal, protecting their investment as much as possible long after we had any hope of getting our money back. Even though it was the worst deal of my life, the relationships forged with the lenders remain one of my best professional references to this day. They know some deals will go south and they'll work with you if you treat them like partners. If you don't, they will nail you to the wall and it will haunt you for your entire career. If you handle a bad deal right, you will live to fight another day.

• *Choose your partners carefully.* One of the biggest lessons of bad deals is to be careful in your choice of partners. The Ceramic City CEO turned out to be a bad partner who took our investment and the company down with him. You cannot be too careful in choosing your partners—both for your management team and investors. When the winds come up and the ship is taking on water, you want to make sure you have all hands on deck. You also want to make sure you can trust the people you are working with. Even if you are initially aligned, it is not uncommon for alignment to shift over the course of the deal. If that happens, you don't want to find yourself sharing a bed with Jack the Ripper.

From your management team to your equity partners to bankers, you will have many partners in the deal. These partnerships will either help you build a stronger deal or lay the foundations for the destruction of the deal and perhaps the company. All dollars are not the same. Some of them have more strings attached than others. Some investors will help you build the business, others will only be looking to cash out quickly. Some will always treat you fairly, others will stab you in the back. Some will let you run the business, others will want to do it for you. For each potential partner, ask yourself: Will this still be a good partnership if we are wildly successful? What will this partner be like if the deal goes sour? Would I want this partner as a friend? Could I survive this partner as an enemy?

Don't Be Blinded by Love for a Deal

The quickest way into deal hell is to have lust in your heart. Passion and dreams are what bring people into deals, but this lovely siren song is also what draws them up upon the rocks. Their fatal attraction, personal emotional investment, and dreams of conquest keep them there long after they should walk away. If I hadn't been so hot to close that Ceramic City deal, I might have paid more attention to the pinkie ring and other glaring warning signs that were there all along.

We all are aware of this problem, yet it happens with deals all the time. The only place people set aside their rationality more quickly is in the bedroom. When you have to have the deal, it is much more likely that it will have you.

This is what happened to two friends of mine who graduated from Stanford Business School in 1987. They were determined to buy a business. It was their dream. They were smart guys who had always been successful. Both were in their late twenties, and they also happened to have the good fortune of being from wealthy and well-connected families. Furthermore, they had the backing of several successful senior professors from Stanford Business School. The professors agreed to help their students find a company, consult on the deal, provide some financing, and serve as directors after closing. It seemed as if they couldn't go wrong.

When these two Young Turks graduated from business school, they moved to Seattle, where their families lived. They formed a partnership, set up a big-hitter advisory board, rented office space, and gave their entity a prestigious-sounding name. They figured they'd give themselves two years, but really expected to close a big deal within six months. They were looking for companies in the greater Seattle area that were profitable with sales of at least $10 million.

That these two under-thirty MBAs had never run a company of that size, or any business for that matter, didn't seem to be a serious obstacle. They should have realized this deficiency and brought in someone with operating experience to advise them on the deal, but they jumped in and started networking. They called every business broker, investment banker, accountant, deal lawyer, and senior operating executive in town. They did meetings, handed out business cards, and schmoozed. They went to industry conferences, hoping to create deal flow.

In short order, they started to see deals. An accountant called and said someone was interested in selling the family company if the price was right. An investment banker called representing a company that wanted to sell a division. They started working through the pile, slowly improving their ability to separate the sludge from deals with potential.

Then an investment banker called with an exciting prospect. The young deal mavens went after it full bore. They fantasized about how this opportunity would make them deal gods. They crunched numbers for three months straight and racked up $50,000 in legal bills, travel, and research. They lined up financing with the help of their advisory board and put in a bid with the investment banker for $15 million. They could almost taste the closing dinner. They fast-forwarded a few years to when they sold the company and retired to Capri.

But the investment banker's next call threw cold water onto their beach. The banker thanked them for their bid and told them they were in the hunt. But they would have to raise their bid by $2 million if they wanted to go to the next round of the auction process. They called their advisers and agreed to raise their bid. "That's it," they said. "Not a dollar more."

The investment banker called back. Theirs was a "strong bid," but there are other strong bids. They would have to "sharpen their pencils." By now the investment banker had them right where he wanted them. They were emotionally tied to the deal. It meant everything to them. It would be unthinkable to just let nine months and $50,000 of capital drop away into expenses on this deal with nothing to show for it. They had to make it work. They had already told their wives and families about it. Their investors might pull the plug on the whole operation if this deal didn't pan out. They were caught, hanging on this deal. They couldn't get free. And the investment banker just let them twist in the wind.

They crunched the numbers again. They squeezed out another million dollars. The investment banker called. "Final bids are due tomorrow. It's you and two other parties. Frankly, you're management's first choice. You could own this thing, but you're going to have to be very aggressive. Sharpen your pencils." Of course, they were sure he told the same thing to the two other suckers, but what could they do? They had to have this deal.

The bid went in at $18 million, way beyond what any reasonable person would offer. But it didn't end there. The investment banker called the next day. "You're close. The bidding is so competitive we decided to hold it open another day." The two young dealers protested, ranting and raving, pounding their fists. It wasn't fair. This is unethical. Then they raised their bid another half-million dollars.

That was Friday. On Monday, they called the investment banker, who didn't return their call. Same for Tuesday. His secretary said he was in meetings. On Wednesday, his assistant called to say they'd signed a deal with a large corporate buyer at $22 million. "Thank you for participating. Your bid was very competitive." In other words, they never had a chance of winning the bid. They were just the stalking-horse to keep the big company honest.

After three years of grueling effort and sifting through hundreds of deals, the two Young Turks disbanded their partnership. One went on to run his family's investment business. The other went into investment banking. I guess he had learned through the process where all the fun and the money were to be found.

Through their own personal deal hell, these two investors learned a critical lesson. They now knew firsthand how easy it was to toy with the emotions of people who were so invested in the deal they couldn't see straight. Additionally, they learned never to get emotionally wed to a transaction. As a manager leading an MBO, you must do the same. Remain detached. It's only a deal, and believe me, another opportunity will come along.

Go in with Your Eyes Open

This is not to say you should avoid pursuing such deals. While some deals like Ceramic City will take you to the hot, lower circles of deal hell, others like Software AG lead to the cool, lofty breezes of deal heaven. Due diligence helps analyze risks inherent in the deal, but even the most carefully analyzed deal still has significant risk. When you're flying hundreds of miles per hour, thousands of feet above the ground, it's best to keep your hand firmly on the stick and your eyes on the terrain. You never eliminate risk. You can either get used to it or go back to a cozy little office at IBM. By understanding what can go wrong with the deal, you have a better chance of avoiding the most common mistakes. As Thomas Edison noted, "People are not remembered by how few times they fail, but by how often they succeed. Every wrong step is another step forward."

In the following chapters, we examine the ways you can structure deals to make them more successful. These strategies and hard-earned experience can help keep you on the straight-and-narrow path that leads you away from Ceramic City to a far better place.

CHAPTER 4

Find or Create Your Opportunity

"It often happens that I wake up at night and begin
to think about a serious problem and decide I must tell
the Pope about it. Then I wake up completely and
remember that I am the Pope."
—POPE JOHN XXIII (1881–1963)

Techway managers were in shock when the news came from headquarters. Their parent company, a large defense contractor, was planning to sell their $300 million information technology (IT) services unit. The parent made large pieces of military and other hardware and no longer wanted to be in the IT services area, a business that has no hard assets and is entirely dependent upon its people. The essence of Techway was its people and their capabilities. The division was a consulting business where professionals billed their time on large, federal government computing contracts. The hardware maker really didn't understand the business and treated it like a stepchild in the organization, denying it capital and applying parent-level policies that made no sense. Finally, the corporate parent decided to cut it loose.

This situation is simultaneously excruciating and exciting for any team. Does this mean we'll lose our jobs, or will we end up with a parent company that actually "gets it"? Or can we buy our firm ourselves? The senior managers of Techway knew they were sitting on an improving asset. What had first seemed to be a dark cloud on the horizon had a silver lining. What was a crisis, they now saw as an opportunity. They would buy the firm. The opportunity had been dropped in their laps.

Throughout the remaining chapters of the book, we will return to the Techway example to explore how these managers tackled key steps in the deal. We'll examine how they developed their strategy, put together their deal with the seller, forged their management deal with investors, and analyzed the expected return for themselves and their equity partners. This running case offers an illustration of the key principles of the book and buyout documents applied to the types of deals you might encounter in your own career.

As Techway managers found, every day large corporations are carving away huge parts of their business that no longer fit with their strategy. There is nothing wrong with these pieces that are tossed overboard, except that they are weighing down the mother ship. Managers whose divisions are tossed into the air in this fashion have an opportunity to either fall rapidly or take flight. It all depends on whether they're prepared to leave the nest. Techway's managers were ready, and when opportunity knocked, they answered.

But other times, opportunities to own a company do not come chasing you down. You have to pursue them. You have to find your own launching pad. You have to dream the dream and follow it— either by buying another company or building a new firm from a series of acquisitions.

This chapter examines the distinctive challenges of each of these approaches. In the first section, we explore leading the revolution from within to buy your own firm. In the second, we look at buying or building a company from the outside.

Leading the Revolution from Within

When companies such as Techway's parent decide to sell business units, the managers running that business usually face a bleak future. Their divisions will very likely be downsized and combined with the existing business of an outside acquirer. Most of the time, the managers will be out on the street. So they hunker down to see what happens. Or, like rats on a sinking ship, they start scurrying out the stern lines, dusting off their resumes and looking for their next company. This is just the time when managers should be thinking about leading a management buyout (MBO). The buyout allows them to go from drowning rats to captains of their own ship.

As the experience of Dan Gillis and Harry McCreery of Software AG shows (see Chapter 1), managers don't have to wait for internal deals to come to them. They can see the opportunity and initiate the process before the parent puts the company up for sale. These buyout opportunities are everywhere, but they are usually hard for managers to see because managers are used to looking at the business as it is today. They are not used to analyzing buyout possibilities, and the world of MBOs is a foreign land.

Why Would a Company Want to Sell to Management?

With all the well-endowed potential suitors out there, why would owners want to sell the business to incumbent managers? Many managers assume they are at a disadvantage in bidding against large corporations and other buyout firms. They don't realize managers actually have several advantages that give them an edge in putting together the deal and pitching it to owners. Among the advantages of selling to current managers are:

• *Secrecy.* Even with the best precautions, having outsiders rummaging through the company and conducting due diligence will expose some confidential information that the seller would prefer not to reveal. Buyers are often large competitors. Most companies would rather not share their client lists or balance sheets for their business units with rivals. This process inevitably gives away trade secrets and tricks of the trade to competitors. As insiders, the current management already knows everything it needs to know to complete the deal. A sale to inside managers maintains the company's confidentiality.

• *Continuity.* When a business is for sale, a lot of the equity walks out the door during the disruption of the sale process. A sale process is painful. It creates uncertainty and turnover among employees and stops long-term investment projects. Customers and suppliers feel the pain and uncertainty, too. And it usually lasts six to nine months, which is now like two lifetimes in corporate America. This period can dramatically erode the overall value of the company, particularly if the process drags on or doesn't go through. An MBO, on the other hand, reduces the disruption of an open sale and ensures continuity of the management. The internal managers understand all the business risks and know how to quantify and analyze them. They're the perfect buyers.

• *Speed.* An inside MBO deal can be put together much more quickly than an outside sale. The process of due diligence and ironing out all the details of the sale move much more rapidly for managers who are already inside the firm. The average buyout can be done in a period of about three to four months rather than the nine months it typically takes for an auction. This speed means more money and less disruption for the owners.

• *Lower Investment Banking Fees.* Investment banking fees for owners who shop the company around for an outside sale usually run between 1 and 4 percent of the overall value. These fees can be avoided through a management-led buyout.

• *Dummy Insurance.* If the business takes off after the sale, the seller ends up looking like a dummy for letting it go. A management deal often offers the opportunity for the seller to take a piece of the new deal. In the SAGA Software deal, German parent Software AG continued to hold 10 percent of the company, so it has benefited handsomely from the company's subsequent success. For managers in the buyout firm, this continued investment gives the new company additional capital and a corporate blessing that reassures customers and suppliers. For the corporate bureaucrats selling the business, however, it serves as a form of "dummy insurance." If they underestimate the value of a business, they can still point to the fact that they share in the upside.

For these reasons, the owners may actually prefer to sell to the current management rather than to an outside bidder, if the price is right. Managers who propose a buyout should point out these advantages to the owners. Particularly if the seller wants to move quickly, these arguments could help avoid an auction for the business.

Even if your persuasive arguments for doing an exclusive man-agement deal are not heeded by senior management and the deal goes to auction, you should still get internal clearance to pursue the deal. In this case, an investment bank will organize an orderly pro-cess and you will be one of a group of bidders for the company. You should pursue the deal if you can, even if you think you may lose at the outset. I've seen many management teams who ap-peared outgunned at the start of the contest go on to win the day. Sometimes the rivals drop out or discover concerns that manage-ment already had factored into its offer. There is a lot that can go wrong, and if managers are in the game, they can quickly step in.

Even if you don't win the bid, you'll learn a great deal in the process, which will be beneficial to your future deal making. While it is expensive to mount a bid, you'll normally, as an insider to the company, learn early on whether your prospective proposal has a chance of success. This gives you an opportunity to bow out early (and gracefully) and save your capital for another day or to com-pete vigorously for the prize. Either way, you'll never win unless you step up to the plate. So pick up your biggest bat and move into the batter's box.

Advantages for Management

In addition to the advantages an MBO offers sellers, there are ad-vantages for the management team and investors that may allow them to put together a better deal. Their biggest advantage is that they really know what they are buying. While outside investors must be content to kick the tires, management has had a chance to test-drive the company. The others have been given the real es-tate tour, but management has lived in the house and experienced the plumbing and electrical system. This is a far better basis for putting together a deal. Usually managers can think of a dozen ways to spruce up the company and strategy, particularly when it is unhitched from the parent. Among the advantages managers have over outside buyers:

• *Strategic Insights.* Managers know how the policies and con-straints of the corporate parent may be holding back the business. They know exactly where they can cut costs or move in new strate-gic directions. Some of these directions can come from fairly subtle observations of customers and astute listening to their concerns. Management is in a far better position to recognize these strategic opportunities than outside buyers. Any strategic buyer will want to assess where profits are lost or strengths are underutilized. Management has the clearest view of the answers.

• *Knowing Where the Bodies Are Buried.* Unlike outside investors, managers don't have to wait for due diligence to hope they identify problems in the target firm. They know the firm inside and out. They know the soft and rotten parts that can be cut out, and they know the fertile areas that can be better exploited. They know where the bodies are buried and how to exhume them. Bottom line: They know the risks and the rewards. This gives them an edge in the process.

• *A Team Standing Behind You.* If management launches a bid, the entire employee base in that unit will typically be behind the deal and energized to gain independence with the team they've known. They know that a management deal will keep the company intact and normally preserve the employee base. This energy will be felt at corporate, which will recognize some of the many intangible benefits of a management-led deal.

Making an Offer

For a company that is already on the block, the approach to the owners is fairly straightforward. After doing homework about the value of the firm and developing a strategy (discussed in Chapter 5), managers express their interest in buying the firm. They then put their numbers up against those of other bidders. In most cases, the managers understand the strategic potential of the business well enough to compete formidably with strictly financial investors. Strategic investors such as rivals, however, may have opportunities to create synergies or strip out overhead that managers cannot hope to match on their own. In these cases, it may be difficult for the management team to outbid the outsiders.

Understand the Seller

You need to understand the motivations of the seller. Be sure there are good strategic reasons for the company to sell the business. Gillis and McCreery knew Software AG needed to raise cash quickly and the U.S. division was the only asset it could sell. Understanding this strategic motivation allowed them to put together a successful deal because the deal met the parent's immediate need for liquidity.

If the seller is motivated primarily by price, it is usually not the best environment for an MBO. The seller will push for the best price, which will likely bring in investment bankers and may bring in other bidders who drive up the price. Then you will be in a strictly price-driven bidding war, which is the worst place to be. If selling to management doesn't add strategic value in the eyes of the seller, you are on shaky ground. Work hard to understand all the motivations of the seller right up front.

Unsolicited Bids

A far more challenging prospect is making an unsolicited bid for the business as Gillis and McCreery did with SAGA. In this case, sometimes asking the question can put an end to your career in the organization. Top management will question your allegiances. But if you are successful and can make a convincing case for going with the management deal, it can lead to a buyout in which the management team is the exclusive buyer.

In making unsolicited bids, the approach to the owner also requires more finesse. Remember that Gillis initially approached then-CEO Schnell through a board member to make the proposal a little less direct, but it also meant that he never really knew if the message got through. Gillis was fully prepared to walk away from the company if the deal didn't work out. This is always a possibility in an unsolicited bid, so managers should have a plan for this outcome.

In making an unsolicited bid, managers often will want to line up prospective buyout partners before approaching the seller. This way, they can present owners with a fully formed, coherent, and at least partially financed proposal. Lining up partners has another important benefit. These partners can be used as straw men in presenting the deal. For example, the corporate development officer of a major corporation wanted to buy a unit of the firm. She didn't want to jeopardize her position, but she did want to find out whether the parent company would be willing to sell the unit. So she found a buyout partner and then told the owners that she had found someone who was interested in buying the firm (which was true, of course). This way, if the owners turn down the proposal, management is just doing its duty in bringing the offer to the table. If the owners express interest, management can then proceed with the deal. Putting the buyout partner forward as the buyer also helps to avoid some of the political forces that can tear apart a deal. Once other managers in the organization get wind of the deal and egos become involved, no one does well.

The obvious issue to be careful about with this approach is to choose your partners wisely and firm up your management deal (discussed in Chapter 7) before you approach the seller. At the point at which the buyout firm discusses the deal with the seller, there is nothing stopping that firm from dumping management and buying the firm or putting pressure on management to give up ground. Most strategic investors wouldn't do this, but some financial investors are notorious for eleventh-hour changes to a deal, and you should be careful to protect yourself.

The Worst Case: A Stay Bonus
If you are careful about the approach and offer a fair price, what is the worst that can happen? The seller may decide not to sell to management for many different reasons. At this point, since you are already in discussions about the deal, you should raise the idea of a "stay bonus" for yourself and your team.

When the sale goes through, the parent company often is willing to pay a percentage of the price to the management team (usually 1 to 2 percentage points) to keep the team motivated in getting the best deal for the unit and providing strong leadership after the sale. A bonus is more likely in a strategic sale, where committed management is an important part of the deal, but corporations only agree to such conditions a quarter to a third of the time. Given how substantial this small cut can be, however, it certainly doesn't hurt to ask. For the sellers, it ensures management will work with them to get the best possible deal and make it work after the sale.

One Foot in the Future, One in the Past
There is an inherent conflict in an internal management buyout. You are both manager and buyer, employee of the organization and negotiator with the organization. You want to get the lowest possible price and the owners want to get the highest possible

price. The best way to address this conflict is to put it right on the table at the outset. You need to state your commitment to continuing to work for the best interests of the company regardless of the outcome.

Most problems occur when managers become greedy and want to put the screws to the owners. In some cases, managers have an ability to create doubts in the minds of other buyers and to reduce the value of the company. But these tactics usually backfire in the long run. The long-term value of the company may be eroded, which hurts the managers after they acquire it. The acquirer may also see through the management smoke screen and it is sure to create bad feelings all around. The acquiring firm would be unlikely to keep the management team around after sale.

The best way to avoid real or apparent conflicts in the process is to be fair and open in your dealings with the seller throughout the process. Disclose all potential conflicts. You need to do a thorough assessment of the value of the business and offer a fair price. If negotiations are fair and fact-based all around, this should minimize conflict. You have to recognize the seller's fiduciary responsibility to get the best price.

You also have to keep doing your job during the buyout process. Particularly early on, the buyout is an extracurricular activity. It can be very time-consuming, but you cannot let it interfere with running the business. You must continue to execute your day job and become a buyout guru at night. You have an obligation to keep running the business. Once the parent has blessed the deal, more of the buyout business can be done during the workday.

While buyout opportunities may sometimes drop into your lap, other times the unit you are running is integral to the company's strategy. You will be stuck here for life if you don't do something. That is when you might consider going out shopping for a new company to lead and own. This is what Stu Johnson did.

Building a Company from the Outside

Stu Johnson had come close to becoming CEO of a major company several times in his career, but every time he saw the prize snatched away. As the youngest vice president at Burroughs, he had a strong shot at the top job before the Unisys merger. Again as a top executive at PRC, his career aspirations were derailed by an acquisition by Emhart. He was given the nod as the designated successor to the CEO of Contel Corporation, but two days later the company was approached by GTE and sold. Johnson set up a new network integration business at Bell Atlantic with the expectation that when he built a great business in this area, it would be spun off as a separate company. But after he built a thriving new business, the parent company found it was reluctant to part with it. Bell Atlantic's merger with NYNEX made it opportunistic for him to leave, so he did.

"I've had a management career that has been satisfying but not totally fulfilling," said the intense former U.S. Navy pilot. "I was a prisoner of business in the 1980s. I was merged or bought out of three companies. It has always been my goal, my ambition, to run a publicly held company, to be the chairman, to be the person who is accountable for the strategic direction and leadership of the company. It was one of my unfulfilled desires. I still had enough years left in the work world and enough ambition to say if I am not going to do it with someone else's company, I'll do it with my own."

This section discusses a second way managers such as Johnson can leverage their expertise to run their own firms. Instead of buying out their own companies, as Gillis and McCreery did, they can lead a buyout of other companies—either buying another firm or rolling up a series of firms from the outside. We look at Johnson's experience in information technology services. We also examine the experiences of Roger Ballou, whom we met in Chapter 2, in leveraging his extensive travel industry experience into a new business that has created tremendous value for him and investors. The remainder of this chapter discusses the importance of matching the business to the skills of the manager, how to set up search criteria, and where to find suitable acquisition targets. Finally, we look at how to analyze potential acquisitions, find financing, and build the business.

Entrepreneurial Skills
Johnson had already started four or five major new ventures within corporations, so he knew how to put together the vision and management team to make it happen. "My modus operandi had always been to create new businesses within the corporate structure," he

said. He launched interactive video and Internet businesses at Bell Atlantic and grew a voice and data network integration business from scratch to a $300 million operation in three years.

Although he had outstanding skills in building and operating companies, Johnson knew he didn't have the entrepreneurial experience he needed to launch a new company. He turned to a friend and golfing partner, Bill Albright, who had successfully started and led several technology-based companies. Albright provided the entrepreneurial vision and track record that complemented Johnson's experience. "Without him, I wouldn't have gotten the company this far. I had a partner who could fill in the voids for me, someone who had done it before," Johnson said. "Knowing what you don't know is important for anybody at any stage in their career. I knew I had someone who had done it before. I had the strategy, vision, and staffing accountability and he had the make-it-happen responsibility."

The original strategy was to take the systems integration experience Johnson had applied to the corporate market at Bell Atlantic and drive down into the middle market in the exploding area of Internet services. In particular, they investigated the possibility of building a leading e-commerce consulting firm via a series of acquisitions. There were other firms looking at this same consolidation model and there was strong interest from investors. Johnson, who is a careful and deliberate thinker, didn't want to jump into it too quickly. He and Albright spent two months driving from Boston to South Carolina talking to customers and suppliers in the mid-market information technology space. They visited companies, met with potential customers to discuss their concerns, and also sat down with several investor groups that were hot to do an Internet services consolidation. He learned the terms "promote fee" and "management carry." And he learned once again that what he was really after was something more than money.

Financial Deals
Johnson was pretty close to moving forward with a quick roll-up* and cash out, but he realized these financial deals would fill his

*A roll-up is a simultaneous acquisition of several companies that then (often simultaneously) target an initial public offering (IPO). This quick slamming together of companies was a hot idea in the late 1990s, but largely proved unsuccessful due to acquisition integration challenges.

pockets but not the hole in his heart. His strength was in building and running companies, not financial machinations. He just had no stomach for it. While money wasn't inconsequential, it wasn't the main reason he was interested in a deal. He wanted to build and run a company.

"I came to the conclusion that if we did a roll-up, we would make some money, have a little bit of fun, but we would not be building a company. We would be building a financially engineered model that was current in the marketplace that was creating no value for anybody. I am not a financial engineer. I need to run things. I need to build things. When we talked to financial investors, we found they had no expectation other than the IPO and running away.

"I probably have made more money than I will spend in my lifetime," he said, a reflection of both his career success and his modest lifestyle. It wasn't money Johnson wanted; it was a legacy. "Stu Johnson isn't going to end up his last real tangible job in the world creating some financially engineered, bandaged company that no one would ever look to and say 'that was a great effort,'" he said. He changed his strategy to look at building a strong operating company and began putting together a management team that could run it. The company, originally called BrightLight and Empyrean (the "highest heaven" in medieval cosmology), was later renamed Iconixx.

Building the Dream Team
In addition to building his own company, a big driver for Johnson was to pull together a team of managers he respected and had worked with over the past ten to fifteen years. This was his dream team. "I saw this [experience] as my petri dish," he said. "I could build a company based on some management tenets and principles I had always thought worked well and now had a chance to test in public markets."

To his surprise, when he approached his team, they signed on to a man. "I was both flattered and a little terrified, because all of them do not have the independence that I have," Johnson said. "They have houses and little children, not ones that are out of college like mine. We made it clear to them that there were risks . . . they needed to be aware of. We gave them our commitment that we would work very hard to [succeed]. Since they had always been successful with me in the past, they just extrapolated that into the future."

Now, not only his legacy but also the careers of his managers were riding on the success of the business. At the end of 1998, with the infusion of some additional seed capital, he brought the team on board. As he and the management team began to challenge and refine the strategy, they looked more closely at the role of the Internet in the midmarket. One of the managers had participated in an Internet start-up and they analyzed the technology adoption curve in the midmarket. It became clear that the use of the Internet was starting to shift for midsize firms. IT, which had primarily been seen as a way to cut costs through reducing accounts receivables or boosting inventory turns, now was being looked upon as a strategic tool. This shift represented a terrific opportunity, and Johnson's team restructured their strategy to take advantage of it.

Building Up
There are additional risks to the type of buildup that Johnson wanted to pursue, compared to the buyout of a single established firm. Roger Ballou, who was already in the midst of his buildup when Johnson launched his company, knew this well. "One is a known entity, with a lot more certainty," said Ballou, CEO of Global Vacation Group (GVG). "The buildup has a lot more risk and complexity. In a buyout, you are taking an existing entity and changing ownership structure. In a buildup, you are taking a number of existing entities and constructively putting them together. You have to have the math work to take one plus one and equal three."

For a buildup strategy to work, there also needs to be a strong flow of deals in the pipeline. In October of their first year, Ballou's GVG was moving ahead with five deals, with the first three scheduled to close in December. By the end of the year, two had failed due diligence. The owner of the third company got cold feet and backed out at the eleventh hour. "We had invested a lot of management time and a chunk of money and wound up with no deals," Ballou said. "It was a downer at the end of the year, but we had two more in the pipeline and accelerated them in the first quarter."

Both Ballou and Johnson had thought long and hard about how to conduct a buildup. But neither had done many acquisitions in the past and neither had ever parallel-processed five to ten acquisitions at one time. This is difficult for any manager, and it takes a well-educated team with significant deal experience. In the case of Johnson, he had a deal expert on his team named Tom Modly who processed the acquisition flow. Ballou relied more heavily on our team at Thayer Capital as his equity sponsor. Both men, however, were able to attract buildup capital because they were (1) successful senior executives with an outstanding record of success; (2) prepared with a detailed plan that demonstrated knowledge of the acquisition multiples in the space and a clear exit strategy; and (3) aware of the significant challenges of integrating several companies.

It is important to note that doing a series of acquisitions of smaller companies is challenging for many reasons. First, a small company tends to have weaker management than a larger company. Often, only one or two managers determine the results of the small company. Taking the helm of a small company is risky, and you need excellent management depth to execute. Second, smaller companies tend to have weak or nonexistent information systems. Often entrepreneurs run these businesses by feel or out of a shoebox. Third, joining employees and disparate suppliers of a series of small companies with different cultures presents many problems. Most important of all is considering the culture of the different entities, which is often overlooked. Are they aggressive and confrontational or collegial and consensual? If you put companies from different cultures together and expect them to work seamlessly, you're crazy. It's like mixing lions and lambs. Be careful on these acquisitions, plan diligently, and go slowly. Given these risks, one must pay lower acquisition multiples for smaller companies. I'd target a 20–30 percent discount to comparable public companies to reflect this "small company risk." As always, valuation is important.

Strategies for Success

What does it take to successfully organize and lead a buyout or industry consolidation from the outside? First, it is a given that the manager must have some significant experience in the industry. As with the internal buyout, you must be able to identify some way you can add strategic value to the company and create value for shareholders.

Setting Your Headings

Before you go out to begin searching for your company, you have to set your criteria. These criteria may evolve as you go through the process, but they must be carefully thought through and written down before you make a single call. You need to find a company that matches your skills and develop a strategy for adding value post-acquisition. This effort will help you establish your search criteria, which you will use to screen potential investment opportunities. If you don't take the time to map this part of your approach carefully, you will be investing your time haphazardly in deals in which you cannot leverage your strengths and will be unlikely to find financial partners.

Finding a Good Fit

The first rule is to know yourself. Make a list of the skills you bring to the table. One way to engage in this process is to update and review your resume, looking beyond the job titles for specific skills and patterns of experience you can exploit. Are you a finance person, a marketing person, or a production person? Do you know a certain industry inside and out? Are you a turnaround manager or a builder? Are you a detail person or a big-picture guy? Which industries are you passionate about? Have you run small or large companies? Have you worked with outside investors? What is your record of success (you must be brutally honest here)? Have you had business failures? What circumstance led to those failures and what do they tell you about your own weaknesses? How can you shore up these weaknesses?

Roger Ballou had run a billion-dollar travel services company before he took on GVG. Stu Johnson was one of the pioneers of the network integration market. When he launched Iconixx to take his insights to the middle market, there was no doubt that he had the experience to do it.

It is possible to start a new business outside of your area of expertise, but your chances of success are far lower. You also will have a very difficult time finding investors who will back you. If you move out of your industry, you need to come up with a convincing story for how your experience can lead to success in your targeted sectors if you hope to raise a dollar of capital from a professional investor or bank.

A manager came in recently to pitch me on a deal in the high-end audio retail industry. He wanted to consolidate the industry. It was a great idea. The strategy was contrarian and well thought out. The industry had performed poorly for three years because of limited new product introductions, and the upcoming shift to digital technology would promote large replacement purchases. He had identified a target company, began negotiating the deal at a pretty good price, and needed equity financing. He had an impressive background as a lawyer who had led successful deals in the cable and radio industries. He was credible and thoughtful. But I asked him one question: "How is this like your prior experience?" He likened the shift to digital in audio to the shift from regulation to deregulation in cable and radio. I had invested previously in retail and knew these were totally different beasts. Cable and radio are oligopolies protected by regulation and license. Retail is fierce, with none of the barriers to entry that protect cable and radio and a need for a more hands-on management style. While his previous experience was interesting, the bottom line was that he had no retail expertise. Before we would participate, he needed to find a partner with extensive retail expertise.

Your acquisition criteria have to fit your expertise. If the largest company you've run is a firm with $20 million in revenue, don't take on a $200 million firm. If you have spent your life running service businesses, don't target a manufacturing firm. Going way off your experience base erodes your credibility and reduces your chances of success.

Assessing Your Background

How do you assess what type of buyout you are prepared to take on? I met recently with a young and aggressive group of managers who were just finishing Wharton's Executive MBA program. They all worked for large concerns, mostly in the chemical and industrial manufacturing areas. Their companies expected them to return after their MBA program, but an exciting entrepreneurial studies professor at Wharton named Terry LaPier had inspired them: They needed to control their own destinies. They were talented managers who wanted meaningful equity positions and were hungry to get going. I had the chance to speak in the professor's class and they pinned me down afterward.

One of the managers knew of a company in the industry that was for sale. It was a $200 million annual revenue company. How could they get started? And what should they look for? Did they have what it takes to get funding and get the project off the ground? Could they pull this off?

To assess the situation, I asked them a series of questions that an investor would ask about the team:

1. *Did they have full profit and loss (P&L) responsibility at their current companies?* One of them did and the other two had only revenue responsibility. This is a typical structure in many large companies. So the manager with the P&L responsibility needed to be the CEO in the group: She was the most backable. These are the types of issues that investors and lenders evaluate immediately. Without full P&L responsibility on the team, they probably won't back you to buy anything. Investors want someone who's been in the trenches before.

2. *How big is that P&L?* The CEO-to-be handled $150 million in revenue. This is an issue. A buyout firm is unlikely to back a team that had run a $150 million business to buy a $200 million firm. It was potentially doable but a stretch, I told them.

3. *Were the year-to-year results for the last three years strong in the manager's unit?* The manager had been running it for two years and the results were good. The manager had improved margins and grown the business at 12 percent while the industry was growing at 6 percent. Could she prove it? Yes, she had the numbers to back it up. Not bad. The story overall was pretty solid.

The size of the business was the big concern. I told them they'd be better off targeting a company with $80 million to $100 million in revenue, which would be a slam dunk given their experience and would make it much easier to attract investors. Again, if you learn nothing else from this book, credibility is everything.

If you have to go outside your own area, bring in partners or advisers who can give you the expertise you need. The team of Wharton managers could have brought in a different CEO with P&L experience at a slightly larger firm. That would have rounded out the team and given them the firepower to take on the larger deal. Just as you need to put together a compelling story for the deal, you also need to put together a team that will make that story credible.

Establishing Search Criteria

How do you sketch out your search criteria? Let's use a real-life example of a search criteria sheet for a CEO we now know well, Dan Gillis of SAGA. If Gillis were to leave SAGA to work toward the acquisition of another company (our firm would back him in a second), sensible acquisition criteria might be:

Dan Gillis: MBO Search Criteria

- *Goal.* To lead a management buyout and become a major equity holder in Newco.
- *Targeted Industries.* IT services and products, specifically targeting middleware, mainframe software, and related services. We will consider hardware-based companies with special characteristics.

> Gillis targets industries in which he has extensive experience, with enough focus so intermediaries and financing partners can help. Managers need to be careful not to define the target industry too broadly. In Gillis's case, "IT services," for example, would be too broad. In the case of the chemical and manufacturing managers in the Wharton program, their primary industry of choice was "light industrial manufacturing." They wondered if this was an appropriate target for their criteria sheet. In fact, it isn't. The reason is that the category is too broad. Industrial manufacturing could include aircraft fasteners, sporting goods, and disposable hospital supplies. The narrower and more specific the criteria, the better. The reasons are twofold:
>
> 1. A more targeted search makes your job easier. You know what you're looking for, which SIC codes to research, and which trade shows to attend.
>
> 2. Specificity is helpful to intermediaries such as investment banks you'll contact about your search. If you're pursuing "light manufacturing," that's too generic, and investors won't think of you

when they hear about opportunities. If you're pursuing "sporting goods," that's much more focused, and when a sporting-goods deal comes through, they'll know you're the team to call.

- *Experience of the Team.* Dan Gillis, president and CEO of SAGA, 1995–present, former president of Falcon Microsystems. Falcon had $250 million of revenue and grew at over 20 percent per annum under Gillis's leadership. He had full profit and loss responsibility.

   This last point seems small but shouldn't be passed over. As discussed previously, full P&L responsibility, not just responsibility for revenue or costs, is critical. If you don't have full P&L responsibility, you should make that clear.

- *Board of Advisers.* Two or three impressive names with relevant industry experience.

   Most successful managers or entrepreneurs know some prominent people in their industry or others who can add credibility to the proposal. They can help advise you as you go forward and serve as a reference. You won't need to pay them anything at this point, but should pay them if a deal closes. Even then, don't give them cash, but give them options in your company and a chance to invest personally in the deals you source. Giving them options on $20,000 to $30,000 in stock, depending on the size of the deal, should suffice. Our firm's advisory board benefits from the support of Vernon Jordan, Jack Kemp, Dan Altobello, Jim Robinson, Drew Lewis, and Frank Zarb, among others.

- *Target Revenue Range.* $100 million to $250 million per annum.

   The range is wide but appropriate. It fits with what Gillis has done in the past and is wide enough to give intermediaries some guidance.

- *Profitability.* 5–15 percent pretax margins; will not consider turnarounds.

   This is common sense but important. Turnaround work requires a completely different set of skills from ongoing management, and if you're not a turnaround person, make it clear.

- *Financing Sources.* Team, Thayer Capital, Chase Bank, others.

  It is important to demonstrate that you also are willing to invest your capital at some level and that you have some preliminary banking relationships.

- *Targeted Equity Rates of Return.* At least 30 percent per annum.

  All private equity firms require target internal rates of return in the 30–40 percent range per annum. If your deal pencils in to only 20 percent, you won't be able to attract investors and you're probably paying too much for the target. If your deal pencils in to over 50 percent per annum, that's exciting to all, but are your projections unrealistic? Do a credibility check on those numbers. We'll examine a model for calculating rates of returns for management and investors in Chapter 8.

- *Geography.* Mid-Atlantic Region.

  Different investment firms focus on different regions. If you have a geographic preference, people really like to know.

Deciding Budget and Time Frame

As you put together your criteria, you also need to determine the budget in both time and money that you are willing to commit to the project. Be prepared to spend at least a year looking for a company and set an outside time frame for yourself. For example, if you don't get a deal signed up within twelve to fifteen months, you may want to reconsider your efforts. If you decide this time frame at the start, it will help when you are deep into the project and more likely to continue flogging a dead horse.

In addition to an overall budget, you should establish a monthly budget with targets for relevant research materials, travel and entertainment expenses, and third-party costs such as legal, accounting, and consulting services for the earlier part of your search. Kicking off this process need not be expensive at all, and you can easily get started while you're still working at your day job. All it takes to get going is a little elbow grease and a couple pieces of paper. Expenses in the early months, including travel, should only be $1,000 to $2,000 per month. The process can get very expensive, however, once you get into "real deal" mode. That's when legal and accounting expenses, perhaps consultants, and certainly travel can start burning up the bucks. By the time real legal and accounting due diligence gets done, you could easily be at $50,000 to $100,000 for accounting and another $50,000 to $100,000 for legal expenses. All of these expenses get reimbursed at closing (if it closes). All in all, be prepared. Buying a company is not cheap.

Setting Strategy

The general investment criteria sketched out previously in this chapter would work for a manager who is still formulating a strategy for acquisitions. This sheet can be the basis for discussions with investment partners and potential acquisition partners. But some executives, like Stu Johnson, prefer to bring a more fully developed strategy and team to the table. They realize that the more complete the strategy and team, the less risk there is for investors, the more value they create, and the greater piece of the pie they can command for themselves. This concept—focusing on the value that management can create for itself by doing the homework and locking up a deal—is key to this book and is discussed extensively in Chapter 7.

The strategy also must clearly target the type of opportunities the manager plans to pursue. It also must clearly show how the management team can add value in the process of evaluating and managing the company. With this demonstrated value, it is much more likely that the team can capture that value when it puts together its term sheet with investors. Developing and presenting the strategy for the business is discussed in more detail in Chapter 5.

Finding Companies to Acquire

Now that you know what you are looking for in an acquisition, where do you look? Potential acquisitions come from networking, either through your existing network in your industry or through investors and other channels. Once you get the word out that you are looking, deal opportunities start to flow in. The clearer you can be about your criteria in the beginning, the more qualified leads you will receive. Going to an investment banker and saying you want to buy anything with revenue above $5 million will get you nowhere. The most important element in the early parts of your research and in meetings with prospective sources of deals is to be well prepared and to have a clear set of deal criteria.

Working the Network

Before you begin beating the bushes for deals, you want to target people with expertise in your area of interest. Make calls to your most senior local advisers and contacts. For example, if you are interested in technology companies, particularly software firms, find out which accounting firms, business brokers, investment bankers, and lawyers have meaningful practices and expertise in that area. Use personal introductions to these professionals whenever you can in order to dramatically improve the quality and timing of a meeting. A blind call to an investment banker will likely be met with derision, catcalls, and cancellations. First the investor's assistant will be reluctant to return calls, then the receptionist will balk at taking messages, and finally you will feel like voicemail doesn't even have time for you.

Each of the different sources of deal opportunities has different qualities and motivations for helping you in your search. The role of each is outlined here:

• *Investment Bankers.* The investment bank is an intermediary, primarily facilitating brokerage trades, equity and debt offerings, and trades of companies (i.e., mergers and acquisitions). All investment banking firms have specialty groups that focus on specific industries. Be sure to get in front of the group that is focused on your part of the world. Their primary motivation to work with you is the collection of fees derived from the completion of these transactions. Fees vary widely depending on the financing or nature of the transaction, but net closing fees usually range between a half percent and 2 percent, depending on the size of the deal. In the meeting with investment bankers, lay out your criteria and discuss ways that they can help you. Do not be shy about committing to pay fees. They are always paid on a success basis and are key to motivating the banker to do work on your behalf. If you have proprietary ideas, do not share them openly unless you feel tremendous trust or have a prior relationship. At the end of the meeting, lay out a specific action and follow-up plan with the bankers. They are usually tremendously busy and hard to pin down, so be specific with follow-up items. Also, while you're there, be sure to ask them for their research on the industry you're looking at. They'll give it to you. Furthermore, ask to be put on their research mailing list for paper and electronic distribution. They'll often do it, and this information will be extremely valuable to you in all facets of the project, now and in the future.

• *Business Brokers.* Business brokers perform similar functions to investment banking M&A departments but focus primarily on much smaller companies (generally below $50 million revenues). Brokers provide little or no service beyond pure brokerage— bringing buyer and seller together and collecting a fee. They are generally small or one-person firms with no research coverage or other investment banking services. Typically, larger firms seek out a full-service investment bank to provide research and analysis. Business brokers typically cold-call numerous private business owners of family-held companies and get the owner on the line. They tell the owner they represent buyers interested in companies such as theirs and ask if the owner is interested in discussing a sale. If the owner says no, they are on to the next one. If the owner says anything that sounds directionally like yes, the broker has a fish on the line. The broker then calls a handful of potential buyers, normally private equity firms, to say the company is available for sale. The broker usually will not say much more until you sign a fee agreement. When you sign it, the broker sends you some information about the company and aims to collect a fee if a sale is consummated in the next year. The broker normally attends the first meeting or two, but in general the heavy lifting on the deal will be up to you.

Brokers are sometimes characterized as the used car salesmen of the deal business because they do almost no work in qualifying the seller. Without checking under the hood, they get the business on the lot and work hard to move it off again. As a buyer, if you recognize that these sellers may be unqualified and perhaps even unwilling, it can still be valuable to have a chance to meet with them. You just need to be careful. Bring in your own mechanic to check under the hood because there are no guarantees. You need to look very carefully for the junky, small, troubled companies that often creep into the mix. You also need to watch out for owners who may want to meet with prospective buyers for fun or pure deal curiosity but have no intention of actually selling their firms. With these caveats, brokers can be an important source of nonauction transactions that are worth looking at. You should work the broker-age community hard and be sure to let them know you'll take care of their fees. In its early days, KKR bought several companies from a business broker in Los Angeles named Harry Roman. Harry did very well and KKR built the foundation for its empire on these early business-broker opportunities.

• *Accounting Firms.* Accounting firms can be another source of transactions. As close tax advisers to business owners through their auditing and consulting practices, they have a direct line on many emerging opportunities. When business owners are contemplating selling the company, the first two people they will likely call to discuss the idea are an accountant and lawyer. When contacting an accounting firm, start by searching out audit partners and M&A partners. Call around the firm until you locate the group that specializes in your industry of interest. Most firms now have highly specialized groups in areas such as technology or retail. In addition to the industry experts, the M&A group sees many potential deals. Contact them next. If you close a deal based on a referral from an accounting firm, you need to find a way to compensate them. Often an advisory fee is acceptable, but more often the best reward is posttransaction audit work on the company you acquire. If you need an auditor anyway, hiring the firm that made the suggestion makes sense.

• *Law Firms.* Law firms generally are not a prolific source of transactions, but they occasionally can be useful and are therefore worth contacting. Seek out the partners in the firms that focus on corporate work such as securities law and financing issues. Trust and estate lawyers may know business owners who are considering selling their companies as part of an estate planning exercise. Again, if they refer you to a successful deal, you should find a way to compensate them in fees and follow-up legal work for their firm.

• *Consulting Firms.* Because consulting firms are also in close contact with senior executives at large corporations, they can be a good source of leads on company units that are going to be sold. Consultants understand the strategic issues facing these companies and industries. Large firms such as Bain have realized the value of this information and set up their own successful private equity groups, but they may still have deals in specific areas that they are not interested in pursuing internally. Smaller, niche-oriented firms that do not have an internal equity financing capability may be an even better source of deal opportunities. When approaching consulting firms, contact people as senior in the firm as possible, use personal introductions where possible, and target people in your area of interest.

• *Active and Retired Senior Executives.* Other executives in your industry are often the best source of opportunities. Even former executives continue to be well connected and usually have fewer conflicts in recommending potential acquisitions. Use your networks in the industry and ask your contacts for suggestions of other executives to talk to. This can be a great source of inside information specifically targeted to your areas of greatest interest.

• *Pure Industry Research.* Conducting research in an industry can be an extremely productive method of generating buyout opportunities. If you're interested in defined sectors, such as sporting goods, begin subscribing to industry trade publications and attending industry trade shows. Nearly every industry of any size has its own association, often based in Washington, D.C. Just go on the industry's Web site to see when and where the leading trade shows take place and the names of the leading trade publications. Through these efforts you'll begin meeting company managers and making helpful contacts. Soon you'll be "living in the space," as they say in buyout parlance, meaning you'll be eating and breathing your target industry, meeting the players, and learning about its dynamics. This is an excellent way of building expertise and developing important relationships, and this method can create lots of knowledge, value for you and your investors, and, I guarantee, meaningful deal flow.

Fee Agreements: The Value of Ideas
If the fee of the investment bankers or other intermediary is not paid by the seller, they will typically look to you for payment at

closing. Before telling you anything about a potential acquisition target, the intermediary will ask you to sign a fee agreement. This is fair in concept, but review the agreement carefully. Fees vary widely, but 1 percent of the total purchase price plus reimbursement of expenses would not be out of line. For smaller deals, investment bankers and brokers often use the famous (or infamous!) "Lehman Formula." The Lehman is 5 percent of the first $1 million of total purchase price (or $50,000), plus 4 percent of the second $1 million, plus 3 percent of the third $1 million, plus 2 percent of the fourth $1 million, plus 1 percent of the fifth $1 million and above. Some greedier intermediaries have tried to push the "Double Lehman," which is the same 5-4-3-2 formula on the first $4 million, but holds at 2 percent until the first $25 million before shifting down to 1 percent. If someone suggests this formula to you, tell them you'll do the standard Lehman and not a ruble more.

Whatever the formula, the most important part of the fee agreement is to make sure it is success driven. If the deal doesn't close, nobody gets paid and all parties eat their own deal expenses. Also make sure all the fees and other expectations are crystal clear up-front. Any ambiguity will only mean trouble later on.

These are the written laws of fee agreements, but there are also unwritten laws. There may be times when an investment banker or other intermediary may suggest an idea to your company but does not overtly ask for a fee letter at that time. In this case you may not be legally bound, but you are ethically bound to pay that intermediary some sort of success fee if the idea they presented to you works out. With investment bankers and business brokers, this is implicit. This is how they make their living. But it should also apply to anyone else who sends a deal your way. Call it doing the right thing, deal karma, or whatever. If someone gives you an idea that leads to a closed deal, they should be compensated for their contribution.

A few years back, my former partner and I were chatting about a company my firm had just acquired in the telemarketing industry. He mentioned that he knew of a Los Angeles–based telemarketing company that may also be for sale. He asked if we'd be interested in meeting the owners, which he could facilitate. I was very interested and he made one phone call to arrange a meeting. That was it. He didn't come to the meeting. He and I had no other conversation about the deal, finder's fees, or compensation of any kind. He just set up a meeting as a courtesy to me. Five months later, we acquired the company for $15 million. My former partner had done nothing at all in that process except share the idea and make one phone call.

When the deal was about to close, I called him to say I needed his wiring instructions because Christmas was coming early. He asked why, protested for exactly two milliseconds, and then I wired him $100,000 as an advisory fee. It was not for arranging the meeting but for the idea. This is an idea-driven business, and ideas that lead to success must be compensated. Of course, this isn't only doing the right thing; it's just smart business. The next time he has a great idea, he'll think of our firm. It is an investment in relationships and brand equity.

In addition to cash, it is important to keep the person in the loop. If someone gives you an idea, call him or her occasionally to mention how things are progressing. You want people to think well of the experience with you so that they'll think of you when the next good idea comes along.

What happens if a banker or broker suggests a company you already know about or are in discussions with? In this case, you owe them nothing, but they may expect something if you don't react immediately. At the moment the suggestion is made, you need to explain to them that you are already in discussions or have knowledge of that situation. If you don't mention it then, it could create bad blood later when the investment banker finds out you are in discussions with the firm. At that point the banker may ask for a fee, and it is not as credible for you to state that you were already talking to the firm prior to the suggestion. These little conflicts often happen in the deal world, so it is always best to state the facts and the nature of any pertinent relationships right up front.

Winnowing the Wheat

Now that you've generated some potential acquisitions, you need to separate the wheat from the chaff. The first thing to look for is the overinflated claims of investment bankers and other sellers. To decode certain phrases, you may need a dictionary or interpreter. The glossary in Figure 4-1 is intended to help you. At a minimum, the presence of any of these statements should be a red flag for you to ask a few follow-up questions. On the other side, when you

begin pitching your own business to investors (as discussed in
Chapter 5), you should also avoid these phrases because they may
be rather unsettling to potential partners.

Figure 4-1. Investment banking glossary.

Term or Phrase	Plain English Translation
Acquisition strategy	The current products have no market.
Basically on plan	There's a revenue shortfall of 25 percent.
Biotech business model	Potentially bigger fools have been identified.
Considerably ahead of plan	We hit plan in one of last three months.
Core business	It's an obsolete product line.
Currently revising the budget	Financial plan is in total chaos.
Cyclical industry	We posted a huge loss last year.
Entrepreneurial CEO	The CEO's totally uncontrollable, bordering on maniacal.
Ingredients are there	Given two years, we might find a workable strategy.
Investing heavily in R&D	We're trying desperately to catch the competition.
Limited downside	It can't get much worse.
Long selling cycle	We haven't yet found a customer who likes the product.
Major opportunity	Last chance.
Niche strategy	A small-time player.
On a manufacturing learning curve	We can't make the product with positive margins.
Possibility of a slight shortfall	There's a revenue shortfall of 50 percent.

Repositioning the business	A multimillion-dollar investment was recently written off.
Somewhat below the plan	There's a revenue shortfall of 75 percent.
Strategic investor	Investor who will pay a preposterous valuation.
Too early to tell	Results to date have been grim.
Turnaround opportunity	Lost cause.
Unique	The business has no more than six competitors.
Upgrading the management team	The organization is in complete disarray.
Volume sensitive	Massive fixed costs.
Well below plan	An outright, unmitigated disaster.
Window of opportunity	Without more money, the company is dead.
Work closely with management	Talk to them on the phone once a month.

Beyond sifting through the hyperbole, you also need to find a business that fits with your criteria. It would all be very easy if the ideal target company fell right into your open arms. The challenge is that the ideal firm you visualize is probably not going to come over the transom. There are always going to be imperfections. It might be a higher price, a difficult seller, or legal problems with the target firm. Like a marriage, you get the whole package, so you need to make a judgment call about which ones are going to be problems that can kill the deal and which ones are personality traits you can learn to live with.

Among the core issues to consider are whether there is a willing seller in the deal. You also need to examine if the acquisition fits with your overall strategy and the culture of the company you are building. Since you are a strategic rather than a financial investor, the companies you buy will be the companies you live with. They will be the companies you lead. If there are insurmountable problems in fit or performance, these companies could be the bane of your existence, not only financially but also psychologically and emotionally. If they are strong acquisitions at good prices that fit well with your strategy, they will represent an important cornerstone of shaping your legacy.

Carefully assess whether the seller is willing to sell or just dabbling with the idea of parting with the company. Then look back at your criteria for the deal and assess how far off track the particular opportunity is on each of the dimensions. If you are examining several opportunities (and you should be), line them up to see how they stack up. As you examine the flaws of each deal realistically, consider which deficiencies you can live with and which ones are signs that you need to walk away.

It's Your Career: Take Charge

When most managers think about their career path or the future of their business, they rarely consider the option of a management buyout. If you have been single-mindedly focused on career advancement within the company, maybe it is time to shift your perspective. That entrepreneurial dream job you are longing for could be closer than you think. The opportunity to lead an independent company could be right in front of you, in fact. And if it is not where you work now, it could be very close by in the same industry or a related industry.

No one will offer you this job. It won't be posted anywhere. No headhunters will come looking to fill it. You have to find it. This search for opportunities is challenging to create and execute, but the financial and professional rewards can be far greater than even the fastest fast track within a company. The opportunities are there for the asking.

Strategy for the Business

"Plans are nothing. Planning is everything."
—Dwight D. Eisenhower

Techway's managers had a strategic vision for restructuring the company. In the past, separate business units were developed around government contracts, creating many duplicated efforts. Managers recognized that these different operations could be drawn together more coherently, generating significant cost savings and thus dramatically increased profits and value. They realized that benefits plans that were uniform across the parent organization resulted in benefits far greater than other firms in the information technology (IT) industry in which they competed. The managers also recognized that a commission structure that was critical to attracting top sales talent in information technology was blocked by the parent's policies.

By rationalizing infrastructure and reducing benefits, Techway's managers knew they could strip millions of dollars from their operating expenses. By offering commissions to salespeople, the company could reduce salaries and boost revenues. There were also growth opportunities as the company, which had concentrated on government contracts in the past, had begun to develop a foothold in the commercial market. Managers expected that they could expand this foothold into a significant area of new business. Opportunities abounded—with the right strategy.

Shaping the Strategy

Developing and communicating a strong business strategy is crucial to selling the deal to investors and to succeeding in the future. This chapter examines various ways to develop and clearly communicate strategic plans to partners, using the Techway strategy as an example. The strategic plan is the living document that you use to build the deal with investors and the business after you close.

The Business Plan

My desk and the desk of any buyout investor is stacked to the ceiling with business plans. Most of them are pretty dreadful, and, surprisingly, some uninspiring plans often represent strong underlying business ideas. They are just poorly communicated. But you have to wonder if managers can't sell the deal to a buyout partner, how are they going to sell it to banks, initial public offering (IPO) investors, or the marketplace? A clear, sharp presentation can't do much to help a bad idea, but it can do a lot to help a good one. Presentation and clear communication counts for a lot throughout the whole buyout process. You can turn an investor or banker off or on in the first five minutes. You are selling the deal all the way along. If you can carefully research and lay out your argument well in the beginning, the deal will sell itself.

What many would-be buyout leaders don't understand is that the first few pages of the business plan set the tone for the potential success of your venture and can either grab or lose a venture capitalist's attention and forever determine the outcome of your financing. Do it right and you might be hanging out with Michael Dell. Do it wrong, and the business plan becomes fire kindling and you'll never see your stock symbol in Section III of *The Wall Street Journal.*

I review a couple hundred plans a year and am always amazed by the many ways managers can damage their own cause by submitting lousy or noncredible (sometimes even *incredible*) business plans. I have several rules for drafting winning business plans. If you follow them, I can't guarantee you'll be on CNN but can be fairly sure your plan won't end up in the round file fifty seconds after the venture capitalist has received it. These are the rules:

1. *Keep it tight.* VCs are swamped with hundreds of plans a week. You need to give them tight, crisp sound bites that clearly convey the potential value of the business. They may take ten minutes, if you're lucky, to get the flavor of the plan. They are impressed by thoroughness but not necessarily by bulk. The business plan doesn't have to be 100 pages to be credible or of interest. It just needs to get the key points across in a forceful way. If your plan is more than forty pages, it probably has too much detail. It takes considerable work to write a simple summary. For Stu Johnson of Iconixx, it took months of personal research on the market, meeting with potential customers, and scouting out opportunities. It also took decades of experience in the industry. The more thinking that goes into boiling down the case for the business, the better it will be and the more easily you will be able to communicate it.

2. *The executive summary rules.* This is a corollary to the first rule. Do not start your business plan with some single-spaced text describing the Java code in your new browser. Start with an executive summary in bullet point form with headers. This may be the only part of the plan the investor ever reads. It should sum up the whole project in a page or two at the most. If it is more than two pages, it is too long. If you can't convey the entire value of the project in two pages of bullets, your idea isn't well conceived. The overview of the plan should give the reasons why investors should invest, what the market opportunity is, and how the management team and the firm are poised to take advantage of it. It should detail how the deal will create value and how that value will be put back into the pockets of investors through a clear exit strategy.

This approach gives potential investors virtually every major fact they need to evaluate the proposal and see its value. It also conveys the information in the tightly focused timeframe required by harried investors. Investors have seen hundreds of plans and have a nose for what works and what doesn't. They've seen most selling points on deals and know what rings true. An executive summary is literally all they need for a first-cut decision. Later, they'll need much more. But for now, this is what it takes to hook them.

Like everything else in our society, all great truths must be distilled into a few important sound bites, and the winners are those who can stay tightly focused on message.

   3. *Do your homework.* Before you write one word of your business plan, complete extensive research. Know your competitors and what they're doing. Know the size and growth rates of the markets you're attacking. As discussed in Chapter 6, all of this information is readily available on the Web or from your investment banker or stockbroker.

Sample Executive Summary for Techway

As an example of a summary, consider how Techway managers might characterize their opportunity in the following executive summary:

- *Objective.* Raise $50 million of equity financing to back Techway's management team in its buyout of Techway from the parent company.
- *Business.* IT services focusing on government sector.
- *Business Model.* Large federal government agency outsourcing contracts for full build-outs of major IT systems.
- *Techway Differentiation.* Large, long-duration contracts with leading government agencies. Highest-quality technical management with more than forty years of combined experience at the company. Substantial margin improvement opportunities. Low employee turnover.
- *Market Overview.* The market totals $40 billion and is growing at 14 to 15 percent per annum.
- *Management.* CEO, Joe Block, formerly CEO of IBM; CFO, Ed Block, formerly CFO of Microsoft, Ford Motors, and U.S. Steel.
- *Competition.* Numerous strong and well-financed competitors including IBM and Oracle's government IT units.
- *Primary Business Risks.* Risk of revenue cutbacks due to potential reductions in federal spending. Highly competitive environment for recruiting and retaining leading IT professionals.
- *Proposed Valuation.* $100 million, representing six and a half times 1999 EBITDA.
- *Summary Financial Projections.* Two-year projections are as follows:

	2000	2001	2002
Revenue	$325 million	$350 million	$375 million
Pretax Profit	$20.6 million	$25.7 million	$27.5 million

- *Projected Equity Rate of Return.* Thirty-five percent per annum over a three- to five-year period.
- *Exit Strategy.* Potential IPO, recapitalization, or strategic sale.
- *References/Board of Advisers.* Andrew Carnegie and Bill Gates.

Sample Executive Summary for Global Vacation Group

As another example, consider an overview of Roger Ballou's plan for Global Vacation Group (GVG). His plan was sharply focused. It may have been summarized with the following bullet points:

- *Mission.* The mission is to create the preeminent provider of leisure travel products to travel agents and consumers in the United States. The plan is to acquire five leading wholesale tour operators to consolidate a high-net-worth customer segment of the package tour business.
- *Team.* Proven executives with more than sixty years of combined experience in the industry, including senior-level positions with American Express Travel-Related Services, Alamo Rent-A-Car, and Holiday Inn.
- *Key Selling Points.* Highly fragmented market, with the largest single player representing only 7 percent of the market. No market leader, therefore excellent opportunity to consolidate the market and build the leading travel wholesaler in the United States. There is excellent growth potential, with steady growth of 5–8 percent over the past decade, which is likely to continue or increase. More than 200 tour operators are the right scale for potential acquisition. There are noncompetitive, private equity opportunities to buy businesses for the roll-up at five to six times EBITDA. There are tremendous opportunities to improve efficiencies through consolidation. Ten acquisition candidates are already identified.
- *Capital/Internal Rates of Return (IRRs).* Seeking $50 million in equity. Projected internal rates of return of at least 35 percent per annum.

- *Competitors.* Some large competitors such as American Express and numerous small mom-and-pop competitors.
- *Exit.* IPO or strategic sale.

In later presentations, the GVG concept was boiled down even further to this statement: "A proven management team and a strong financial sponsor combine to create economic value by executing a leveraged buildup of travel wholesalers and packaged tour operators in the highly fragmented $400+ billion leisure travel industry." Now that's punchy!

What *Not* to Say

Credibility is everything. In making a compelling case, it is absolutely crucial not to try to spin investors. First, experienced investors will see right through it if you start swaggering and talking about how you will achieve growth at double the industry rate or your historical patterns. You had better have quite an argument. Second, it would be even worse if they do accept your fish tale hook, line, and sinker. Then you will be committed to reaching these impossible objectives. Keep the projections honest because you will live with them for a long time. Once you've eroded your credibility, you will never get it back. Far too many business plans I've seen blow this credibility by page three and end up in the dustbin. Every day, I read plans that make one of these classic credibility mistakes:

- *"We have little or no competition."* This is just a joke. Instead of making the deal more attractive, this statement makes the deal less attractive. The reader knows that everyone has competition—fierce, real competition. There are no attractive parts of the U.S. economy that are not highly competitive. This statement means that either the managers are too dumb to recognize that they have competitors, or they believe the reader is too dumb to know better. There are competitors in every sector and often threats from outside the sector. Name them and get on with it.
- *"We want a valuation of $300 million (when it's really worth $100 million)."* Unless you truly have the Midas touch, there's just no way investors will buy this line, and it only sends your plan into

the bin. Be aggressive, but be realistic. What is your plan worth? How are comparable companies valued? Have you sufficiently discounted the public comparables to get to your value?

• *"We conservatively project third-year revenues of $700 million (up from $3 million today)."* These types of financial "hockey sticks" only land you in the penalty box. They're just not credible. Make projections that can be supported by real-world math, not astronomical aspirations. It would be credible on revenue projections if you argued that the total market for your product or service is $500 million and you expect to gain a 4 percent share through 150 customers, generating third-year revenue of $20 million. Now I know you didn't just pull the number out of the air.

• *"We plan a year-two IPO with Goldman Sachs and Morgan Stanley as lead managers, with the closing dinner scheduled for Sparks Steakhouse."* Don't build your case around your initial public offering. One of the worst dings to credibility is to make the future IPO a selling point. The IPO is no magic bullet. While it's a good idea to have an exit strategy, it is bad taste to tout your IPO before you've even raised your initial capital. This drives investors crazy. Your goal should not be an IPO. Your goal should be to build a great, long-term business. The IPO is a by-product of your business success, not an end in itself. Potential investors know that you have the potential to do an IPO as part of an exit strategy. The IPO is part of the dessert menu, but no one is going to walk into the restaurant without an appetizing main course. You need to convince investors that the business can be successful before they will start salivating over the prospect of some future offering.

The summary of the plan should clearly lay out the strategy. Bottom line, it should give investors reasons to do the deal and not offer them any reasons to reject it.

More Elements of the Successful Plan

The executive summary should be followed by all the information necessary to make the case to investors—and no more. If you throw in everything but the kitchen sink, potential investors won't be able to spot the important items. So pick and choose from the following list of elements of the plan as necessary to make your specific case.

Every element should be accretive to the overall case for the deal. Make your arguments in hard-hitting points, and keep it tight.

Company Overview
This section should describe the company and its position in the industry in more detail. In the case of GVG, the summary provided a description of what "wholesale tour operators" do and the composition of the company. The plan went on to give more details about the deal structure of the platform acquisitions.

Financials and Trends
The plan must include company financials for at least three years back and projections for three years into the future. Techway managers discussed their recent record in turning around the firm. In just two years, they had turned a $2.8 million operating loss (EBITDA) into a $14.8 million gain. This enormous operating improvement was a great reflection on management's capabilities and a key selling point in the deal.

For GVG, because it was created from the acquisition of five companies, presenting financials was somewhat complicated, but they worked up financials for the five companies in the platform acquisition and the combined company afterward.

Industry Growth and Trends
The plan should discuss the overall potential for the industry. It should describe the aggregate market size and the size and growth rates of niches within the total market, overall growth, and projections for future growth. It could also present information about the structure of the industry (e.g., number of players and size). Techway's industry analysis focused on the growing government market for IT. It noted that the $40 billion government market is one of the largest IT markets in the nation and is growing at a compound annual rate of 14 percent. The market is part of a $325 billion total IT market that is also growing very rapidly at rates of over 25 percent. The expansion is driven by the growth of government agencies; the acknowledgment that, even for the government, IT systems have become a key competitive weapon; the replacement of equipment; and the prolific growth of the Internet. Techway identified $10 bil-

lion in potential new government contracts that it was positioned to bid on. It's a strong story.

For GVG, since its strategy was to consolidate, showing that the industry was fragmented and that there were a substantial number of potential acquisition targets was crucial to making its case for the roll-up.

Strategy

The plan should also delineate the company's strategy for taking advantage of the opportunities for growth in the industry. It should describe the advantages of the new firm or buyout in capitalizing on these opportunities. In Techway's case, its strong customer relationships were a tremendous asset in the arena of government contracts. Its long-term contracts locked in these customers and made it harder for rivals to move into its existing market. At the same time, Techway intended to leverage its strengths in government contracting to move into new commercial markets.

GVG stressed the experience of its founders in the travel industry and the opportunities for consolidation. The summary profiles of the key executives are always included in the executive summary, and resumes of the senior managers are always included in the appendix of the plan.

In his book *Competitive Strategy* (New York: The Free Press, 1980), Michael Porter describes "five forces"—customer power; suppliers; competitive, dynamic substitutes; potential entrants; rivalry among existing firms—that offer a good framework for looking for potential strategic advantages. These forces also help identify threats to the firm's current advantages.

Competitors

The plan should give a careful review of current competitors in the industry. It should also look at potential competitors who may be expected to enter the market in the future. The plan should clearly describe the competitors, their size, and their current strategies. It should also offer strategies for countering the expected competitive moves. Techway managers noted that the market for government IT services is highly competitive, and they bid against a range of other contractors. The company then listed its key competitors.

Exit Plan

The plan needs to explore the potential for exit by investors from the deal. (Chapter 10 explores the options for exit in more detail.) In the case of Techway, the exit plan was to either take the company public (there were numerous public competitors of similar size), sell the company to a larger buyer (there was a very active M&A market in this sector), or recapitalize the company to pay out capital to shareholders. In the case of GVG, the exit envisioned (and ultimately realized) was an IPO that allowed investors to return some of their capital. The IPO could be followed by secondary stock offerings or a distribution of publicly traded securities. The plan noted that if the public offering was not possible or preferable, the business could also very likely be sold to a strategic buyer. Managers strengthened the credibility of the statement by noting that the company had already been approached by several strategic buyers.

Financial and Return Analysis

In addition to providing a way out, the plan also has to show that money invested will be well spent. The plan should outline the potential returns from the deal. The model for analyzing the deal, discussed in Chapter 8, should help you give investors a credible estimate of the returns for your specific deal.

You should provide base-case, best-case, and worst-case examples, with equity returns based on different time periods. This information allows investors to get a sense of what they could take away from the deal. The model discussed in Chapter 8 allowed Techway managers to show investors that they could potentially earn 16–40 percent return on the investment, with the base case at 32 percent. This is certainly in the range of 30–35 percent returns these investors are seeking. In the case of GVG, the projections were done for a three- to six-year exit period, showing the IRR and return multiple for each scenario.

Risks of the Deal

Finally, the plan needs to identify and discuss some of the key risks for the firm and investors. For Techway, some of the risks include the loss of government contracts (long-term contracts help mitigate this risk), departure of key employees (the structure of the deal addresses this concern), entrance of aggressive commercial competitors such as Oracle, or further government downsizing yielding lower prospective revenues. For GVG, the risks included the challenges inherent in execution of multiple platform acquisitions (the company had letters of intent), the integration and realization of synergies, the ability to complete the IPO and additional acquisitions, concentration of the core business in Hawaii, and the reduced role of travel agents because of electronic disintermediation. It also considered the standard bugaboos of exogenous shocks (e.g., airline strikes or acts of war) and exposure to economic cycles. For each risk, management discussed potential problems and offered strategies for addressing them and strengths that may help the company avoid them. GVG set out a list of mitigating factors, including management experience, attractive purchase prices, attractive consolidation economics, and a stable Hawaiian market that help reduce many of these risks.

As mentioned previously, all investors know there are risks in any deal; you only strengthen your credibility by laying them out in a detailed and comprehensive way.

Product Literature

If the company has product literature, it should be included as an appendix. It can be briefly summarized in the company overview up front.

Professional References

An overview of the experience of the key players must be included in either the opening summary or the company overview (or both), but the actual, detailed CVs are included in an appendix. Since the management is a big part of what you are selling, these resumes should be carefully developed and presented.

Be Tenacious

No matter how good it is, the plan cannot sell itself. Once you've developed your tightly focused business plan and put it in front of the VC, be tenacious in following up. Do not take an unreturned call as a "no." Believe me, they won't call you back the first time and probably not the second. Remember, they're swamped. Your expectations should be as follows:

Level A   If the VC or investor is your spouse, she *may* return your first call.

Level B   If the VC is an in-law, he won't ever return your call.

Level C   If the VC is your very best friend's spouse, he will return your fourth call.

Level D   If you met the VC at a conference and got her card, she may return your seventh call.

Level E   If you just cold-mailed the plan to the VC, you will have to call at least six times before the secretary will consider calling you back. You may need to stalk her at the grocery store.

Making a clear and compelling case gives you a greater chance of success. A powerful plan with a crisp summary has the power to make a VC pick up the phone and call you, even if it was cold-mailed out of the blue. But don't bank on it. And some investors want to see a little hunger for the deal on the side of the managers involved. They know how much you'll have to push to make it a reality and want to see these traits in their first interactions with you. Of course, after the seventh call, you probably want to take the hint and give up. Tenacity shouldn't turn into harassment, and you may have another, better idea to float by these investors someday.

CHAPTER 6

The Deal with the Seller

*"There are two fools in every market;
one asks too little, one asks too much."*
—RUSSIAN PROVERB

"There are more fools among buyers than sellers."
—FRENCH PROVERB

When Stu Johnson sought to buy out Bell Atlantic's network integration business that he had built years earlier as a senior Bell Atlantic executive, he found an equity partner, but it turned out the seller wasn't willing. After months of exploring the deal with Bell Atlantic, it was apparent that the company could not get comfortable with selling a business that now had perceived strategic value for the firm. "They couldn't put a price on something that was a keystone to their data strategy," Johnson recalled. "It was an activity trap. As long as they can continue to study something, they don't have to make a decision for which they will be accountable." After five months, Johnson walked away.

Johnson didn't have a willing seller, and he wisely pulled the plug on the deal before he wasted more time and money on it. The willing seller is just the first requirement for putting together a successful deal. The buyer then has to determine a fair price, approach the owner, and structure the deal. This chapter explores how to structure the deal with the seller, including approaching owners or senior managers, avoiding a bidding war, and valuing the company.

Avoiding a Bidding War

The problem with auctions is that the auctioneer, usually an investment banker, knows how to squeeze top dollar out of the bidders. Even if you stay calm in the auction process, it is likely that at least one competitor will become obsessed with the deal. It takes only one emotional buyer to ruin a sane market. Auctions tend to be painful.

If you have to participate in an auction, be clear about your maximum price and stay with it for as long as it makes sense. Discipline is absolutely critical. Don't get emotional about the transaction. If you do, the process will get the best of you and you will overpay. Work through the personal impact of the numbers (as discussed in Chapter 8) so you know where you stand. Be careful not to let your emotions take over and always be willing to let the deal go. *There will be other opportunities.*

How do you avoid auctions? There are a number of strategies:

• *Find your distinctive advantage.* Identify some special advantage you bring to the table. If you are a strategic buyer, is the company worth more to you than financial investors because you have unusual opportunities to build the firm or remove costs from the income statement? As noted in Chapter 4, managers buying their own firm offer sellers a number of advantages over outside suitors, such as speed of diligence and confidentiality.

• *Offer a fair price.* Another way to potentially avoid an auction is to offer a fair price early on, based on careful research. You may be inclined to low-ball your bid early on to get the company on the cheap. This is always tempting, but is rarely successful. There are few bargains in the competitive deal environment. Instead your low-ball bid may hurt your credibility and push the seller to conduct an auction. If the price you put forward is rational and fair and you can convince the seller of it, he has little incentive to spend the time and effort looking elsewhere, unless he's convinced there is some sucker out there waiting to pay more.

   • *Get there first.* As discussed in Chapter 4, you can attend industry trade shows and talk to industry insiders in an effort to create a deal opportunity. Read the industry trade publications and call people in the industry for their advice. Look for companies that fit your profile and then go after them. A wide range of sources are available for identifying potential businesses to purchase. Some of these businesses may not even be for sale until you make an offer. That gives you a tremendous advantage in getting there first. If you avoid the crowds, you avoid the auctions.

Determining a Fair Price

Determining a fair price for a company is never a simple task. While it would be nice to apply mathematical formulas to get a point answer, math is not enough. Valuing a company is, in fact, part science and part art. The science is determining what similar companies are worth, where the industry is headed, and what kind of multiples a company of this size and shape can command. The art is then adjusting that mathematical number to reflect the characteristics of the actual firm.

   The science part is well known, and there are many good books on valuation that can help you refine your approach. Many of them utilize esoteric valuation approaches that are not very useful in practice. If you are a financial guru, it may be to your advantage to make it as complicated and precise as possible. Highly detailed analysis can be useful. If you like to play with advanced mathematics, there is probably no limit to the gyrations you can go through to calculate the value of a firm. But if you are interested in closing a deal, most of the time some fairly simple analysis can give you a good ballpark estimate for what the company is worth. As with most things in life, the simple and straightforward is the best approach. Most of the time this is all that's needed, but it takes a little bit of savvy in coming up with enough information to put a price on the table.

The Science of Valuation
Just as you comparison shop for prices on cars in an overall automotive marketplace, there is also a "market" for companies that deter-

mines overall value. In most cases, this is the public stock market. These markets drive the science for corporate valuations worldwide, and these markets will shape your thinking in valuing a firm.

The science piece of valuation is based upon getting your hands on the research analyzing trends in similar companies and across the industry. Companies in an industry usually trade in public markets along certain valuation lines, and many in specific sectors tend to have similar characteristics. Some companies break out of the pack due to terrible performance, in which case their multiples are much lower. The multiples of other firms soar above the crowds, usually because of excellent growth or performance beyond the norm. It is important to look at the metrics for firms in the industry and to decide which are the important multiples.

In general, the multiple that is watched most closely is the ratio of overall enterprise valuation (i.e., value of equity plus interest-bearing debt) divided by the company's latest annual earnings before interest, taxes, depreciation, and amortization (EBITDA). EBITDA represents pretax cash flow before maintenance capital expenditures. It provides a measure of the cash flowing out of the company before the capital expenditures required to be made on equipment, systems, and facilities to maintain the business's market position. It is a primary focus of the commercial banking, investment banking, and Wall Street research communities.

However, it is important to look beyond EBITDA to EBIT multiples (i.e., earnings before interest and tax but after depreciation). From the buyer's perspective, cash flow after maintenance capital expenditures (EBIT is usually a proxy for this figure) is also critical. Other multiples such as revenue multiples and net income multiples are useful but supplementary. Usually, you want to track all of these metrics for twenty-four months of trailing EBITDA and EBIT and projections for twelve to twenty-four months ahead. The core EBITDA multiple used in valuation is based upon actual trailing twelve-month EBITDA generated by the business. Sellers often attempt to get buyers to pay multiples based upon *projected* EBITDA, but it's the historical EBITDA that really matters. If you find out all the companies in the sector are trading at seven or eight times EBITDA, or nine or ten times EBIT, this is the range you would expect to pay for the firm in question, unless there are extenuating circumstances.

Where you fall in the range depends upon the "art of valuation," as discussed later in this chapter.

For example, Techway managers determined that their comparable industry multiples were six to eight times EBITDA. This implied that for a company with EBITDA of $17.1 million, the ballpark value of the company would be $103 million to $137 million. So when managers made an initial offer of $100 million, they were making their initial offers in the right spot, at the low end of the range.

Do Your Homework

Where do you come up with these industry numbers? It used to be that any manager with a half-decent stockbroker could access the industry research analysis pretty easily. With the Internet, it is literally at your fingertips. Anyone with a connection to the Web can come up with the information you need to evaluate the metrics of the industry.

Most investment banks have a strong research department where a bunch of very smart propeller heads immerse themselves in the details of specific industries. These research analysts are the rock stars of the investment world, earning millions of dollars per year. They are poached by other banks for multimillion-dollar signing bonuses. Their word literally moves billions of dollars in the market. They are hardwired into their industries, making recommendations on whether to buy, hold, or sell stocks in those areas. Institutional investors trade based on those recommendations (which means trading, investment banking, and M&A fees for the investment banks). If you decide to take your software company public, you will want the leading software industry analysts to write research reports on your company. To do that, you need to do investment banking business with the firm where the analyst works.

But right now, what you need more than anything are the reports these analysts produce. Everything you need to know about the industry sectors you're targeting is in these reports. Analysts' reports give you an understanding of industry trends, an overview of competitors, and an understanding of how Wall Street values these companies.

Moreover, since these analysts are well respected by investors, when you meet with buyout firms and banks, you will dramatically enhance your credibility if you can quote from them. When some investment banker is doing a condescending, superficial rap on the software industry, you can turn to the banker and say, "Yes, but have you seen Rick Sherlund's most recent report that says . . . ?" (Sherlund is Goldman Sachs' software industry guru. This is a guy who wouldn't have time to return Bill Clinton's call because he is spending so much time talking to Bill Gates.) The investment banker will pale, fidget, and say, "Er, I think I saw it . . . what did he say?" From that point on, the banker will treat you with newfound respect.

How do you get your hands on this valuable information? It is really quite simple. Start by looking at the annual All-Star Research issue of *Institutional Investor.* (If you subscribe to it already, you are twenty steps ahead of me and I am concerned about your social life.) This report lists the top research analysts sector by sector. Review the list to find the best minds in your part of the world and identify where they work.

The next challenge is getting your hands on the analyst reports. This research is so valuable to investment banks that you can't simply call Goldman Sachs blindly and ask them to pop the report in the mail. Start with your own stockbroker. Stockbrokers often can get you some research generated by their own firm or others. If you are lucky, the broker may have just the reports you are looking for. If you know someone who has access to a Bloomberg service, you can often get research there. Just keep plugging away until you get your hands on it. It will greatly enhance your own understanding of your industry and strengthen your strategy and credibility in presenting your ideas.

While getting some of the more impressive analyst reports may take a little finagling, getting the multiples and other numbers you need takes almost nothing. All this information is available online. Many investment sites offer industry analysis and metrics. In a matter of minutes, you can have a fairly good sense of what companies are trading at in your sector.

When working to obtain this research, look for several elements. First, look at the date of the research. Wall Street research that is more than a year old is probably of limited value, particularly given the blistering pace of change in the economy. Second, research generally comes in three different forms: "macro" surveys on overall trends in the economy, company-specific reports, and industry analysis. The macro analyses generally cover economic trends or policy and are interesting to read, but they are not the most useful for valuation or competitive analysis. Company-specific reports are quite helpful, and you should seek out pieces that analyze the largest and most direct competitors to your target. These reports not only tell you the competitive context in which you need to make your case, but they also may indicate the factors and issues that are of key concern to investors in the deal.

The most useful pieces, however, are the industry analyses that evaluate all the major trends in a specific sector, such as Internet Services or Corporate Training, and analyze all of the prevailing growth rates, margins, and valuation multiples of the primary competitors in the sector. Most analysts put out significant competitive compendiums once or twice a year, and when you're calling your friends or surfing the Net to get research, request some competitive industry pieces, even if they are six or nine months old. Because these reports are very valuable, you should study them carefully and commit key industry metrics to memory so you can blow your bankers away with your knowledge in meetings.

By the way, not doing this level of research is simply not an option. This research, the financial metrics, and competitive analysis together provide the basis for your valuation of the company and will be key to demonstrating to your financial partners the credibility of your effort. You must do the homework and do it well.

Preliminary Valuation

As I've mentioned, valuation basics do not need to be complex. I'd like to give you a couple of generic ways to think about it. First, in the heady times of the 1999 and 2000 buyout markets, the average purchase multiple for all buyouts completed was approximately 7.5 times trailing EBITDA. This is a useful, though not perfect, benchmark. As it is an average, it reflects deals done at ten to eleven times EBITDA, which are prevailing multiples in the radio and media areas, for instance, which reach such lofty heights because of their growth characteristics and because they are generally extremely stable and predictable businesses. The more predictable (and thus less risky) the cash flows, the higher price one can pay. So a good target for a more normal operating business with traditional risks is six to seven times EBITDA.

If you only think of this conceptually, it makes sense. Just think of rates of return and risk. U.S. Treasury bonds are perceived to be the least risky of any entity and generate an essentially guaranteed rate of return today of about 5 percent per annum. A $1,000 Treasury bond yields $50 per year. To buy the bond, then, you're paying twenty times the cash flow of $50. That's your cash flow multiple. Now, think of the risks inherent in purchasing a living, breathing, operating company. Customers come and go. There are industry shocks, and people come and go as well. This is normally a risky situation, and your cash return on your purchase should reflect that risk.

There was once a rule of thumb in the buyout business that one should never pay more than six times EBIT for a company. This rule has long since been broken in this highly competitive investment environment, but it was a rule that made sense. If a risk-free rate of return was 5 percent, or twenty times cash flow, paying six times cash flow for a much riskier asset makes sense, because this implicitly generates an unlevered yield of 16.7 percent per annum.

If you then put 50 percent leverage on the transaction (thus reducing equity capital required by 50 percent), you would see future equity returns of 30 percent per annum. As you can see, these numbers work and are sensible as risk/reward ratios go. The leveraged internal rate of return that most buyout funds target is 30–35 percent, and you should, too. The 30 percent target makes sense because on an all-equity basis, you get a 16.7 percent return, which reflects the underlying operating company's business risk. Then you layer a high level of debt, creating substantial financial or balance sheet risk, and you have a risky situation for which you should be paid a higher rate of return to commit capital. That moves the figure up from 16.7 percent to 30–35 percent, depending on the overall level of risk.

That's why, generally, it makes no sense to pay ten times EBIT for most businesses (the exceptions to this rule are extremely predictable and extremely high growth businesses, which can justify the higher multiples). This implies an unlevered return of 10 percent on your capital, which to me is not enough return to reflect the risk of buying and managing an operating company. Remember, you can buy many corporate bonds in stable companies that yield nearly 10 percent and are much less risky than the cash flows from an operating company.

The Art of Valuation

Once you have done the research, you have gathered a range of multiples on comparable firms. You have a generic image, but you still need to paint in the actual features of the company in question. This is where the art comes in. Now that you've crunched the math, you turn your attention to the critical nonfinancial issues to determine where you should sit in (or outside of) the multiple range. Among the issues that may adjust the multiple are:

• *Pretax Margins.* If the company has lower margins than the industry average, you should likely discount the multiple. If it has higher margins, it may command a premium.

• *Growth.* If all companies are growing at 12 percent and this company is growing at 20 percent, it should command a higher multiple. You must be careful that the growth rate hasn't been artificially inflated (e.g., by special selling programs implemented by the company) and that it is sustainable. If it survives these tests, the company should command a higher price.

• *Future Prospects.* If the company has some tremendous future events coming up, such as the award of a large contract, you might boost the multiple. At the time of the deal, Software AG was valued at 8.5 times trailing EBITDA, which was above the prevailing industry standard. But the prospect of cost-savings and an expected ramp-up in sales meant that on a projected basis our value would actually be just five times EBITDA, which was a low valuation. Although you don't want to get too caught up in the glowing picture the seller may paint for the firm, if there is a solid basis to expect strong future growth, this could be cause to offer a higher price.

• *Customer Diversification.* If half the company's business comes from a single, dominant customer, this increases risk and should decrease the value.

• *Scale.* If the company is generating revenues of $200 million or higher, you should expect to pay public market multiples. If it is a $20 million firm, the purchase multiple should represent a 15–30 percent discount to public market multiples to adjust for the smaller scale (and therefore more risky company). A smaller firm typically doesn't have the quality of management, systems, customer relationships, or clout of a much larger company.

• *Control.* Sellers of private firms often argue that buyers should pay a "control premium" because the buyer gains operating control over the company, rather than an investment in it. Sellers contend that buyers should therefore pay extra, but it is usually countered by the fact that the investment, unlike stock in a public firm, is an illiquid security. It can be a catchy argument and sometimes will bump the multiple a tad, but today's buyout markets are so competitive, buyers of private firms generally pay multiples very close to the public market.

• *History.* As noted previously, you want to look for several years of history in growth and earnings to make sure they are not just sleight of hand. You don't want to set the value from peak earnings. If the company has earned 6 percent historically and the year preceding the sale the earnings spike up to 10 percent, be very skeptical. You would be better off setting the value based on the 6 percent historical earnings level.

• *Seller's Motivation.* The motivation of the sellers also affects the price. Are they desperate to sell? Do they need something particular out of the deal? SAGA's offer was based on its understanding of what the company needed to pay off the banks, not on a careful analysis of multiples in the software business. Managers inside a company have an advantage because they have a better understanding of the seller's motivations and the company situation. The "art" of adjusting the price becomes a little more refined because it is based on a detailed understanding of the specific company.

• *Rival Bidders.* The psychology of rival buyers also plays a role in determining how much a business is worth. One management team bidding against an outsider for their business was surprised at how high a premium the other company was willing to pay. It just didn't make sense. It turned out the CEO had lost out on a previous deal and decided he had to have this one, no matter what. There is no bidding against a competitor with that kind of motivation.

All these factors, and others that may be idiosyncratic to the deal, are used to adjust the value of the firm. How much of an adjustment should be made for each? This is where the art comes in. In addition, some of these factors interact with one another. A company with a dominant customer may also have lower margins due to this customer, and these issues should compound a reduction in value against prevailing market multiples. You just need to systematically identify the issues, look at ranges for comparable companies, and then adjust your initial "scientific" estimates accordingly.

The outcome of this process is never a single price but rather a range of prices. You decide at the outset what the top dollar is. When you reach top dollar, you need to be able to walk away.

Why Not Use Price/Earnings Ratios?
The price/earnings ratio we always hear quoted on the news is the ratio of the price of the stock of the company to its net income per share. It is also equal to the total equity valuation of the company divided by its net income. Buyout investors should certainly consider net income in their valuation review, but it is not often the driving multiple because the net income at the bottom of the income statement does not equate to cash flow. Net income comes *after* noncash charges such as depreciation and amortization and taxes. These metrics may be different at each company and not useful because they may be wildly affected by old acquisitions or irrelevant amortization. Also, tax rates for all companies differ. Cash flow is what matters: It's cash that you'll use to pay the piper, not net income. That's why buyers use EBITDA minus average capital expenditures to value their companies. As always, true cash flow is king.

The Balance Sheet Matters, Too
Most business valuation analysis rightfully focuses on the income statement. This is appropriate, but don't forget to carefully evaluate the target's balance sheet. First, do not simply focus on the most recent balance sheet. Just as with the income statement, look at the last three years of historical data. Analyze the key working capital accounts and see how they've been changing. Have the days of accounts receivable outstanding been getting longer or shorter over time? If the receivable days outstanding are getting much longer over time, you may have a collections issue. If they've gotten

much shorter in recent months, perhaps the seller has accelerated the collection of receivables in advance of a sale and you may have a financial hole to fill.

This same type of analysis is critical as it relates to inventories and accounts payable. Have the inventory days lengthened or shortened recently? If they've gotten much longer, perhaps there's lots of old inventory that you'll have to eat. If they've gotten much shorter, perhaps the seller has been tightening inventories to take cash out of the business. Same with payables: Are they stretched? If so, you may have some angry suppliers out there and a financial gap to fill. If the payables are very short, perhaps you have an opportunity to generate cash by extending the payables.

Look carefully at all these metrics. If they're consistent over time, you're probably in good shape. If they're bouncing around, you've got issues to analyze and questions to ask. Again, seek out industry comparables to see where competitors have inventory turns, days of receivables, and days of payables set. If you find there's a working capital deficit at the company, that means you need to reduce the purchase price. There is always both opportunity and risk in balance sheet management, but in my experience, there's usually more risk than opportunity.

Along similar lines, beware of capital investment deficits in a company that's for sale. Just as it's natural for a seller to try to optimize the cash on the balance sheet before a sale, it's natural for a seller not to invest heavily in capital equipment right before a sale. Sadly, it's a little bit like when you sell a car: You won't put in a new stereo right before you sell it. So beware and carefully check to see that the capital expenditure rate matches historical levels. If it does not, you'll likely have some extra investigating to do going forward.

The next important element on the balance sheet is the debt outstanding. When you buy a company, you're buying its balance sheet. You should expect to purchase a balance sheet with certain working capital accounts as discussed previously. There's a natural working capital level for any business, and that's part of what you're buying. You may also be buying a company with some existing bank debt on the balance sheet. This is fine, but it certainly affects valuation. Remember the old, simple formula:

Total enterprise value = Equity value + Debt value

Therefore, if you're looking at Techway and you value the enterprise at $100 million, the sellers get the $100 million only if you get the company debt free. If there's $20 million of bank debt, then you pay the sellers $80 million for their equity value. This is all very simple and straightforward, but you must discuss the balance sheet with the sellers early on to make sure you're on the same page on valuation. You may value a company at $10 million and the sellers may tell you they want $10 million for their company and you think, hey, we're ready to go. But the sellers "forgot" to mention the $5 million of bank debt they're carrying. Later, they say they expect you to assume the bank debt. They meant $10 million for "the equity," so it turns out you really weren't on the same page, because you were thinking $10 million overall and they were thinking $15 million for the debt and equity. Again, get the facts out early and make sure everyone's on the same page before putting lots of time into the project.

Balance sheet analysis is complex, so it pays to have a good finance person on your team. Other issues that may arise are the seasonality of the balance sheet. Many companies have highly seasonal working capital needs (e.g., a swimming pool company or a florist), therefore it's important for you to understand these seasonal fluctuations. In general, you want to buy using a twelve-month *average* working capital and debt level as your baseline. If you can buy the business when the balance sheet is at its fullest, that's fine. But beware of buying in the quiet months, since you'll have to plan carefully the ways to finance the growth of the balance sheet accounts in the high seasons.

Finally, there are more esoteric questions, such as how to define debt. Are leases debt? Should leases on the balance sheet reduce the purchase price? In general, the answer is no. Most leases can be rolled over in a sale and behave more like working capital. But all forms of bank debt and subordinated debt are clearly debt and are therefore a dollar-for-dollar reduction on equity proceeds in a transaction.

What If There Is No EBITDA?

We've talked a great deal about valuation based on EBITDA, but what if the company is losing money or is currently a not-for-profit business and there is negative EBITDA? In this case, naturally, you rely on metrics other than EBITDA to value the business. As always, look at all the industry comparables to see which metrics make sense. Do most companies in the sector trade at some multiple of revenue, such as 50 percent of annual revenue? If so, that's a guideline that can be useful. One rule of thumb in a situation where the company is not making money is to go to the balance sheet for valuation guidance. In this case, the net worth or net equity line on the balance sheet is a good guide for valuation. You might also look at liquidation value of all the assets and liabilities as a guide.

Of course, if the company is losing money, you must be extremely careful. I'm no turnaround expert, but I've seen many tough situations and know that turning a company around is always harder than it looks. It requires an especially tough and unemotional demeanor to successfully pull it off. It almost always requires swift and massive action that entails firings and potential litigation. Suffice it to say that it's not work for the faint of heart. Furthermore, there are businesses that simply have no value or negative value. If the company is losing money and has a poor balance sheet, perhaps the seller has to *pay you* to take the company. Believe it or not, there are hundreds of deals done that way every year.

If the business happens to be a not-for-profit company that is converting to a for-profit model, the same rules apply, such as looking at comparable multiples of revenue as indicators of value. In this instance, though, matters other than financial would be of paramount importance, such as asking whether a previously not-for-profit company has the mentality, human resources, and capital base to venture into the for-profit world to take on long-standing for-profit competitors.

Negotiating Strategy

After you've determined the price for the company, you need to test this value against the seller's expectations. Now that you know what the company is worth, you don't just march into the seller's office and put the numbers on the table. There are better ways to approach the deal. If you can, you want to always make the seller put the price on the table first. Discuss the deal informally, and get a ballpark figure. If you know from analyzing multiples that the business may be worth $55 million to $60 million and the seller is looking for $100 million, you know you have a long way to go. In fact, you may not even have a "willing" seller. (Any seller is "willing" if the price is high enough.) Perhaps you should use your crucial time wisely and walk away at that point, knowing you'll never come together.

Start out informally. Set up a lunch with the seller and say, "I haven't looked at the numbers as much as I'd like, so can you give me a range of what you are thinking about?" Get the seller to talk first. Sometimes you can find a "bluebird"—a wildly favorable deal that lands on your shoulder like the bluebird of happiness. Don't let it fly away. These bluebirds fly in when the seller underestimates the value, hasn't done the homework, or is in a personal bind and needs to sell quickly. There aren't many bargains out there, but a lot of money has been made in the buyout world by dealing with unsophisticated sellers. A lot of money has also been lost on sellers that appear to be unsophisticated but are actually crazy like a fox, so use some caution. If the seller is way under market, the first question to ask yourself is, Why? Is there some hidden reason why it is not such a great asset? If you've gotten a bargain and it all tests out, though, close the deal fast and thank the stars. You've just made money on the buy.

An unsophisticated seller is the exception, however, because a prepared seller usually has a pretty good idea of what the business is worth. Most of the time, the seller is willing to talk at pretty close to market metrics and you know you are dealing with a rational person. Sometimes, however, these initial discussions indicate that the seller is off in a distant part of the stratosphere. You now know that you'll have a harder time bringing this deal to earth than guiding back *Apollo 13*.

It may help to use a good guy, bad guy approach in negotiations. One person maintains a close and friendly relationship while the other plays the heavy. If there is a silent partner, it's easier to say, "I ran this by my partner and these are the five things he's concerned about . . ." In other words, you love the deal but these tough partners are throwing up roadblocks.

This approach often makes it much easier to develop and maintain a good relationship, which makes the work much more constructive. If you are a sole manager negotiating, your silent partner could be your lawyer or a friend in private equity, or even a tangentially involved lawyer or accountant who acts as your negotiating foil. That foil is so important. When you're making a deal, always begin the negotiations 10–20 percent lower on all the parameters than where you want to finish at the end of the day. If your top dollar on the deal is $50 million, put $40 million to $42 million in as your first indication. Never lead with the deal you want to make. Start at a level where you know you won't insult the seller, thus losing the fight before it gets started, but start below your best deal.

Some straight shooters just want to cut through the "negotiating crap" (a technical finance term!) and put their one and only deal on the table. This is a nice concept in a perfect world, but in our world it loses 90 percent of the time. The reason is that it's human nature for people to want to win or improve a negotiation. Believe me, even if the seller seems to want to cut to the chase, the seller's lawyer or banker will want to extract some pain from you. It's a well-honed game and everyone likes to play. You should play, too.

Give the seller some points to win, and be prepared to raise your bid to make him feel like he's winning some big points. A term sheet always has a lot of points on it, and there are some that are critical to you and some that are critical to the seller. It is certainly possible that one term critical to both parties may blow up a deal. But when you go through all of the fifteen to twenty terms on term sheet, decide which three or four you want to win. Present a couple of straw man points on which to lose, then complain like crazy to the seller about getting beaten over the head. Then hold tough on your "must have" points and you'll have created a true win-win.

At the same time you are hoping to trap a bluebird, sellers are dreaming the same dream. Only you are the one they hope to trap. They will push to get you to put a number on the table. In general, you shouldn't do it, at a minimum, until you see their financial information. If you put a number on the table before seeing the hard numbers, it will be guaranteed to change and then create the prospect for bad feelings of "retrading" between yourself and the seller. It is a 100 percent lose situation. And when sellers drag their feet in showing you the financials, this is another red flag that there could be problems later in the process. Sellers normally don't want to show you the numbers for a reason: They are not pretty. It's one of the rules of the buyout business: Good numbers arrive early. If they're late, they're ugly.

You want to see at least the last three years of income statements and balance sheets, as well as plans for the current year and following year, if possible. This gives you three years of trend lines and shows what the plan is for the future. The current year will often look much higher and there will be aggressive projections for the future. It is up to you to use your judgment, but the three years of history provide a reality check.

It is particularly important to have audited statements. Many family-owned companies, even fairly large ones, do not want to spend the money for audited statements. Even here, most sellers at least put up the money for an audit when they know they want to sell. Unaudited statements could be a sign that the owner just didn't want to spend the money, or that there is something to hide. If you have to work with unaudited statements, there should be some discount on the valuation for this meaningful added risk. You can reconstruct an audit, but it is a lot of work and time that is sometimes not possible within the timeframe and budget of the deal.

As amply illustrated in the discussion of Ceramic City in Chapter 3, even audited statements are not airtight. There are plenty of places to hide problems, particularly if sellers are determined and unscrupulous. But the audit at least gives you a fighting chance of recognizing severe problems.

In analyzing the price you could pay for the company, you also need to be aware of the implications of the price for what you and other investors will get out of the deal. The deal won't work for you or other investors at any price. We examine how the selling price affects returns for management and investors in Chapter 8. Will investors earn their expected return of at least 30–35 percent? Will you as managers earn enough to make the risks worth taking? With this analysis handy, you'll be able to see early on whether the deal makes sense and assess whether higher bids for the company are worthwhile. You have to know where the deal pencils out. If you ever reach a point at which you feel you cannot walk away, no matter what, you need to get away from that deal as quickly as possible.

The Family Seller

Particularly with sellers who have built a business from scratch or who run a family-owned business, there is a tendency to feel that the company really is "their baby," meaning that they feel a very strong emotional as well as financial attachment to the company. The company is like a child they have reared for many years. These sellers also often feel the child is much more beautiful than she really is. Their customers are great. The business is a miracle. Buyers should be paying a premium for a business this great. You don't need detailed agreements and representations, the proud parents argue. You may no longer be dealing with a reasonable business owner. You are trying to wrench a child away from a protective parent, which takes tremendous time and patience. Be prepared for a very long negotiation.

For many sellers, there is a lot more at stake than money. They have put their heart and soul into the business, and usually its future success and viability is very important to them. They care greatly for their employees and usually want to make sure that the loyal staff continues to be treated fairly. You may hear many a long, boring story about the company's history, particularly from a family-owned company chieftain. Don't doze off. These tales could give you insights into ways you may be able to add unique value to the deal to make yourself a more desirable buyer. This strategy will keep the whole deal from devolving into a pure price discussion. Even if it becomes a competitive bidding situation, bringing compassion for the seller's situation to the table can give you a far greater advantage than cold cash.

Is the seller reasonable on price? Is the seller reasonable on other issues? Is this someone you can negotiate with? Ask your law firm to review their litigation databases to see whether the seller has been litigious in the past. It is a pattern that will probably continue into the future. If getting a signed letter of intent from the seller is harder than scaling Mount Everest, the chances that the deal will break down in later-stage documentation are about 80 percent. A good price without a strong agreement that has real representations and warranties is not a good price. You need to be sure the sellers are willing to stand behind the representations they are making about the business.

The Documents of the Deal

You've identified a willing seller, discussed a price, and begun to explore terms of the agreement. After the initial verbal conversations have been completed, you now move into various stages of documentation for the deal. This is a process that first kills small forests of trees and then clutters your office or home with stacks and stacks of paper. As you will soon see, the paperless office is more a dream today than ever.

There are three phases of documentation with the seller:

1. The term sheet
2. The letter of intent (LOI)
3. The purchase agreement(s)

These documents are an evolution in complexity from the amoeba-like simple term sheet to the sophisticated and highly evolved legal documents that comprise the purchase agreements.

The term sheet is a discussion document outlining primary terms with the seller. From the term sheet, you move to a letter of intent. This longer document begins to nail down all the key issues of the deal. It is the last stage in negotiations before you start running up large outlays of time and money. The letter of intent should address every major issue that will be in the final purchase agreement. If you raise major new issues during the creation of the purchase agreement, it is guaranteed the seller will balk, and it could blow the whole deal. Once you have signed the letter of intent, the serious work begins. There is the accounting review, the legal review, and the start of diligence, as discussed in Chapter 9.

The letter of intent is not binding in most of its provisions, except that it legally locks up the deal for a period of time, usually sixty to ninety days. This means the seller cannot shop the deal or enter into discussions with prospective buyers. Both sides agree to make serious good faith efforts to put together the deal sketched out in the letter. The deal is, of course, subject to final documentation, but if all goes well in that process, the details of the term sheet become the provisions of the deal. The letter of intent also becomes the governing document for the deal that you show to financing partners and bankers. The Techway term sheet and letter of intent are annotated and presented as examples in this chapter; a copy of the letter of intent also is presented in Appendix B.

In negotiating the term sheet, you don't need lawyers and accountants. An operating and financial person in the firm can probably do most of the calculations well enough for this stage. There will be plenty of time for the lawyers and accountants to get their hands into it in the next stage. It keeps the process much simpler if both sides can sketch out the broad outlines of the deal. Sellers also can be scared off if you bring in too much firepower too early. A seller who has not already put the business on the market often starts out as a reluctant seller and gets more comfortable with the idea over time. The chemistry and key points of the deal can be worked out without significant expense and complexity.

I am not a lawyer and make no representation to you that the sample documents in this chapter are complete. They are presented only so you can familiarize yourself with their key features. You must have your own counsel on each deal, and certainly your counsel should be involved from the LOI phase forward. You'll be seeing a lot of your lawyers during this process, and in the end, I guarantee you'll either want to kiss them or kill them. There are seldom in-betweens. (As for the other side's counsel, I can almost guarantee that at the end you'll only have one of the two reactions. And it won't be a kiss.)

The Term Sheet

The term sheet is usually two to four pages outlining the broad conditions of the sale. Though short, it should be relatively thorough. It should specify price, whether the consideration is in cash or stock, the major diligence issues, and timeframe. The draft of the term sheet becomes a starting point for negotiations.

As discussed earlier, with your first term sheet, start about 10–20 percent lower on valuation than where you want to end up. If it is a less competitive situation, start even lower. Always put some items in the original proposal that you are willing to give away later but that you could live with if they stay. Sometimes these straw men stay in the deal. In one deal, for example, we put in a much higher performance hurdle than we expected the managers to agree to. It stayed, and now their higher returns are based on stellar performance that will reward all of us well. You will never get something unless you ask for it. The worst that will happen is the seller will say no. If the price is relatively close, neither side is likely to walk away over these tertiary issues.

There are no set standards for term sheet provisions. The following is an annotated sample term sheet for the Techway transaction that we prepared to send to the parent of Techway as a first-cut proposal on the deal. As you see, it's quite straightforward. As I reiterate often in the book, it is critical for you to get important issues on the table early. As such, if there's an important issue on your mind, put it in the term sheet at the outset.

Seller Term Sheet
Techway, Inc.

We have completed a significant analysis of this opportunity and are prepared to make an aggressive offer to acquire Techway in a management-friendly transaction on an expeditious time line. We have discussed the following proposal with the management team at Techway and believe that it represents a mutually beneficial opportunity for Techway, the parent company, and management.

1. Consideration
Our proposal will generate total proceeds to the parent of $110 million to $115 million. This will include $95 million in cash and 10 percent equity stake in Techway, which we believe will yield an additional $15 million to $20 million.

> The value of the offer and how the buyer will be paid is crucial. There are many ways to structure this consideration, including direct cash payments, seller notes, earn-outs, and consulting or noncompete fees, as discussed in more detail below.

2. Structure
We would propose that the buyer acquire approximately 90 percent of the stock of Techway from the parent company in a leveraged recapitalization, with the parent retaining approximately 10 percent ownership stake. The remaining equity will allow the parent to retain upside potential in the investment while allowing Techway to avoid the creation of book goodwill. We believe that the company could be an attractive candidate for a public offering and the avoidance of goodwill charges will benefit all equity holders. Additionally, the reten-

tion of an equity stake by the parent company is important to Techway's customers as evidence of the parent's support of the transaction and a vote of confidence in the future of Techway.

> This information gives the seller a compelling argument for keeping a small investment in the company going forward. As noted, structuring the deal this way adds to the credibility of the new company, but also gives the parent a stake in the upside, or "dummy insurance" in case the transaction turns out to be a home run.

3. Valuation

The all-in value of $110–$115 million to the parent company represents a fair value when compared to prevailing public market companies in similar businesses. The primary public competitors of Techway and the respective EBITDA valuation multiples are as follows:

Company	EBITDA
Company A	6.4%
Company B	7.6%
Company C	5.7%
Company D	7.7%
Company E	7.6%
Company F	7.8%
Average	7.1%

Based upon these multiples, the implied value of Techway is approximately $90–$120 million. Our offer is consistent with this implied value. This represents a particularly strong value when considering Techway's inconsistent historical returns and its customer concentration. More than half of Techway's revenue and more than half of Techway's profits are generated by one contract, which expires in three years. This customer concentration and projected revenue decline places risks on the buyer at these levels and is a further indication of the strong value the seller will receive in this transaction.

> This is one approach to making a proposal that gives the seller lots of information supporting the bid. This approach demonstrates your work and justifies your offer. It works through your reasoning both by comparing the valuation to industry multiples but also explaining how those multiples need to be adjusted for the particular weaknesses of the company being

sold. This approach empirically shows that your offer is a fair price for the business. If you have done your homework on valuation, this should be a fairly easy process. If, however, there are no direct market comparables or you do not wish to show your analytical approach to the seller, cut this valuation section back to bare-bones information.

4. Confidentiality
None of the parent company's proprietary information available in the data room will be reviewed by rivals and will remain confidential to the buyout firm and management.

Most sellers will require buyers to sign a confidentiality agreement at some point in the process. This type of language may also be included in the term sheet.

5. Exclusivity
The parent company agrees that until the termination of this letter as provided herein, neither the parent nor its representatives will submit, initiate, respond to, or discuss any proposal or offer from any person relating to any sale of Techway's securities or any part of Techway's assets.

This is an important provision that gives you exclusivity on the deal. It is also called a "no-shop" provision.

6. Binding Effect
Except for paragraphs 4, 5, and 7 of this letter, and this paragraph 6, this letter is not a binding agreement between the parties hereto and is only intended to be an expression of mutual understandings until definitive agreements are executed and delivered. Notwithstanding the foregoing, paragraphs 4, 5, and 7 and this paragraph will bind and inure to the benefit of the parties hereto.

This agreement, including the offer made and structure of the deal, is largely nonbinding. Only the confidentiality, exclusivity, and termination clauses are binding. It doesn't mean you can act with impunity. The term sheet sets the stage for more binding agreements to come, and a significant change in position in these later agreements could scuttle the deal.

7. Termination
This letter shall terminate, unless extended by the mutual agreement of the parties hereto, upon the earlier of a) three weeks, b) the execution of the defin-

itive agreements contemplated by this letter, or c) mutual agreement of each of the parties hereto to terminate this letter. Upon termination, this letter will be of no further force or effect and no party hereto will have any liability hereunder, except as set forth in paragraph 6 above and except with respect to breaches hereof prior to termination.

If you concur with the terms set forth above, please sign this letter in the spaces provided below and return an executed copy to us. Upon receipt of an executed copy of this letter, we will proceed with our due diligence and negotiations. We look forward to working with you on this important process.

Very truly yours,

_____

Buyer signature

_____

Seller signature

Letter of Intent

The seller will want to negotiate several of these major points set forth in the term sheet. If you reach a positive conclusion on the term sheet, this document evolves into the next phase of the document process—the drafting of the letter of intent.

The letter of intent is usually seven to ten pages. It is the first legally binding document in the process, so it is the critical document that sets the deal in place. You will want to have a highly detailed letter of intent with the seller that covers all major issues related to the purchase of the assets or the stock. If you have a detailed letter of intent, you are in good shape and the rest of the process won't be too painful. If you have a letter that doesn't tackle the hard issues up front, the subsequent negotiations are guaranteed to be brutal and you may be investing your precious time and money in a doomed negotiation.

What follows is an annotated letter of intent for the Techway transaction. This is a critical document that provides the foundation for all future negotiations and sets the major parameters of the deal in place. Although every LOI is different, this one should provide a decent working example on which to base the LOI for your deal.

Techway Letter of Intent

Investor
1515 Big Hitter Lane
Cash Flow, Wisconsin

Techway Parent CEO
Street
City, State, Zip

Dear Ladies & Gentlemen:

This letter agreement (the "Letter") sets forth the general terms pursuant to which Investor (the "Purchaser") is prepared to purchase all of the outstanding capital stock of Techway and any majority-owned subsidiaries of Techway (collectively, "Company") from the Techway Parent Co. ("Seller") (the "Transaction").

> This is a straightforward preamble. If you wish to add other introductory language with issues related to the specifics of your transaction, you should do so.

1. **Form of Transaction.** Subject to the terms of this Letter, Purchaser will purchase 100 percent of the Capital Stock of Company for the Purchase Price (as described in paragraph 2). As a result, Company will become a wholly owned subsidiary of Purchaser. For purposes of this Letter, "Capital Stock" includes all of the Company's common stock, preferred stock (if any), and any other securities (whether contingent or not) that are convertible into common stock or preferred stock. Purchaser will use its best efforts to structure the Transaction in the most tax-advantageous manner possible, which does not result in a tax or other economic detriment to Seller or Purchaser.

> This section lays out whether this transaction will be an asset or stock purchase. In this case, it's a stock deal and you need to make sure that all forms of stock are included. If it's an asset deal, it should lay out specifically which assets and liabilities are included. The tax-planning piece is included here to be comprehensive. If there are no specific tax issues to be highlighted in your deal, you can drop it.

2. **Purchase Price**. The purchase price ("Purchase Price") shall be the sum of the following:

(1) $95 million in cash.
(2) $5 million in the form of a performance-based promissory notes (the "Notes"). The Notes are described in detail in Section 3 of this Letter.
(3) Common stock in Purchaser equal to 9.2 percent of Purchaser's common stock that is currently outstanding (after giving effect to unexercised options in Purchaser).

Purchaser will work with Seller to provide at least 3 percent of the Purchase Price to the Company's key employees, as identified by Seller. (It is anticipated that the entire $95 million cash amount go to Seller, that the Notes be payable to the Company's key employees, and that the common stock in Purchaser be divided in the same 80/20 percent proportion among Seller and Company's key employees.)

This is obviously an important section that lays out the exact consideration, in detail. As this Techway example was an information technology services deal, which was totally dependent upon the people running the company, we wanted to make sure that they were receiving some compensation in the deal. This is typical in service company transactions.

3. **Notes**. The Notes shall have the following features:

A. **Priority**. The Notes shall be:
   • Senior in liquidation only to the amounts that Purchaser owes to its parent company, Techway Parent Co. ("Parent") (except for indebtedness described below in this Section 3).
   • Junior to any acquisition debt that may be incurred in connection with the Transactions contemplated by this letter.
B. **Performance Feature**. The Notes shall be payable in three equal installments: 12, 24, and 36 months after the closing of the Transactions contemplated by this Letter, provided, however, no amounts shall be due and payable under those Notes whose original holder is not employed by Company or one of its affiliates as of the scheduled payment date.

This section spells out some key provisions of the seller paper. As always, be detailed, direct, and specific.

4. **Sources and Uses.** In summary, cash sources and cash uses of funds are as follows:

Cash Uses (millions)		Cash Sources (millions)	
Purchase Price		Senior Bank Debt	50.000
Cash	95.000	Performance Equity	3.000
Note	5.000	Cash Equity	50.000
Transaction Exp's	3.000		103.000
	103.000		

It is very important to clearly delineate the cash in and cash out in the deal so everyone can review it and sign off. This is also important because people often forget or omit the transaction fees, which are usually 3–5 percent of the total deal and can have a big impact at the margin on your financing.

5. **Purchaser's Due Diligence Review.**

(a) Purchaser's due diligence review ("Purchaser's Due Diligence Review") will consist of a general review of the business and prospects of the Company, including an investigation of Company's historical financial statements, its products, and competitive position, and the sustainability of its originations, revenue, and cash flow, as well as customary legal, regulatory, tax, accounting, and investment structure due diligence. As part of Purchaser's Due Diligence Review, Purchaser will evaluate Company's future business prospects, will review its direct marketing and advertising processes, will assess the Company's ability to securitize its products, and will review loan files and underwriting procedures. Concurrent with Purchaser's Due Diligence Review, parties providing financing and their respective agents and representatives may also conduct due diligence reviews. Purchaser's Due Diligence Review will begin on the date upon which Purchaser and its agents, representatives, and financing sources are granted access to the Company's books, records, portfolio tapes, facilities, key personnel, officers, directors, independent accountants, and legal counsel in accordance with Section 9 below. The Seller agrees that such access will be granted promptly to the Purchaser, its agents, representatives, and financing sources following execution of this Letter. The Purchaser will complete due diligence within thirty days thereafter.

(b) Seller's due diligence review ("Seller's Due Diligence Review") will consist of a general review of the business and prospects of the Purchaser, including an investigation of Purchaser's historical financial statements, its products, and competitive position. Seller's Due Diligence Review will begin on the date upon which Seller and its agents and representatives are granted access to the Purchaser's key personnel, key officers, directors, independent accountants, and legal counsel. The Purchaser agrees that such access will be granted promptly to the Seller, its agents, and representatives, following execution of this Letter. The Seller will complete due diligence on the earlier of (1) the date on which Purchaser completes its diligence or (2) thirty days after execution of this Letter.

> This is an important section that lays out your diligence plan. Be detailed and comprehensive. Set out all major pieces of your work plan so there's no ambiguity.

6. **Definitive Purchase Agreement**. The Purchaser will prepare and deliver to the Seller within ten days of the conclusion of Purchaser's Due Diligence Review a definitive Purchase Agreement (the "Purchase Agreement"). The Purchase Agreement will contain terms and conditions customary in transactions of this type (including standard representations, warranties, covenants, and indemnifications) or which are reasonably necessary as a result of the Due Diligence Review. Representations regarding the Company will, for most items, survive closing for three years, and for other items, including without limitation environmental, taxes, ERISA, and title, the survival shall be for longer periods (and in some cases indefinite).

> This section could be even more comprehensive and is extremely important. It looks ahead to the creation of the purchase agreement and lays out major issues such as the survival period and what items will survive longer. Ask your counsel to assist you in being specific here as to which issues you will need representations for in the purchase agreement. Some standard provisions that could be put into the LOI include representations that all financial statements are true and accurate, that there is no known litigation threatening the company, and that the company has continued to be run in the ordinary course of business (e.g., no one has recently changed any major procedures at the company). These issues are covered in more detail later.

7. **Closing Conditions.** Purchaser's obligation to consummate the Transaction contemplated by this Letter is subject to, among other things, the following conditions:

i. Completion of, and Purchaser's satisfaction, in its sole discretion, with the results of Purchaser's Due Diligence Review;

ii. Negotiation and execution of a Purchase Agreement and all other necessary Transaction-related documentation mutually satisfactory to the parties thereto;

iii. Receipt of third-party financing on terms and conditions satisfactory to the Purchaser;

iv. Negotiation and execution of employment agreements with the CEO and other selected executives of the Company, identified by Purchaser during its due diligence, which agreements will contain noncompete/nonsolicit/confidentiality provisions. A draft employment agreement for the top five executives is to be provided as an attachment;

v. Absence of a material adverse change in the financial condition, results of operations, business, assets, properties, or prospects of Company since June 30, 2000;

vi. Compliance of the Transaction contemplated hereby with all laws and regulations applicable thereto, including (a) obtaining all necessary governmental and third-party approvals and consents (including consent by all applicable state licensing authorities) and making all necessary filings with regulatory authorities (including Hart-Scott-Rodino filings and approvals), and (b) the expiration of all waiting periods during which objections to the Transaction contemplated hereby can be raised; and

vii. Compliance by the Seller with its obligations hereunder.

The obligation of Seller to consummate the Transaction contemplated hereunder is subject to, among other things, the following conditions:

i. Completion of, and Seller's reasonable satisfaction with the results of Seller's Due Diligence Review (provided, however, Seller shall only be able to terminate this Letter based on this paragraph if Seller's Due Diligence Review reveals items that would reasonably cause Seller to believe that the Purchaser will lack the financial resources to repay the Note);

ii. Negotiation and execution of a Purchase Agreement and all other necessary Transaction-related documentation mutually satisfactory to the parties thereto;

iii. Compliance of the Transactions contemplated hereby with all laws and regulations applicable thereto, including (a) obtaining all necessary governmental and third party approvals and consents (including consent by all applicable state licensing authorities) and making all necessary filings with regulatory authorities (including Hart-Scott-Rodino filings and approvals), and (b) the expiration of all waiting periods during which objections to the Transaction contemplated hereby can be raised; and

iv. Compliance by the Purchaser with its obligations hereunder.

As you can see, this is a comprehensive section that delineates many issues. List all issues that are important conditions that must be satisfied before you will be willing to close the deal. Be specific. If there's a big customer concentration issue at the company and you need to meet face-to-face with that customer to satisfy yourself on the relationship, list this visit and your satisfaction as a closing condition. Hart-Scott-Rodino is an antitrust filing with the Securities and Exchange Commission (SEC) that costs $40,000 to file. Your counsel will help you prepare this filing.

   8. **Schedule.** Purchaser, Seller, and Company agree to use their reasonable efforts to adhere to the following schedule of events leading up to the closing (assuming acceptance of this Letter by September 5, 2000):

September 15, 2000:	Hart-Scott-Rodino filing will be prepared and filed, if necessary.
October 6, 2000:	Purchaser's Due Diligence Review will be completed.
October 16, 2000:	Purchaser will deliver a first draft of the Purchase Agreement to Seller.
October 29, 2000:	Purchase Agreement will be executed, and closing will occur was soon as practicable thereafter.

This section lays out major scheduling milestones to be achieved to meet the deal time line. These should be the major milestones that are a subset of your detailed time and responsibilities schedule (see Appendix G for an example), which you use as a tool to manage deal progress.

   9. **Cooperation.** Upon the Seller's acknowledgment of and agreement with the terms and conditions set forth in this Letter, the Seller will permit

the Purchaser and its agents, representatives, and financing sources (including attorneys, accountants, and any financing sources, and their agents and representatives) access to the Company's books, records, portfolio tapes, facilities, key personnel, officers, directors, independent accountants, and legal counsel in connection with Purchaser's Due Diligence Review.

This statement seems like a given in any deal, but it is important to spell it out. Some sellers may have a peculiar security or confidentiality concern, so it's important to address those issues up front.

10. **Exclusivity.**
    A. **Cessation of Other Acquirer Activity.** Company and Seller agree that from the date of their acknowledgment of and agreement with the terms and conditions set forth in this Letter through the closing of the Transaction contemplated by this Letter, or the earlier termination of this Letter, neither Company nor any of its record and beneficial shareholders, officers, directors, affiliates, agents, or representatives will, directly or indirectly:
       i. Submit, solicit, initiate, encourage, or discuss with third parties any proposal or offer from any person relating to any (a) reorganization, dissolution, or recapitalization of Company, (b) merger or consolidation involving Company, (c) sale of the stock of Company, (d) sale of any assets of Company outside the ordinary course of business or in connection with whole loan sales or securitizations unless consented to in advance by Purchaser, or (e) similar transaction or business combinations involving Company or its business or assets including without limitation any debt or equity financing thereof, or
       ii. Furnish any information with respect to, or assist or participate in or facilitate in any other manner any effort or attempt by any person to do or seek the foregoing.
    B. **Notification.** Company and Seller will, and will cause Company's officers, directors, affiliates, agents, and representatives, to terminate all discussions with any third-party regarding the foregoing and will notify Purchaser of the fact of receipt of any proposals or offers.
    C. **Representation and Indemnification.** Company's and Seller's acknowledgment of and agreement with the terms and conditions set forth in this Letter also constitutes a representation and warranty

that neither Company, Seller, nor any of Company's record and beneficial shareholders, officers, directors, affiliates, agents, or representatives have entered into any executory agreements or accepted any commitments concerning any of the foregoing transactions. Company and Seller hereby agree to indemnify and hold harmless Purchaser and each director, officer, investor, employee, and agent thereof (each, an "indemnified person") from and against any and all losses, claims, damages, liabilities (or actions or proceedings commenced or threatened in respect thereof), and expenses that arise out of, result from, or in any way relate to the breach of the foregoing representation and warranty. The obligations of Company and Seller under this paragraph will survive any termination of this Letter and will be effective regardless of whether a definitive agreement is executed.

Overall, this exclusivity section is key because it locks up the deal for you and ensures that the seller will no longer discuss the transaction with any other third parties.

11. **Conduct of the Business.** Upon acceptance of this Letter and until the earlier of closing the Transaction contemplated by this Letter or the termination of this Letter, Company agrees to preserve substantially intact its business operations and assets and to conduct its operations in the ordinary course of business consistent with past operations. Without limiting the generality of the foregoing, Company shall not, without the prior written consent of Purchaser, (i) make any material capital expenditures, (ii) make or pay any dividends or distributions of any kind, (iii) enter into any material contracts, commitments, or arrangements (except in the ordinary course of business), (iv) change any compensation plans or pay any bonuses, (v) change any underwriting guidelines, or (vi) launch materially new products.

This section further ensures that the business will be managed in the ordinary course and that nothing unusual will be done with any assets.

12. **Management.** It is anticipated that Company will be a stand-alone subsidiary of a holding company to be formed by our counsel for the purposes of consummating this acquisition. The CEO (named) will remain President and

CEO of the Company for three years, pursuant to an employment agreement, a draft of which is attached to this letter.

> This section denotes the acquiring entity and sets forth any required senior management employment agreements.

13. **Reimbursement of Fees and Expenses.** If the Transaction is not consummated by reason of a breach by the Seller or Company of any obligations under this Letter, the Seller and the Company hereby agree that Seller and the Company will jointly and severally reimburse the Purchaser and its affiliates for their out-of-pocket costs and expenses, including legal and other professional fees and expenses, incurred in connection with Purchaser's Due Diligence Review, the preparation, review, negotiation, execution, and delivery of this Letter, the definitive agreements and other documents relating to the Transaction, and the financing of the Transaction. If the Transaction is consummated, Seller and Purchaser will each bear their own expenses (and Seller will bear Company's expenses). No party to this Transaction has any liability to brokers in connection with this Transaction, or to which any other party to this Letter could become obligated. No employees of the Company will receive any payment, bonus, or other extraordinary compensation as a result of this Transaction.

> This is an excellent clarifying paragraph on who is responsible for which expenses. Again, it's helpful to be specific.

14. **Termination.** Purchaser's offer hereunder will expire at 12:00 noon, Wisconsin Time, on September 5, 2000 ("Expiration"), unless the Seller and Company agree to the terms and conditions of this Letter by signing and returning to the Purchaser the enclosed counterpart of this Letter and the Purchaser receives such signed counterpart prior to that time. The Purchaser may terminate this Letter at any time if: (i) any information is disclosed to or discovered by the Purchaser or its representatives, after the conclusion of the Purchaser's Due Diligence Review, which the Purchaser believes in good faith may be materially adverse to the Transaction or to the financial condition, results of operations, business, assets, properties, or prospects of the Company, or (ii) the Purchaser believes in good faith that one or more of the conditions to closing set forth herein will not be fulfilled. The Seller shall be permitted to terminate this Letter at any time after sixty days from the date hereof in the event that the Purchase Agreement is not executed on or before that time. Notwithstanding

the foregoing, (i) this Letter shall not be terminated if the closing is delayed solely due to delays in obtaining regulatory approval, (ii) the Reimbursement of Fees and Expenses section shall not terminate even if this Letter is terminated, and (iii) the obligations under subparagraph "C" of the Exclusivity section of this Letter shall not terminate even if this Letter is terminated.

This provision spells out exactly how long this offer stands. It is often important to have specific drop-dead times to move the process along.

15. **Binding Effect.** Subject to the conditions set forth herein, the obligations of each of the parties under this letter shall be binding at the time this letter is executed; provided, however, that the parties acknowledge that not all terms to be reflected in the Purchase Agreement and related documents have been discussed and agree to negotiate in good faith to finalize these agreements setting forth such additional terms.

This is a binding letter, still subject to final documentation and financing.

16. **Announcements.** All press releases and other announcements relating to the Transaction shall be subject to prior approval by Purchaser, Company, and Seller.

This is an important provision that is often overlooked. Will any press releases be issued? Who will respond to press inquiries? How will communications with employees, suppliers, and customers be conducted? These communications issues are very important to the reception of a deal announcement, set the tone for the merger, and can have an impact on the outcome of the deal. They should be carefully considered.

17. **Governing Law.** The Transaction shall be governed by the laws (which shall mean all laws other than conflict of laws) of the State of Delaware.

Although this isn't usually a big issue, make sure that the jurisdiction is not in a state with odd laws (such as Louisiana) or one that is overly unfriendly to corporate matters. The normal prevailing legal domains are New York or Delaware.

Please sign and date this Letter no later than the time of Expiration (as set forth in the "Termination" Section, above) in the spaces provided below to confirm our mutual understandings and agreements as set forth in this Letter and return a signed copy to the undersigned. By signing this Letter, you are representing that you have authority to consummate this Transaction and that you are the sole shareholder of the Company (and that no other shareholders exist whose approval could be necessary to consummate this Transaction).

PURCHASER

By: _____
Investor and Management

ACKNOWLEDGED AND AGREED TO
AS OF SEPTEMBER _____, 20_____

_____

Selling CEO *(or person with authority to sign for the corporation)*

There's obviously a great deal of important detail implicit in this agreement, so it's vital to have excellent counsel working with you through a successful conclusion on this document. The key issues to be carefully considered in this document are discussed in the next section.

Key Issues of the Sell-Side Agreements

In examining these agreements with the seller, among the most important issues to consider beyond the price are consideration, confidentiality agreements, and the representations and warranties to be made by the seller to you.

Consideration
Obviously, in these early documents, price is the fundamental issue. But another important issue to address is the so-called consider-

ation (meaning how payments will be broken out between cash, notes, earn-outs, or equity). For example, there may be a provision for the seller to take 20–30 percent of the deal back in a debt instrument of some type, which can be advantageous for financing and boost the credibility of your new company.

Of course, the consideration has serious implications for the deal. Let's discuss some of the options for the consideration. The cash portion is, of course, straightforward: You give the seller cash for a piece or all of the business. There are several other primary vehicles that may be used as consideration, each of which is discussed next.

Seller Notes

Seller notes are used when the seller of the company takes a note or debt instrument, which he holds as an asset, for a portion of the purchase price. These notes are used very frequently in deals, particularly in family-held companies or in companies that have had bumpy financial histories. There are numerous advantages for a buyer to have the seller take notes as part of the payment:

1. The notes generally reduce your overall cost of financing the transaction. It's usually cheap debt that you now do not need to go to a bank to finance.

2. The notes demonstrate the seller's support for the business and willingness to keep some skin in the game. This conveys the seller's sense of confidence in the business, which is usually a very positive signal for your lenders and other partners.

3. The use of notes shows continuity. This may be important, particularly in family-held companies, to show suppliers, employees, and customers that the prior owner still has an ongoing interest in the business.

While there are advantages to having the former owner involved, in conserving cash and ensuring continuity, there are also disadvantages. The new buyer must evaluate whether he *wants* the former owner to have a financial stake in the new company. This generally means that the former owner will have a right to see financial information and to look over your shoulder to a certain extent. Also, if things do not go well, the former owner is now a noteholder and you may end up negotiating with him in a restructuring, so you must think carefully about whether the cash and continuity are worth this potential price.

Why should the seller take notes as consideration? From a seller's perspective, cash is almost always better. The notes can provide a deferral of some capital gains taxes if the notes can be treated on an installment sale basis. Current tax laws are tough on this provision and should be reviewed with your accountant.

The structure of the notes is almost purely a matter of negotiation. The current market approach is to pay interest at a value of close to the prime lending rate with perhaps a 1 to 2 percent premium to acknowledge the risk implicit in the situation. These notes can either be structured as cash pay or as "accruing" interest, which means the interest is paid in more notes. About half the cases are cash pay. Accruing interest saves you cash in the future. Obviously, you should ask for accruing interest if the seller is willing.

The notes usually range between 5–25 percent of the overall purchase price, but again, it depends on what you negotiate. The only requirement on the term of debt will come from your banks, which require that the seller's note have a longer term than their bank debt. From the bankers' perspective, they want to make sure the seller can't get paid out before they do. Thus, if the bank debt term is five years, the seller term will need to be six.

Earn-Out

The earn-out is a common approach that partially pays the seller out of the future earnings of the business. The theory here is that a buyer and a seller do not know exactly how the business will perform in the future, and if it performs very well, the seller should get a piece of that upside. For example, if the company is making $10 million in profit and you're buying it for $60 million pretax, the seller might get 20 percent of pretax profits above $12 million for the first three years. Earn-outs are used often. From a buyer's perspective, it seems to make sense. If the business goes great, the seller gets something. If not, he doesn't. It sounds so simple and beautiful that many deal makers jump at the chance. But I *hate* earn-outs and believe they should be avoided like root canal work without anesthesia. How much do I loathe earn-outs? Let me count the ways:

1. *The seller is now your partner.* With an earn-out, the seller now has a huge interest in seeing you maximize profits and use the most aggressive accounting tactics to do so. If you decide to accelerate depreciation on a piece of equipment (which may be the right thing to do, though it lowers profits), the seller will be screaming bloody murder. If he doesn't like your accounting results, he'll accuse you of cooking the books. Now the seller earn-out becomes a ball and chain, weighing down the business. Sellers know the business inside and out, and so can be expected to have an informed opinion on virtually every decision, which they will be only too happy to share if their interests are threatened. Also, with a long history of relationships within the firm and outside, an angry seller can cause you many problems.

2. *Earn-outs misalign incentives.* While it seems as if you and the seller are in the same boat—an aligned goal of maximizing profits—you're not. Suppose you decide in the middle of year one that you need to make a larger investment in your plant. That may be lousy for the first year income statement and great for the year-four income statement—after the earn-out. Here, the best interests of the company and the new owners may conflict with the earn-out of the seller. Now the seller is your partner and you can't optimize decisions.

Overall, earn-outs sound fine, but they almost always lead to accounting questions, seller audits of the books, and poor decision making for the business. Also, what if you make an acquisition in which the former seller has no interest and you wish to consolidate plants to cut costs? As you can see, it's a mess. I'd take the root canal any day.

Covenant-Not-to-Compete/Consulting Contract
There are two vehicles for paying out additional cash to the former owner that also, in general, have the benefits of lowering your up-front accounting goodwill and being tax deductible over time. They're simple purchase price financing mechanisms, which are generally beneficial to the buyer because they lower cash up

front and give the seller an ongoing, if mostly symbolic, financial interest in the company. They both get you to the same place, which is that rather than paying the seller $750,000 cash up front, you pay the seller $250,000 per annum to consult to the company going forward. In the covenant-not-to-compete, you pay the seller an amount each year as an inducement not to compete with you. You must have the accountants opine on both of these approaches, but they are viable ways to distribute purchase price over time rather than to pay it up front.

Purchase Structures

On every deal there are complex accounting and tax issues at work. As such, you must have excellent tax and accounting advice when you approach your structure. Your buyout partners are experts here and should add great value in this area. Entire books have been written on the nuances of purchase structures, so I will only highlight two major structures and some issues related to each.

From an accounting and tax perspective, there are fundamentally four ways to purchase a company. Earlier, we discussed one of those, the asset purchase, which can be applicable in some situations. The asset purchase is beneficial to the buyer because it eliminates purchase goodwill and allows you clean title to the assets with none of the liabilities of a stock purchase. But the asset sale can be very tax inefficient for the seller, and as such is used in a small minority of deals.

Other purchase approaches all entail the purchase of a company's stock. When you buy stock, you also acquire all of the liabilities associated with such stock, which is why you need a comprehensive and exclusive purchase agreement to protect you after closing. In a normal stock purchase, you generate accounting "goodwill," which is the amount of your purchase price in excess of the net book value of the company. Because goodwill is amortized against earnings, it is not tax deductible and as such is not desirable. However, it also often cannot be avoided. Most deals are structured as straightforward stock purchases.

There are, however, two ways to avoid goodwill in the purchase. The first is a "recapitalization" of the company, which can only be achieved if the seller of the company is willing to hold at least a 10 percent stake in the new company. This dynamic has its own set of pros and cons similar to the seller note. Although it shows commitment to the new company, it also means the seller is your "partner" for life. The "recap," as it's called, though, has become very popular in deal circles, particularly in low tangible net worth industries such as technology.

Because of the elimination of the goodwill earnings drag, it is usually worth having a minority partner, particularly if you plan to go public. The details of accomplishing a recap are complex (and you should seek detailed tax advice here), but in general what it entails is funding the bank debt and equity dollars into the target company, which then repurchases up to 90 percent of the stock directly from the current owner. Thus the company is "recapitalized," not "purchased," and you have no goodwill. I'm not sure how long this approach is going to escape SEC/FASB scrutiny, but it works today and should be actively pursued if it works on your transaction.

The last way to afford a purchase without goodwill is in a "pooling" transaction, but to complete a pooling you must already own another company which is "poolable." The pooling rules are highly complex and cannot be utilized in a stand-alone buyout and won't be addressed further here. Also, the issue of pooling is at the center of a raging tax debate (particularly in the technology world) and FASB has said that poolings will no longer be acceptable after December 31, 2000.

Confidentiality Agreements

To see the company's financials, you normally will need to sign a confidentiality agreement. (For a sample, please see Appendix D.) Sellers are understandably nervous about their strategic information getting into the hands of rivals. Usually these agreements are routine. They make sure that only you or your representatives review the information. Once the deal is terminated, all the material must be returned or destroyed. The information needs to be kept in confidence for a specified period, usually a year and sometimes longer. The agreements usually also require the potential buyer not to solicit employees from the company during the period covered.

The company can sue you to hell and back if you breach this agreement. People have become very cavalier about these documents. My advice: Don't be. These are serious and meaningful agreements and should be treated as such.

What do you need to watch out for? Very long "tails" on the agreement can significantly constrain your actions. If sellers ask for confidentiality for more than a year, they should have a good reason. With the pace of change in business today, most information is pretty useless within a year. In addition to a nondisclosure agreement, public companies often also ask for a "standstill agreement." A standstill agreement means you can't buy company stock during negotiations, so you may need an even shorter tail on this agreement, maybe three to six months. The nonsolicitation of employees clause should not be too broad. It should clearly read that the potential buyer should not actively "solicit" or recruit employees. If, however, employees quit and wish to come to work for you, you should have the right to hire them.

Remember that the confidentiality agreement, like all agreements, is negotiable. As with all negotiations, you need to clearly identify the points that are important for you to win up-front and be prepared to give a little on points that are less important, so the other side can feel good about winning a few points.

The negotiations related to this simple agreement tell you worlds about how the deal is going to go, whether the people you are negotiating with are realistic, and whether there will be a deal. You will have to work out very tricky issues with the seller for a few months, so don't just look at the numbers. Look for signs that the seller will be easy to work with. Pay attention to body language and signals.

Representations and Warranties

Among the primary issues covered in both the LOI and the final purchase agreement are the seller's representations and warranties. Here the seller represents that the assets are of good quality and that the financials are accurate. The seller also affirms that he controls the assets and has the right and ability to transfer assets to you; has done nothing out of the ordinary to impact the assets or liabilities; has no specific litigation outstanding, other than litigation specifically raised; and has no specific material changes on the horizon other than those written out in closing schedules that are appended to the final purchase agreement. On the buyer side, you represent that you are a buyer in good standing and have all the authorizations and capital necessary to close the transaction.

Of course, as a management team, you may not currently have all of the money "committed" to do the deal. This is a very typical situation and is simply fully disclosed to the seller as a "financing out." This means that you disclose that you do not have the capital today to do the deal and that you are currently seeking committed capital for the transaction. A capital commitment, by the way, is a serious matter and has clear meaning in financial circles. Having a "commitment" means that you have third parties legally committed to fund to you. It means you have, in your possession, "commitment letters" from financial institutions that are prepared, *now*, to fund your transaction. These are detailed letters that are difficult to obtain. The point is, of course, that unless you are prepared to cut the check yourself, do not tell the seller or any party that you have committed capital unless you can back it up. That said, capital commitments normally come together at the end of a deal, and buyers almost always have financial outs until very near closing, or at the time of the signed purchase agreement.

The selling documents also specify how financial disputes related to the company and the deal are handled after closing. Even if you have a strong and detail-oriented lawyer, you need to pay attention as a manager, because many thresholds and timeframes vary by industry and business. For example, many documents have a dollar threshold for taking action against the seller or a time limit on seller responsibility. In general, there is a "basket" of stuff that is too small to bother with. The seller doesn't want the buyer coming back to argue over nickels and dimes after the deal. On a $100 million deal, you might set up a $250,000 basket, below which the buyer group agrees to assume incremental costs. As a manager, you may know that this amount is either too low or too high.

There are also very important survival issues for representations and warranties. In some deals, the seller may make the representations for one year, beyond which you can't call the seller to pursue any misrepresentation and monetary damages. Several representations, such as those relating to environmental issues and tax issues that can haunt you for many years to come and are hard to evaluate normally, stand in perpetuity or for a ten-year period. Again, as a manager, you may know because of your business cycles that problems might not surface until eighteen months after the transfer. In that case, you must push the seller to extend the representations and warranties to at least twenty-four months.

These are just a few of the cases in which managers can identify strategic issues that will affect the shape of the deal. For every document that comes by, carefully consider its strategic implications. Will the document bind your hands in any way as a manager? Are there strategic risks created by the agreement?

Deal with the Hard Issues Up Front

The next lesson is one of the most important in the book, and it is one that I've learned the very hard way, through losing literally millions of dollars on dozens of broken deals. The worst part is this: All of these expenses and the associated pain could have been avoided by following a seemingly simple lesson: Deal with the hard issues up front.

Sadly, it's human nature to wish to defer pain and conflict until a later date. We all know in our hearts, however, the truth, which is that we would be much better off in the long run if we dealt with the hard issues early and decisively. Then we could move on and enjoy our lives with much less stress from looming dark clouds. This is the same in the deal business. Only here the price is not just psychological discomfort. The price is big dollars and the value of lost opportunity as well.

In every deal, there are hard issues. There are always bumps in the road, and many will come up unexpectedly. With most of these difficulties, you can do nothing about them other than tackle them energetically as they arise. However, there are also hard points in every deal that are apparent on day one. Your deal may require key people in an organization to sign employment contracts. Or perhaps there is a dominant customer whose contract you'll need to review. Or perhaps you require full environmental indemnification from the seller. Whatever the issues are, many people wish to leave these challenges until the end of the negotiations. Then, they believe, the seller may be more "pregnant" with the process and unable to walk away. This kind of wishful thinking is simply foolish and can only lead to difficulties. Bringing up the hard issues right up-front, in a detailed letter of intent, provides many benefits. It allows you to:

1. *Smoke out deal breakers.* By discussing the hard issues early in the process, you find out which issues are deal breakers and which are not. You'll usually be surprised that even the tough issues may not be deal breakers if put on the table early. By finding out if your key issues are deal breakers, you'll save enormous amounts of time and money.

2. *Create trust.* Everyone knows there will be hard issues, and by getting them on the table right away, you let the seller know that you're prepared to discuss the issues in a sensible and trusting way. If you conversely bring up new, challenging issues late in the process, the seller may believe you are trying to retrade the deal by raising new issues when you have most of the leverage. This is simply a destructive dynamic that can quickly erode much of the trust you have created in wooing the seller.

3. *Avoid "issue anxiety."* If you wait until the end of a protracted negotiation to bring up a major issue, you will be living with the uncertainty of that result and the inherent "issue anxiety" every day. It is much better to get the issue on the table and leave that part of the unnecessary anxiety behind you, so you can focus on the *necessary* anxiety of the deal. You will sleep a little better at night.

Some buyers dismiss problems in putting together the letter of intent, hoping things will get easier. Or they avoid dealing with the difficult issues just to move the letter along and avoid conflict with a difficult seller. This is a huge mistake, one which is often made by even the most seasoned deal maker. The same issues will come back with a vengeance during the development of the purchase agreement and other more extensive and binding documents. At that point, the issues will be harder to deal with and you will have sunk more money into the deal that you likely will never see again if it goes sour.

If there is going to be bad news, get it out as quickly as possible. Smoke out whether there really is a deal. If not, then you can move on the next opportunity. At my firm, we sift through some

500 deals per year that are proposed as bona fide transactions to pursue six or seven good ones. That is pretty much the ratio—one in a hundred. You cannot do every deal that comes along, even if you are excited about the idea and the deal is for the company where you currently work. Some deals don't work at any price. If you are evaluating external deal opportunities, you should plan on spending at least a year and looking at fifty or more deals to get something teed up.

If the deal with the seller determines what goes into the deal, the agreements with a buyout partner determine what comes out of it. That's the topic of Chapter 7. Financially, whatever terms the management team agrees to with the buyout firm will determine the returns they get out of the deal. Strategically, whatever strategy is agreed upon will be the one managers will live with for years to come. And, as far as personal chemistry, whatever devils or angels you bring into your life with the management deal will be there to haunt you or bless you for the next few years at least.

CHAPTER 7

Show Me the Money

"Many things are lost for want of asking."
—English proverb

Iconixx Corporation founder Stu Johnson had met Tony Forstmann when Forstmann came to Johnson's offices to discuss Bell Atlantic's interactive video operation. They became friends, and Forstmann said he'd like to find a company to pursue together if Johnson ever left Bell Atlantic. When Johnson was looking at buying out the Bell Atlantic network integration business he had built, he looked up Tony and met with his brother Nick, the cofounder of the legendary buyout firm Forstmann Little & Co. At his first meeting, Nick Forstmann wanted to discuss the management deal. Johnson put him off, saying he wanted to find out whether he could put the deal together with Bell Atlantic first. He was actually just stalling. He had never done a deal of this type before and had no idea what to ask for.

"I said, let's see if we can put together a deal first," Johnson recalled. "I was just treading water because I didn't know enough about it." He learned quickly.

Thus began Johnson's education in the buyout world. Bell Atlantic ultimately decided it didn't want to go through with the deal, but Johnson learned a tremendous amount about working with buyout partners. Several years and a dozen potential equity partners later, he probably knew as much about the buyout business as most prospective investors. He and his partners had talked to a wide range of equity partners. Johnson had progressed pretty far in putting together term sheets with some of them. At this point, he knew what kind of investor he was looking for and under what kind of terms.

This chapter will provide you with a head start in your first meeting with buyout investors. It offers an overview of buyout firms and examines the kinds of deals you need to strike with them. We also explore some of the key documents needed for those deals. Finally, we look at diverse aspects of bank financing. You will still learn much more from your own direct experience than from reading about the process, but this overview can help you make better deals and hit the ground running.

Hard-Won Lessons

What were the primary lessons about working with equity partners from Johnson's perspective? He identified several key insights:

• *Experience pays.* As with any skill, you get better with practice. Johnson knew a lot more about the investment business by the time he reached his tenth firm than when he started. He knew what partners wanted, what the best terms might be, and how he could most favorably position the deal. He learned this partly through conscious effort and partly through long-suffering experience. "By the time we put together the deal, we knew what they were looking for and how we were perceived by investors," he said. "If you don't talk to at least two potential partners, and ideally at least a half dozen, you are doing yourself a disservice." Buyout firms differ greatly in their goals and operations, and you will learn things about them and about the industry that you can only learn through experience. Many firms focus on specialized industry groups and most only pursue deals in a certain size range that is normally dictated by the size of the fund they manage. You should understand the quirks and special interests of each of the firms well before you approach them. You can find out a lot by getting recommendations from your own networks. Then you can ask for information from the firms or go to their Web sites to assess whether there is a good match with your deal and objectives. Some firms will say they will only work with you on an exclusive basis. Unless they are already your last resort, there are usually enough others around that you should walk away from these deals. If they were good partners, they wouldn't want to handcuff you to the furniture at the outset. As with all deals, it is critical to have several irons in the fire so you're not relying on one party.

• *The more you bring to the table, the more you take away.* Prospective investors are concerned about all levels of risk involved in pursuing transactions. Their time and money are extremely valuable, so they are constantly assessing your deal against the backdrop of thirty other deals they're pursuing. Can this team get it done? Does the deal yield the necessary return? Is there a real seller here? Can we finance the deal? Do we want to be in this industry? When and where can we exit? The more risk, the harder it will be to sell the deal to investors and the worse terms management will receive. And the converse is also true: If you tee up a sweetheart deal for the buyout firm and you've already got a credible, signed letter of intent (LOI) at five times EBITDA ready to go, you've just created huge value for them and should be asking for 25–35 percent rather than the customary 15 percent. When Johnson found investors were concerned about the integration risks of joining together fifteen companies, he reduced his target to just three core companies. By putting together an outstanding management team and a solid strategy, he was able to add significantly to the attractiveness of the deal. "Try to do as much of their work for them as you can," he said. "Look at the competitive landscape and tie down the strategy." On the other hand, the price of this preparation was that Johnson and his partner Bill Albright had put up more than $30,000 of their own capital for the initial research and start-up. At the point they needed to hire young managers, Johnson wanted to ensure that they could cover salaries and expenses for fifteen months to get the business going, so he needed to come up with an additional $3 million of seed capital, which he ultimately sourced from a Virginia-based venture capital firm.

• *Understand the competition.* Equity firms see many deals, but managers often act as if theirs is the only one. "You think you are the only deal these guys see because you live with it day and night," Johnson said. "There is another bus along every fifteen minutes. You have no appreciation for the deal flow and the work that is involved in analyzing the deal flow." The strategy for the business needs to be well reasoned and clearly presented.

• *Understand your leverage.* Johnson was surprised at how valuable his own experience and his team actually was. He remembered one investor who commented that he never lost money on technology or on betting on the long-term in the market. The investor only lost money betting on the wrong management. "I started to see I had more leverage than I thought I had," Johnson said. "The strength of the management team casts a larger shadow than even I thought it would."

• *Understand your worth.* When another equity partner told Johnson they never did a deal above 15 percent, Johnson countered: "You have never done something with a company this far along. I've done most of the work that you perceive as risk and it is ready." Johnson had a good strategy that was executable. There was no market risk, no technology risk. There was only execution risk, and they had a great team. The buyout partner settled on a term sheet at 22 percent.

• *Know what you are looking for.* Find an investment partner with a compatible philosophy and probe to understand the philosophy. Johnson once came close to signing with an equity firm that initially talked like a long-term strategic investor. Weeks later, they started discussing cashing out in six to nine months. "I had to hear that their philosophy was to build a strong operating company," Johnson said, "and there wasn't a gun to my head to get this company into the public markets." Johnson passed on the churn-and-burn partner in favor of a longer-term investor.

What Do Buyout Firms Really Want?

Through a careful study of the industry and interactions with different buyout firms, Johnson gained an understanding of the buyout business that he could use in developing his deals with equity partners. Understanding how buyout firms work and their various motivations is very important to your approach and interaction with them. In this chapter, we offer an overview of the industry and discuss sample agreements between managers and buyout firms. We also explore the other principle source of financing for the deal: banks.

Although buyout firms differ based on their particular character and investment strategy, they generally have told their investors that they will generate a minimum 30 percent annual rate of return. A deal that comes along that falls well short of this level is likely to go quickly into the dustbin. Most firms are also looking for a credible management team and the ability to get their money out within three to five years. They are looking for money makers and good leaders with a proven profit and loss record and an established record of success who have run all facets of a business. Above all, they are looking for people they can trust.

A Brief History of Private Equity (Buyout) Firms

Contrary to popular belief, the buyout industry wasn't started by KKR in the 1980s. The management buyout industry was started early this century when financiers such as J. P. Morgan, Charlie Allen, and John D. Rockefeller used money borrowed against the assets of a target company to acquire a series of companies and build a large business. In those days, the deals were called "bootstrap" deals instead of leveraged buyouts, but it was essentially the same structure as used today (though in those days they probably paid only three times cash flow!). The buyout business became institutionalized by a number of today's largest and best-known masters such as KKR and Clayton, Dubilier & Rice in the mid-1970s. The private equity industry expanded rapidly through the 1980s. The massive leveraged buyout (LBO) deal growth of the 1980s, driven partly by Michael Milken's junk bond business at Drexel Burnham Lambert, culminated with the race to acquire RJ Reynolds for $25 billion in the biggest buyout ever at the time (as wonderfully detailed in the book *Barbarians at the Gate*). In 1989, when Drexel collapsed and the debt markets dried up, the industry hit a big bump in the road, and growth slowed dramatically until 1992.

At the time, no one ever expected to see another "era of greed" like we saw in the late 1980s. But, to paraphrase Mark Twain, the rumors of the death of the industry were greatly exaggerated. Surprisingly, the stable economic growth of the 1990s led to a resurgence in the buyout industry that makes the deal velocity of the 1980s look like child's play. For example, in 1996, the buyout industry as a whole raised around $18 billion to invest in deals. This was more than was ever raised in any one year in the 1980s. Industry watchers thought this level would never be matched again. Amazingly, from 1996 to today, the dramatic growth has continued such that during 2000, buyout firms will raise over $90 billion! Industry estimates are now that there is more than $200 *billion* of uninvested equity standing by to pursue *your buyout.*

It's important to understand the mechanics of buyout firms so you can further understand their motivations. Most of the money used to fund deals doesn't come out of the pockets of the buyout firm managers. Buyout firms raise funds primarily from large institutional investors, particularly corporate and state pension funds. These are huge funds made up of retirees' pension dollars. (The California Public Employees' Retirement System, CalPERS, had more than $168 *billion* of assets in early 2000.) The funds put most of their assets into stocks and bonds, but generally are allowed to invest in the range of 5–15 percent of their funds in "alternative assets." These alternative investments include LBO funds, venture capital funds, and real estate funds.

These investments offer higher rewards and higher risks than traditional equity and debt instruments. Although it is a tiny part of a fund's overall portfolio, these small percentages generate huge amounts of capital for which buyout funds aggressively compete. For example, the State of Michigan's employee pension fund of approximately $40 billion has about $4 billion committed to "alternative assets." These investors are the masters to whom the buyout firms must answer. When a buyout firm sets up an $800 million fund, each of these institutional investors has made a commitment to invest at a certain level (usually $20 million to $50 million) for a five-year period. They realize these riskier investments can have their downside, but if the returns are not generated for investors, the money will not come back to the buyout firm. Thus, buyout firms face intense pressure to invest the large sums of capital at high rates of return, or they will be put out of business.

Buyout firms pay their own overhead and deal expenses through a management fee of 1.5–2 percentage points per year charged to the investors for managing the capital. The professionals at the firm generally get 20 percent of the profits (the "carry" or "carried interest") generated by the investments they make. This piece of the action is the buyout firm's Holy Grail and provides a massive upside incentive for them to do successful deals. You'd be surprised, but buyout firms generally have fairly small staffs. KKR, among the largest in the world, may have forty or fifty people. Our firm has just sixteen professionals, and the usual range is ten to fifteen employees. Everyone is extremely busy managing the existing portfolio of ten to twenty companies and looking for the next big winners.

This means that whenever a new potential deal comes in, there are probably thirty to fifty other deals sitting on the table. Buyout firm professionals are highly compensated, very busy, and have short attention spans. Managers who want to put together a deal need to be very tenacious in contacting buyout partners. As discussed in Chapter 5, when you are trying to get a firm's attention, it behooves you to have a tight presentation. On paper, it should be boiled down to a few pages. On the phone or in person, it should be a direct ten-minute pitch. After that, if the buyout partner isn't interested, he is already thinking about the next deal.

Obviously, it's also important for you to know which firms to contact and why. Like any increasingly mature industry, the buyout world has become segmented into a number of different niches. You must match your deal to the type of deals that buyout firms do and the size range each firm prefers to target. In Appendix I, we provide a selected list of buyout shops with some notes as to their specific interests, but you should study each firm further yourself. All the firms have Web sites, so that's the best place to start looking.

The primary reasons for their potential interest in a deal will be location, size, and industry. Location is obvious. Firms like to work on deals that are nearby so travel times can be minimized. For the same reasons, you should seek out local firms so you travel less and have a more accessible partner. Second, on size, most firms only work on deals of certain ranges. This is typically driven by the amount of money that the firm has under management. In our case, with more than $800 million under management, we need to do deals that require at least $20 million of equity and preferably $50 million. We're located in Washington, D.C., so we prefer deals in the Mid-Atlantic region. To work on smaller deals, we have established a $75 million partnership that targets $3 million to $10 million investments. If your deal requires $5 million, target suitable funds. If it requires $200 million to $500 million of equity, now you can get the attention of Henry Kravis or Ted Forstmann.

Finally, many firms specialize in investing in particular industries. Our firm, for example, targets information technology, electronics manufacturing, and the travel industry because these are the industries in which the firm's partners have expertise. Other firms specialize only in information technology, health care, or consumer products, or even low-tech industries. Some firms, but only a few, focus on turnarounds. Others target industry consolidation plays, backing teams in a series of acquisitions. As I mentioned, check the firm's Web site first to determine which sectors they target and align your interests with theirs. Again, a list of selected buyout firms from diverse regions and with diverse interests is also given in Appendix I.

Create a Mini-Auction for Your Talent
Be sure to line up at least five or six firms to pursue, for two reasons: first, to be able to create an auction for your talents and, second, you'll need several potential partners because even the most logical firm for the project may be too busy at any given time to take on your buyout. Managers with a proven track record will command more attention. But you cannot rest on your laurels. The buyout firm is not looking at how impressive your resume is, but whether you have a plan to do something that is worth investing in. You need a credible plan that spells out the strategy, the potential returns, and exit strategies.

If none of the firms likes your deal, you've got to reevaluate. But if more than one firm expresses interest, there is no reason why you can't set up a bakeoff among them. If you get your term sheet in front of two or three firms, you can haggle with them over different provisions and play them off one another to create the best deal for yourself. ("Your competitor is offering us three-year vesting. Do you think you could match it?") Of course, this means more headaches and lost deals from the investor's side and for managers, but managers will end up with a better deal. And buyout investors know it goes with the territory. The only way you will know you are getting the best possible deal is if you have shopped it around.

Drawing Up the Management Term Sheet

Your relationship with the buyout firm is defined by a set of agreements. The management term sheet is the starting point for negotiating the management deal. These few pages will likely represent the most important single financial deal you as a manager will make in your career, and they should be treated as such. This is it. This is the negotiation for your piece of the pie. As we learned in the case of SAGA, this piece can be worth tens of millions of dollars—or much less if the management deal is not a good one. The management deal will ultimately become very complex, but the bottom line is simple: How much of the company will you as a team own at the end of the day? How much upside will you have? What do you need to do to get it? You'll also have to address specifically how much each team member individually owns. This is challenging, too, as discussed later in this chapter.

In the past, the management deal used to be relatively straightforward: The management team would get 5–15 percent of the company in options to acquire stock in the future. Simply put, if the investors made money, managers made money. This was pretty simple. But two factors are driving a change in the way the management deals are structured today. The first is the amount of money chasing deals. Because capital is so ubiquitous, there is much more competition for good management. And, by the law of supply and demand, competition leads to better deals. Buyout shops don't like the trend, but it's happening, it's not going to stop, and you as a manager should be aggressive in taking advantage of this strong dynamic. The second change that has driven a shift in deal structure in favor of managers is the recent change in the tax code, which significantly lowered the capital gains tax. As such, it is now imperative from a manager's wealth-creation perspective to structure a deal that generates capital gains (roughly a 20 percent tax) on all the manager's equity rather than simply structuring the deal with traditional equity options that lead to taxes at ordinary income rates (usually near 40 percent). This tax differential is now so large that deals must be structured to accommodate these powerful tax considerations, as discussed in more detail later in the chapter.

The Summary Term Sheet

The documents that define the relationship between managers and the buyout firm become increasingly more specific and more binding as they evolve. The first term sheet between Techway managers and the buyout firm was a one-page agreement. It summarized the key points of the relationship as shown in the sidebar example below. It is a broad-brush view of the relationship that defines the key terms of agreement, including the equity, vesting, and investment of both sides. It is primarily a discussion document, but once it is agreed to, it forms the foundation for the more complete agreements to follow.

Techway, Inc.
Management Incentive Package
Summary Term Sheet for Discussion Purposes

The following outlines the principal terms of the agreement between Investor and the senior management of Techway (the "Company"):

Equity:	Promoted interest of 15 percent of equity, structured as a common stock to preserve capital gains treatment.
Vesting:	The equity will vest 20 percent at closing and 20 percent per year thereafter, becoming fully vested at the fourth anniversary of closing.
Investment:	Management will invest a total of $750,000 in the transaction on the same terms as the investor.
Current Compensation:	Subject to discussion, Investor will preserve the current compensation programs.
Benefits:	The nature and issues of the benefits need to be understood more clearly.
Closing Fee:	Management will be paid a closing fee equal to 15 percent of Investor's fee; 100 percent of the after-tax portion of this fee will be invested in the transaction in addition to the pre-mentioned personal commitment.
Investor Fees:	Investor is to be paid a closing fee of 1 percent on the total transaction size and a $250,000 annual management fee.

Investor's Role:	Investor will invest 100 percent of the equity in the transaction and will arrange the debt financing with one of its lending partners.
Agreed in principle:	——————————————— ———————————————
	Management Signature Investor Signature
Date:	——————————————— ———————————————

This example term sheet for the Techway deal is short and sweet and straightforward, as it should be. There's obviously a long way to go between this term sheet and a closed deal, but it establishes some basics. Who drafts this first term sheet? Normally, the buyout firm produces a draft for management's review. Should you negotiate this term sheet? Absolutely. The same rules apply: Create a bakeoff and, believe me, you won't get something if you don't ask for it. At this point you still have plenty of leverage, so it's a good time to be aggressive.

Fleshing Out the Term Sheet

From the initial version, the next step is to flesh out the term sheet. The managers and investors will go back and forth with revisions, offers and counteroffers, clauses inserted and removed. Each of the elements of the original agreement is still represented, but each exchange adds a little bit to the mass, until you end up with a much more substantial "memorandum of understanding," as shown in this second example. It takes more time and attention and a higher level of detail as we move to a more complete document. One important piece of advice: Do not agree to go with one buyout firm on the deal until you see *all the language* in the memorandum of understanding. Keep your options open until then. This is common sense because the term sheet is just a starting point and is obviously too skimpy a document on which to base the most important deal of your career.

Ask the buyout firm repeatedly whether there are any other issues they wish to put in the term sheet. Is it comprehensive? Is there *anything* else? Get it all out on the table. There are many issues to consider on this critical document, as noted in the annotations in the following sample memorandum of understanding.

Techway Management Term Sheet
Memorandum of Understanding

I. **Introduction**

Techway will be recapitalized by a group of investors led by Investor and certain other side-by-side investors, Seller, and the key executives (each individually, an "Executive" and collectively, the "Executives") for the purpose of building and operating a leading information technology services company.

> This is an overview section that has limited important content. It points out, as discussed in Chapter 6, that this deal will be structured as a "recapitalization," which is functionally a purchase but is an often-used structure, particularly in technology deals, that eliminates the goodwill on the purchase balance sheet. To achieve a recapitalization the seller must continue to own at least 10 percent of the company postclosing. This has its own set of pros and cons as discussed in Chapter 6, but it can be a useful accounting tool. Look to your accountants to tell you if a recapitalization will work on your deal.

II. **Investor's Role**

Investor will provide significant equity capital and support in forming and developing Techway. Investor would initially commit the necessary equity capital to consummate the recapitalization of Techway (the "Recapitalization"), and Investor would provide or arrange for up to 100 percent of the cash required to purchase the portion of equity in Techway not purchased by the Executives or retained by Seller. In addition, Investor expects to work closely with the Executives in formulating a business plan, securing bank and other financing for Techway, visiting and analyzing initial acquisition prospects, and helping to negotiate and close initial acquisitions.

> This section is also straightforward. One thing to make certain when dealing with investors is that they have a committed fund and the capital available in the fund to do your deal. If the firm does not have committed capital or is between funds, be very careful and expect a

clear dialogue about where the money is coming from. It's difficult to raise equity capital, and you'll be best off working with firms that have plenty of capital available for them to call.

III. Executives' Role

The Executives will serve in their current offices of Techway except as otherwise agreed by the Executives and Investor. Each of the Executives will report to the board of directors of Techway. Executives would initially collectively invest not less than $750,000 of the equity invested in Techway (including the Management Carry described in Section VI below) or such greater amount as Executives may wish to commit. All of such equity investments by the Executives will be made at the time of Recapitalization.

The big issue here is your $750,000 investment. Whatever it is, it's a lot of money. This raises many issues. First, how much should you put in the deal? Put in what's comfortable. Do not mortgage your house or dramatically overextend yourself to fund the equity. These deals have big upside and downside, too. Put in an amount that will convince investors that you have some skin in the game and are serious. Some firms like managers to lever themselves up to make a huge personal capital commitment to the deal. Have frank discussions with the investors on this point so you know their philosophy. Finally, if you have limited liquidity but want or need to put some money into the deal, the buyout fund will usually arrange for the new company to loan you the capital at a relatively attractive rate close to the prime rate of interest. The loan will be a recourse loan, meaning that if the deal goes bad you'll need to pay it off personally. So be careful as to your level of financial exposure.

IV. Board of Directors

The Board of Directors of Techway following the Recapitalization and each subsidiary thereof will consist of one Executive and four Investor representatives. A representative of the Investor will serve as Chair of the Board. The Board may grow in size as appropriate as Techway grows and could in the future include the executive officers of major acquisitions or other strong outside directors, subject to Investor's right to elect a majority of all directors. The Board of Directors shall have the right to approve all material transactions involving Techway, including without limitation, acquisitions and dispositions, material credit facilities, executive employment agreements, budgets, capital expenditures, and major contracts.

In addition to the composition and role of the board, there are a variety of other governance issues that can be addressed here—or in the formal purchase agreement—as discussed later in this chapter. One obvious point here is that inasmuch as the investors put up most of the money, they will control the board. Make no mistake about it: They control the company. And as I've said before, the deal is like a marriage, and you'd better know well the people you're in bed with.

V.   **Funding**

A.   Commitment. Investor will commit to invest up to $45 million in Techway for the Recapitalization and for acceptable acquisitions. Investor will have the right to assign up to 25 percent of its commitment to an affiliate or any other investor(s) (including Techway and sellers of other acquired business (collectively, the "Selling Shareholders").

You should not be overly concerned about this ability to assign a piece of the deal to another affiliated investor, but you should ask why they want this provision in and about whom specifically they are thinking.

B.   Future Investments above Commitment. If Investor invests additional moneys above $45 million, such dollars invested shall be made using the same ratio for preferred and common stock set forth in paragraph C below and all purchased equity and the Management Carry (as defined in Section VI below) will be diluted on a prorated basis.

This is an important point, and it's good and comprehensive to have it in the term sheet. The key item to understand here is that if the deal requires further equity because it's doing poorly or is pursuing another acquisition, you will be diluted down in your ownership percentage.

C.   Form of Investments. Except for the Management Carry, all investments by Investor, Seller, and the Executives shall be in a combination of convertible preferred stock (the "Preferred Stock") and common stock (the "Common Stock"). Such investments shall be allocated on the basis of $34 invested in shares of Preferred Stock for each $1 invested in Common Stock. The Preferred Stock will be subject to conversion or redemption upon the earlier of (i) an initial public offering or (ii) a sale of Techway.

This section evidences the split between Preferred and Common Equity in the structure. The structure is pursued only to get the managers capital gains tax treatment on their invested dollars. This structure is a give-up on behalf of the investors and a big benefit to you. All of your money goes into the common stock, which is how you get a 15 percent ownership stake for $750,000 in a $100 million deal. This is an approach to simply leverage your relatively small equity dollars into large ownership.

One important concept to understand here is that the Preferred Stock has no voting rights but is normally accruing at a relatively high rate of interest (in this case 15 percent, which is typical). The common stock gets no such coupon. This means that the Preferred builds each year at 15 percent, and if you as a management team do not generate returns of at least 15 percent per year on all the equity dollars (in this case, $50 million), your investment in the common stock will be diluted and could end up being zero. This is reasonably fair because if the investors do not get 15 percent rates of return, you have not succeeded in the management of the deal. This demonstrates how the leveraged equity structure works both for you (gets you capital gains on all of the equity) and against you (if you don't hit your numbers, you can lose it all). Live by the sword, die by the sword.

VI. Management Carry

A. Management Common Equity Carry. A total of 15 percent of the total common equity of Techway (exclusive of the Executives' purchased equity) will be reserved for the Executives and other members of Techway Management (the "Management Carry"). The Management Carry shall be purchased out of the $750,000 aggregate investment to be made by the Executives. The Management Carry will be subject to "time vesting" (50 percent) and "performance vesting" (50 percent) and will dilute all purchased equity on a pro rata basis. The Management Carry is intended to provide the Executives with a significant upside opportunity at a reduced capital commitment. Because we are issuing the Management Carry up front in shares as opposed to options, it also has the additional benefit of being taxed at capital gains rates as opposed to ordinary income tax rates.

The most critical portion of this agreement is the "management carry," the pool of common stock (in this case 15 percent) available to current executives. This pool will vest based on passage of time and/or the achievement of certain performance objectives. As discussed, this provides management with the opportunity for a significant upside investment with a reduced capital commitment.

Why is it a 15 percent interest for management? This, of course, is the most important number in your entire deal. As I mentioned earlier, the traditional range for management is 5–15 percent and is driven by many factors, such as the value that management has added in creating the deal. Should you ask for more if they propose 15 percent? Absolutely. Again, you won't get it if you don't ask for it. And ask for home run warrants, which are discussed later in this example. Be aggressive. This number will drive your gains on the deal.

Let's discuss time vesting and performance vesting. Obviously, time vesting is better for you than performance vesting, because with time vesting you must merely survive for your equity to vest. The split of 50 percent to time vested on the equity is purely arbitrary and is a matter of negotiation. Try to get it to 60–70 percent time vested if you can, but it cuts both ways as the more you put into performance vesting, thus aligning your interests fully with the investors, the more equity you will get overall.

B. Time Vesting. Fifty percent of the Management Carry will be subject to Time Vesting. Generally, the time-vested shares of an Executive will vest over a five-year period from the Recapitalization at the rate of 20 percent per annum on each of the first five anniversaries of the Recapitalization Date as long as such Executive remains employed by the Company as of such dates. All time-vested shares will become 100 percent vested upon either (i) a sale of the Company, (ii) a termination of such Executive without "cause" or "performance cause" within one year following an initial public offering, or (iii) a change of control of Techway.

The important point for this piece of the management carry is that it only depends upon the passage of time. In this case, the management carry vests over a five-year period. Vesting provisions such as this are important to the investors and central to any management deal. This obviously is a retention tool, encouraging managers to stay with the firm. The vesting usually occurs over four years but it could go as high as seven years. This result is a matter of negotiation and in some cases you could get three-year vesting, but four is typical. For example, Microsoft's vesting period is four and a half years.

Vesting schedules can be complex. They can vest daily, which is better for you, annually, or even on a "cliff" basis at the end of four years (a deal you shouldn't agree to). Ask for shorter schedules with daily vesting and see how you do. In addition, you should have some protection on your equity against ill will. This protection arises because, due to their board control, investors have all the cards and could essentially turn around and fire you the day after the deal closes. For this reason you must negotiate all of your severance protections up front (such as getting one year of salary upon severance), and there should be a provision that if the manager is asked to leave involuntarily, without cause, the vesting schedule is accelerated. A standard approach would be to vest 20 percent of your equity if you are terminated without cause in the first year after closing. This way you still get some of the management carry that you worked so hard to get during the deal process.

C. Performance Vesting. Fifty percent of the Management Carry will be subject to performance vesting. Performance-vested shares held by an Executive will become fully vested if either (i) Investor receives a specified return on its investment compounded annually (Internal Rate of Return) or (ii) such Executive remains employed by Techway on the tenth anniversary of the Recapitalization. The Performance Vesting Shares shall become vested on the following schedule:

Percentage of Performance	Investor Internal Rate
Shares Vested	of Return
20%	30% IRR
30%	31% IRR
40%	32% IRR
50%	33% IRR
60%	34% IRR
70%	35% IRR
80%	36% IRR
90%	37% IRR
100%	38% IRR

This portion of the management carry vests upon meeting predetermined performance objectives. For example, all of this second part will vest when the firm achieves a 38 percent rate of return to investors. You should ask why 38 percent was chosen. It's totally arbitrary and is a matter of negotiation. Some of our deals vest the performance piece at 40 percent and some at 50 percent. This piece of the carry is absolutely critical, as investors love this section because it aligns your incentives with theirs. "Show me those high IRRs!" they're thinking. As such, this is the place in the management carry dialogue with investors where you should do your heaviest negotiating, and hopefully you've got more than one firm bidding for your services. As we've discussed, most buyout investors have 30–35 percent annual rate of return target. If you generate 50 percent per year, you're a hero, so you should be compensated like a hero.

Investors can often be quite generous with incentive equity, particularly if the firm really takes off. But you've got to ask for it up-front to get it. To win the lottery, you must first buy a ticket. Many managers don't think to ask for "home run warrants," but their partners usually have little trouble agreeing to them. If you are buying the company for $1 per share, management might get warrants to purchase shares for $3–$5 each once a certain performance level is reached. If the investors earn 50 percent return on the deal, management might get another 5 percent of equity. Why not 10 percent? You won't get it if you don't ask for it! This is a lot of money, but given that the whole pie is so big, it is not hard for the buyout partners to put this on the table. They know this added incentive might just provide the nudge for managers to actually produce those extraordinary returns. So go for it. This is the place in the document to swing for the fences.

The agreement should also specify dilution and repurchase rights. In general, if the executive's employment contract is terminated, the investment partner will have the opportunity to repurchase the manager's interest. This is a complex but important part of the agreement, and as with all of these documents, you should have your lawyer read it carefully and give you appropriate advice. This way the equity works on your $750,000 investment in that if you leave, the time vesting and performance targets kick in. And if you're only 20 percent vested at the time (meaning you've likely served for only one year), the investors have the right (unilaterally) to buy your equity back from you at your cost. This is your punishment for leaving the firm. If the deal's going gangbusters, the investors will repurchase your unvested equity at cost, and if it's going badly they'll leave you owning the equity. They normally have a month or so after you resign to decide whether to buy your equity or to let you keep it. Big stakes, big risks, complex structures; such is the buyout world.

C. Sales of Equity to Third Parties. If in the event Techway sells or issues shares to third parties (i.e., to lenders, in a public offering or, if necessary, to raise equity to gain compliance with debt agreements), all current equityholders and the Management Carry will share dilution on a pro rata basis.

This is a straightforward provision but important to make clear in the document that all parties share in future dilution. Some investors/managers believe they should be protected against this potential future dilution, but dilution protection simply doesn't exist in these deal markets.

VII. Ownership

A. Recapitalization. At the closing of the Recapitalization, Investor and the Executives will purchase approximately 90 percent of Techway's Common Stock from Seller. This will leave the Techway Common Stock owned as follows:

Investor/Management   90%
Seller   10%

Immediately after such acquisition, Techway will recapitalize into two classes of stock: Preferred Stock and Common Stock. Each existing share of Common Stock of Techway will be exchanged for 10 shares of Common Stock and 90 shares of Preferred Stock. The percentage ownership of all shareholders (including Seller) will be the same in each class as set forth above.

Immediately following such acquisition, the Executives will purchase their Management Carry Common Stock. Upon acquisition of their shares, the Executives will make an 83(b) election under the Internal Revenue Code of 1986, as amended.

This is just a big reminder for all executives to file their 83(b) elections with their tax returns in order to guarantee capital gains treatment on their investment. Make sure your personal accountant is aware of your deal and makes this filing for you.

B. Ownership. Fully diluted ownership of the Techway capital stock upon consummation of the recapitalization (including the Management Carry) will be as follows:

	% Acquired Com. Shares	% Acquired Pref. Shares
Investors	76.50%	90.00%
Seller	8.50%	10.00%
Management Carry	15.00%	0.00%
Total	100.00%	100.00%

This section delineates the preferred/common ownership split.

C. Repurchase of Stock. If any other member of management leaves Techway for any reason, Techway has the option to acquire the former employee's unvested Management Carry Common Stock at its original purchase price. However, the repurchase price shall be the fair market value per share (to be defined, i.e., to be equal to recent acquisition multiples × EBIT + cash − debt − preferred shares or the public market price following an IPO) for the applicable percentage of all time-vested shares and all performance-vested shares (but only to the extent such time-vested shares and performance-vested shares are then vested).

This provision spells out the ability of the investor to repurchase shares at cost or market as discussed previously.

D. Right of First Refusal. Techway and the Investor will have a first right of refusal on the sale of any equity shares by the Executives or management.

This is a standard provision. The company always gets the first right to purchase third-party stock.

VIII. Management Team/Compensation

A. Employment. Each Executive will enter into a customary employment agreement with the Company mutually acceptable to the Executive, the Investor, and Techway. The terms of each Executive's employment by Techway will begin on the date of closing of the Recapitalization and shall continue for a period of three (3) years thereafter, provided, however, that such employment shall automatically renew for additional one-year terms unless either party gives the other a nonrenewal notice six (6) months prior to the end of any term.

Employment agreements (see Appendix A for a sample) are back in vogue and offer certain protections to both sides. Most private equity firms don't like employment agreements because of the restrictions they place on investors, but if managers want them the buyout firm will generally go along. For the managers, the agreement ensures that they will continue to work for the company and be treated in a predetermined manner upon separation The equity partners also want to make sure management will not jump ship after the deal is completed. The management term sheet usually specifies the period the executive will serve as CEO and a member or chair of the board of directors of the company. Techway managers negotiated a three-year minimum, automatically extended one year at the third anniversary and at each anniversary thereafter unless sixty days' written notice is given by either party. The agreement should also specify the initial salary and bonus of the executive, as well as the process and criteria for annual review.

This agreement also may specify a noncompete/nonsolicit agreement with the company for a certain period, usually the remaining term of the contract or two years from termination.

B. Compensation. Subject to a detailed review of the existing compensation structure, all current compensation levels will be maintained at current levels or, if appropriate, raised to reflect market compensation for comparable positions at similar firms in the IT industry. Executives will be compensated with a Base Salary and a Bonus Opportunity. The Base Salary for each Executive will be subject to annual review by the Company's Board of Directors. The Bonus Opportunity will be calculated as a range based on a percentage of an Executive's Base Salary commensurate with his or her position. Generally, we would expect that the Bonus Opportunity would range from 50–120 percent of an Executive's Base Salary (depending on the position of Executive) with attachment of agreed-upon financial goals being the primary determinant and individual contribution the secondary determinant. The total Pool Available for bonuses will be determined in cooperation with the Board. The Company's CEO will have primary discretion in establishing individual performance goals and bonus awards.

It is important for the managers to discuss this issue up front because some investors like to tinker with current compensation packages, often looking for ways to cut them. Like all matters in a buyout, you should discuss all open items early on so there are no ambiguities after closing.

C. Benefits. Subject to a detailed review of existing plans, all Executives will be entitled to all standard benefits, including health insurance, retirement/401(k), vacation, and other benefits and perquisites that may be established in consultation with the Board of Directors.

Standard stuff, but worth understanding. What are the benefits packages like? Ask your partner to let you know.

D. Termination. If an Executive is terminated after closing of the Recapitalization without "Cause," he or she will receive twelve months of severance pay and benefits allowance. If terminated for "Performance Cause" (to be defined as missing 80 percent of any operating budget for any twelve-month period), then he or she will receive three months of severance pay and benefits. An Executive can be terminated for Cause without payment of any severance.

The employment agreement also details severance arrangements for termination without cause, typically salary for the remaining term of the agreement or one year. Termination for poor performance usually continues salary for a shorter period, and termination with cause or resignation usually offers no continuation of salary. It helps to know when you are in trouble. This is a critical discussion to have with your buyout partner. When will they be dissatisfied with the numbers? Get specific with them. It doesn't mean you lack confidence, it just means you'll all know where you stand if things get tough. Note that the Techway agreement specifies a definition for how far off plan the company needs to be (below 80 percent). This gives great clarity to discussions if the company does, in fact, miss its target. In some cases, investors may consider 10 percent to be behind plan and in other cases, it could be 5 percent. But these expectations need to be clearly articulated up-front or they will cause problems later. In general 10–15 percent is the upper limit, because that is the point at which you are going to have trouble with the banks.

IX. Expenses and Fees

Techway will pay Investor's reasonable legal expenses in connection with any financing and any later enforcement of the rights of Investor, as well as any out-of-pocket expenses incurred by Investor in attending Board and other company-related meetings. Investor will also receive a transaction fee equal to 1 percent of all funds (debt and equity) raised by Techway. Techway will pay the Executives' reasonable legal expenses related to entering into definitive management agreements upon close of the Recapitalization.

One important issue to address in developing the management term sheet is fees and fee sharing. Most (though not all) buyout firms take closing or advisory fees as part of the deal, but it is important to get these matters out on the table so there are no surprises. Normally, the buyout firm takes 0.5 percentage point to one percentage point on the deal in fees at closing. But some private equity firms take massive fees. You'll need to get these fees out on the table as early as possible and have a full discussion on the subject.

Negotiating with several buyout firms particularly helps in this area. As noted previously, if you have term sheets from several private equity firms, you can set up a mini-auction and play them off one another. The fees, equity, and other factors will become bargaining chips in these discussions. If investor A plans to charge a fee that investor B doesn't charge, you can go back to A and ask to remove the fee. Firms may say no, but they won't remove the fee unless you ask.

Some managers take the next step. They say, if the buyout firm is getting a closing fee, why shouldn't managers also get a closing fee? After all, managers are also doing a lot of work on the project. Some managers will ask for a half-point closing fee as well. Again, they may not get it, but they have a better shot if they actually ask for it.

X.   Other

A.   Non-Binding Letter. Except for paragraphs B and C below, which shall be binding, this agreement is not binding until execution of definitive legal agreements by Investor and the Executives. Such agreements will be negotiated and completed in conjunction with the Recapitalization. Notwithstanding the foregoing, in the event that the parties hereto agree that the principal terms of this letter agreement shall govern any such definitive legal agreements between them.

B.   Terms Held in Confidence. Terms of this letter of understanding will be held in confidence by Investor and the Executives.

C.   No Shop. In consideration for the Investor's advancing expenses in connection with the Recapitalization, each Executive agrees that following acceptance of this letter and until ninety days from the date hereof, he or she shall not offer to buy, entertain, or discuss an offer to buy, or solicit any proposals regarding the sale of all or any part of Techway, with any party other than Investor (except as contemplated by this letter).

D. <u>Investment Agreements</u>. The parties will enter into investment agreements consistent with this understanding and containing customary private equity terms such as information rights and drag-along rights and appropriate noncompetition provisions.

The parties to this letter agreement hereby agree to execute and deliver this letter agreement as of the last date set forth below:

By: _____   _____

   Name: _____

   Title: _____

_____   _____
                                 Date

_____   _____
                                 Date

Key Issues of the Management Deal

The sample memorandum of understanding agreement is quite comprehensive, but if you or your counsel have other issues you wish to include, do so. Usually everything presented in our example is subject to negotiation. One important piece of advice is that you should negotiate hard as a team for the best deal you can get. It may upset your buyout partner that you're being so aggressive, but, on the other hand, he or she will be pleased that the team is tough and aggressive. That tells the buyout firm a lot about the team's mentality and sends the message that, hey, we're all on the same side of the bargaining table; these managers will be tough out there, making tough deals and creating value.

Among the issues on the table in negotiating the management

deal, there are several that were touched on in our discussion of the management agreement that deserve further consideration.

How Much to Ask For?
The most important area of the agreement is the provisions for management ownership. This is the management Holy Grail. This section of the document is where the team's big economics reside and should be the focus of your dialogue. This agreement outlines the equity structure for the deal (i.e., what is invested and what stock is received for that investment). This section also specifies the amount executives of the company will coinvest in the buyout and the terms.

This equity portion is the piece you're fighting for. The amount you end up with, whether 5, 15, or 25 percent, is entirely a matter of judgment and negotiation with your equity partners. It doesn't always depend on the depth of your experience or the quality of your deal, although these are certainly factors. Like any negotiation, it depends on what you bring to the table, but also what you are skilled enough to take away from it. Whether you end up at the high end of the scale or the low end will largely be determined by your actions and will have a huge impact on your ultimate gains. Several factors drive the equity share for management. The key issues are:

• *Management Value-Add.* This is, of course, a vague and general concept. But the value-add *perceived* by the buyout firm in the transaction is critical in negotiating this provision. One key driver of management value, discussed many times in this book, is how far managers have taken the deal before they bring in the buyout shops and banks. The buyout professionals are swamped and the value of their time is enormous. And getting deals done is hard. Thus, if your management team delivers a "fully baked" deal (i.e., a signed LOI with a seller of a company), you've just increased the odds of success for the buyout investors and have saved them lots of time. You will be paid handsomely for it.

One management team recently brought us a largely baked, highly interesting deal and wanted 35 percent for management. We had never done a deal at more than 25 percent. But they had a deal teed up and convinced us that other credible buyout investors were prepared to do the 35 percent deal, so we did it. And if the deal works, they will make more than $100 million. They got the deal because they were smart, knew the process, and brought a deal with a lot of value added. In addition to their preparation, they had many key elements that made them an attractive team to back: a track record of success in the same industry, a credible plan to deliver excellent returns, and a full management team. However, five years ago they wouldn't have even considered asking for 35 percent. Now that they've broken the ceiling, today you can go for it.

• *Management Fit.* This is hinted at in the discussion of the way buyout firms assess deal opportunities. If the buyout firm determines the likelihood of success by the management team is very high, they are likely to give management a better deal. As such, if your background is a perfect fit *and* you have a strong record of prior success in the same industry, you will be able to negotiate a better deal. If the industry is not one where you have experience, or if your record is unproven, your deal will not be as good.

• *Deal Size.* The deal size has an impact on the equation as well. This is a pure mathematical equation. The deal is structured to make management a certain amount of dollars. If the deal is very large (e.g., $500 million and above), managers will get a lower percentage of the deal but still have a large amount of money working for them. Conversely, if the deal is much smaller, the team can credibly ask for a larger percentage of the upside such that they have the chance to earn the necessary absolute dollars to be highly motivated.

Tax Considerations: Moving away from Options
As mentioned previously, the form of the management equity incentive also has changed. The upside used to be provided as simple stock options, but given recent capital gains tax law changes, most of management's share of the deal has moved into other forms. Nearly all options, when exercised, are taxed at the ordinary rate, whereas direct common stock ownership receives capital gains treatment, so any management deal in the current tax environment must be structured to give managers outright common stock ownership instead of simple options.

For example, for a $100 million deal with $50 million in equity and $50 million in debt, the approach before tax reform would have been to treat the $50 million in equity as 85 percent of the company. Managers would be given the additional 15 percent in options, which would have an exercise price equal to the investor's buy-in price. Managers would then invest $750,000 to buy slightly more than 1 percent of the company ($750,000/$50 million). The new leveraged equity structure is to break the $50 million into $46 million of preferred stock and $4 million of common stock (where the votes are). Managers put up $750,000 to own 15 percent of this common stock. (If they can't afford to put up that much, the company can arrange to loan them part of the capital on a recourse basis.) This direct 15 percent ownership, of course, has a tax-friendly vesting schedule and is partly based on future stock per-formance.

To illustrate what a powerful difference these structures make for tax considerations, consider what that $50 million equity stake in a company would be worth down the road. If the equity doubled from $50 million to $100 million, the management's 15 percent share would be worth $9 million before taxes. Taxed at 40 percent, managers would receive $5.4 million after taxes. On the other hand, with a stock structure that falls under the capital gains tax rate of 20 percent, the $9 million of pretax value would put $7.2 million into the pockets of managers after taxes. That's almost $2 million extra (an amazing 40 percent more than the tax inefficient structure) simply because managers thought carefully about tax is-sues and put a smart structure in place. This demonstrates the criti-cal importance of recognizing that Uncle Sam is a silent partner in every deal, so you need to evaluate all income tax considerations carefully when structuring the deal.

These are, of course, general observations. The tax arena is highly complex, of course, so it is critical to have strong tax advice in putting the deal together. All of the major accounting firms have dedicated tax departments.

Governance
Governance is the structure that defines how decisions will be made after closing. It is important *before you sign the deal* to have detailed discussions with your partner about governance issues. You need to

deal with these tough issues right at the outset or you will have to deal with them later under circumstances where you no longer have any leverage. The term sheet should describe the governance structure for the new company and address some of the key issues you may face going forward. The equity partner usually wants a few members on the board to be actively involved in the firm's progress. The agreement should specify how many people are on the board, who will serve as chair, and the respective responsibilities of the board and the CEO.

The term sheet should also discuss whether you can be fired and on what basis, and the nature of decisions that are handled by management versus those that are handled by the board. Among the key governance issues are these:

- *Termination.* If you are the CEO, on what basis can you be fired? The equity firm usually controls the majority of the company and can make these decisions. Though it is unlikely, it is possible the buyout firm can turn around and fire you the day after closing. Because they control the board and most decision making, you need to define the bases upon which they would have those kinds of conversations. Usually they only consider firing you if you are meaningfully off plan, but you need to negotiate all severance arrangements up-front to make sure you are fully protected.

- *Severance.* Negotiate your severance deal to make sure if they fire you, you have one full year of salary for the CEO or CFO. If they fire you early on, without cause, a small portion of your equity should vest upon that termination.

- *Board.* You need to have clear conversations about how the management team is going to interact with the board, and which investment professionals at the firm will be your daily contact. Who will be on the board? How often is the board going to meet? Typically, in the first six months, the board meets monthly and moves to quarterly meetings after the critical postclosing period.

- *Scope of Control.* You need to specify what issues the board will control and which ones management will control. For example, you might negotiate specific clipping levels on expenditures. The CEO may be able to approve expenditures under $250,000. Anything above that goes to the board. These levels depend very much on the size of the company and the nature of its business. Can the CEO unilaterally hire and fire key executives and enter into supplier or customer agreements? Who is responsible for approving acquisitions, divestitures, and sales of stock and issuances of debt? (Hint: Almost always, it's the board.) Make sure all governance issues are clear to avoid setting up flash points for later conflicts.

• *Points of Contact.* Discuss with investors how their points of contact are going to work. Can they call your direct reports without your knowing? Typically, the investor would call the CEO and CFO directly, who would route calls through to directors. Most investors feel they can call anyone in the company anytime they want to. This is an issue that needs to be clarified.

• *Board Composition.* Who is going to represent you on the board? For example, a seven-person board may have two members from management and five from the investor team. The CEO and CFO often sit on the board. The investor may bring in three people from within the firm and two outsiders with specific industry experience. You also need to determine whether these investors and directors are going to have compensation. Will they receive options or draw board fees? Any compensation going to the board is coming out of the company, which means it is taken from your hide. Typically, representatives from the investment firm do not receive compensation. The outside directors get some stock in the company, which is dilutive to managers. Directors may receive $50,000 in stock that vests over three years if they serve on the board. Members who leave the board forego a portion of the stock due to these vesting provisions.

When to Bring in the Financing Partners
At what point should you bring in the financing partners? In the case of Software AG, Dan Gillis and Harry McCreery set up the deal with our firm before approaching the seller. In this case, it was very important to have a quick and compelling deal queued up at the right moment. Sometimes, particularly if the managers need to move quickly or if they have little experience in developing such deals, it may be to their advantage to begin by building a relationship with the buyout firm before going to the seller.

On the other hand, Stu Johnson put his team and strategy together before coming to us with it. The advantage of that approach is that it gives the managers much more leverage in negotiating their terms with the buyout investors. At that point, a lot of the risk and uncertainty have been worked out, so the deal is more attractive to investors and can command more attractive terms. The further along the deal is, the better your leverage will be, but the more sweat and equity you will have to invest up front.

Shifting Negotiating Leverage

The reason it sometimes pays to wait to contact the equity partner is that negotiating leverage shifts away from management throughout the life of the deal. As these documents evolve, it is better to drive all the important economic decisions early in the process. If your investors wish to "defer" some of these decisions while the deal gets "closer to fruition," politely push back and tell them you'd like to deal with these issues now. By the time you get deeply into the detail, it may be too late. Once you select a partner, your leverage goes down. By the time you get close to closing, the private equity firm has all the leverage. At that point, what's to stop the partners from changing the deal or going behind your back to work directly with the seller?

You have to be sure you can trust your partners. It may not be apparent at the outset, but it will be very apparent as you move toward closing. You may be willing to put aside your reservations and grab a slightly better offer from a questionable firm, but it will almost always cost you in the long run.

Take plenty of time to get to know your investors. Drink wine, go out to dinner, play golf with them. They say you can learn just about everything about a person's character by playing a round of golf. If you don't like golf, throw horseshoes or go for a run. Visit their homes and meet their families. You simply can't spend too much time getting to know them. It really is like a marriage. You'll spend months of intense work leading up to closing and then you will live with them and make difficult decisions for years afterward. This marriage can either be bliss or a living hell.

As I've mentioned, do your homework. Do reference checks on equity partners in advance. Talk to managers of deals that have gone well and ones that have gone badly. Every buyout firm has CEOs they have fired. Ask for their names and contact them. They can give you a sense of what the equity partners are like to work with when things go wrong. Do your research on how these guys behave in a downturn.

The Deal with the Banks

Once you've struck your deal with the equity partner, the next hurdle is meeting with the banks. Banks provide your debt capital. They are the "L" in LBO. The buyout partner always has extensive banking relationships and usually guides you through this process. But you may be doing the deal without a buyout partner. Fortunately, most managers, particularly good CFOs, have more experience in dealing with bankers than with equity partners, so you'll likely be more comfortable here.

Because debt finance is fairly straightforward and contractual, and the banks tend to take a more hands-off approach to the business, managers often ignore them. Worse, they sometimes treat them as "dumb money." This is a mistake. It is important to get to know your bankers and to keep them in the loop as issues evolve at the company. Banks will be an important part of your success, and their assistance can give you the breathing room you need to get out of a tight bind or help pave the way for a smooth exit from the investment.

If there is a problem with the business, let the bankers know immediately. If there is a success, also let them know. Treat them as partners. That's what they are. Inevitably, there will come a day when you'll need them to do something for you. If you haven't treated them like partners, they can hurt your business very badly. If they get upset, they can normally find a way to shut down your business if they don't advance money when you need it.

Almost every buyout firm has five or six banks they work with frequently. These relationships help ensure the best possible terms because the banks know they will deal with the equity investors over and over. Managers wouldn't have the same kind of history on their own. Usually managers and the buyout firm pitch the deal to these "partner" banks. If it is a strong deal, several bankers will be interested, giving you the opportunity to set up one of those mini-auctions we love so much. The banks will offer different terms, and the buyout partner, along with management, will evaluate the terms to select the best offer.

The Banker's View of the World

Before we go further to talk about bank issues, you need to be able to see the world as bankers see it. They are mostly very conservative by nature and are much more concerned about the deal's risks and downsides than the upside. Whereas equity investors can make a large multiple on their money if a deal goes well, a banker cannot. Bankers in a deal can only recover one times their money plus accrued interest. But just as equity investors can lose all of their money, so can the banker. Since they have very limited upside potential and significant downside, bankers are almost always highly focused on risks and potential problems. They are constantly thinking, "How can we get hurt on this deal?" and "How can we lose our money here?" As such, they will care less about your grand, expansive vision than analyzing all of the ways the deal can go wrong.

Because of the risk/reward ratio of their position, the bank's capital is the senior capital in the structure. This means that if things go badly, theirs is the first money out of the deal. Conversely, you as a common stockholder are the *last* money out. There's a simple capital structure for the Techway deal that illustrates the situation (see Figure 7-1).

Figure 7-1. Techway capital structure.

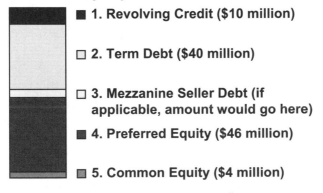

■ 1. Revolving Credit ($10 million)

☐ 2. Term Debt ($40 million)

☐ 3. Mezzanine Seller Debt (if applicable, amount would go here)

■ 4. Preferred Equity ($46 million)

▨ 5. Common Equity ($4 million)

(In order of liquidation, from most senior to least senior debt.)

What Figure 7-1 illustrates is that if things go badly, and you're forced to sell the company for $60 million, the banks will get their entire $50 million paid off (the top two layers of the chart). The preferred stockholders will get $10 million back against their $46 million and the common stockholders will get nothing. Conversely, of course, if things go great, the common stockholders have the most upside and can earn a huge multiple on their money.

Risk/Reward: Live by the Sword, Die by the Sword

Why do bankers take the risks for limited upside? Well, there are several reasons. First, in their senior piece of the capital structure they don't often lose their capital. A wipeout is extremely rare. Second, they do take extensive fees on these LBO loans, which implicitly increase their yield on the loan. Third, the interest rates they charge produce high margins in the banking world. They often charge an interest rate of 250 basis points (2.50 percent) to 300 basis points over LIBOR (the London Interbank Offered Rate) on the loan while they, as a large banking institution, are borrowing the money themselves at closer to LIBOR. Therefore the spreads and fees are decent and the risk justifies the reward.

Revolving and Term Debt

We've talked a bit about the equity, but let's briefly consider the two most common types of debt facilities. First is the revolving facility ($10 million in the Techway deal), often called the "revolver." Nearly all LBOs have a revolving facility, which is the loan they draw upon on a daily basis to run their business. As such, the loan goes up during some months when they're using cash and down during other months when cash is coming in. Think of it as the checking account for the company. It's generally secured by the company's most liquid assets, such as inventories and receivables, and as it is the most senior loan it usually has the best interest rate. Revolvers usually have a one- to three-year term and are renewed if things are going well.

The second part of the debt facility is the "term debt," so named because it is due to be paid down at specific dates over a finite period of time, usually five to seven years. It is longer term than the revolver; has annual requirements to be partially paid off (i.e., amortized); is normally secured by the company's equipment, buildings, and real estate; and, because it is longer term than capital, carries interest rates that are normally 25–100 basis points higher than the revolver.

There are many permutations of term debt and hundreds of types of debt structures. Some firms pursue very esoteric debt structures, whereas most prefer plain-vanilla structures.

Mezzanine Debt

While we did not have "mezzanine" or "junior" debt securities in the Techway deal, there are other debt facilities that can be used to finance transactions that are junior to the revolver and term debt. This is normally known as mezzanine or high-yield debt. It's called mezzanine because of where it falls in the capital structure (see Figure 7-1), which is below the senior debt but above the preferred stock. You can think of it like the mezzanine level in a building—it's just above the ground floor (the equity) but not very high up in the building.

Mezzanine debt is similar to term debt in that it is paid back over a fixed period of time (usually seven to ten years, which is longer than the senior term debt), but because it's much riskier in its liquidation position, it must have a much higher yield, normally 18–25 percent. This yield is achieved by the mezzanine getting a much higher coupon than the senior (usually 12–15 percent per annum) plus receiving some equity in the company, usually in the form of options to purchase common stock (or "warrants") at some price in the future, such that if the deal's a big winner, the mezzanine investor will win big, too.

Many equity investors like to use mezzanine debt in the structure because it allows them to use fewer equity dollars to do the deal. For example, in Techway, we could have considered using $10 million of mezzanine debt to replace $10 million of our preferred stock, thus increasing our equity returns. This is often doable in a deal but creates its own challenges. It takes time and effort to identify and "pitch" mezzanine investors on the deal, requires extensive due diligence, and places additional financial risk on the deal because of the high mezzanine coupon. As a manager, looking at potential mezzanines can help you leverage your equity more, but it also increases financial risk.

There are many permutations of all pieces of the debt financing structure that require substantial analysis and can be found in finance texts. For managers, though, be open to using mezzanine debt and looking at your computer model (discussed in Chapter 8) to see how it influences your rate of return. Be open to mezzanine or the use of high-yield securities (which can be publicly traded or privately held), but be cognizant of the inherent risks, rewards, and time requirements.

Bank Covenants

All bank lending comes with strings attached. A full copy of a sample bank agreement appears in Appendix C. Banks want covenants and liens on all of the assets of the firm. They set these covenants from a financial computer model with all of the deal's assumptions built in and tend to be fairly conservative. They also generally take 2 to 3 percentage points on the total debt capital up front in closing fees along with a legion of smaller fees. They normally limit the size of the loan from 2.5–4.5 times trailing EBITDA.

You may be familiar with covenants from other dealings with banks. These are basically different financial tests the banks set up for you that you have to perform against, typically measured on a quarterly basis. All of these covenants are negotiated up front. And like the biblical covenants, if you break them, you could end up in a very hot place.

Since the covenants are based on your plan for the business, you should always work from a fairly conservative plan with the banks. They use these projections, usually discounted 10–15 percent to set the covenant levels. This gives you a little breathing room, but not much, because every quarter they are testing whether you've met these covenants. These tests usually include interest coverage ratios (i.e., quarterly EBITDA/total interest paid) and total leverage coverage (i.e., total bank debt/pro forma run rate EBITDA). There are also minimum net worth levels that you cannot fall below. The bank agreement also will usually specify that all new equity that comes into the company goes to pay down debt first, though this point can often be negotiated.

What happens if you miss a covenant? If you've treated your bankers as partners and communicated along the way, it won't come as a big surprise to them. That works in your favor. If you miss a covenant, they rarely take the company away from you. Technically, they do have some draconian options, but they don't exercise them if they can help it. Banks don't want to ruin or own the company. They just want to be sure they can get their money back.

If you miss your covenant, it just means you are now in negotiations with the bank. If you miss by a little bit, they may work with you to reset the covenant and will not charge a fee. They will work with you to find ways to fix the problem if it's a near miss. If you break your bank covenant by a lot, you will need to renegotiate it. Banks will charge a fee for this work and your interest rates will usually go up. This often comes as a shock to managers, who think the bank is hitting them when they are down. But it makes sense from the bank's perspective, because of the extra work and risk the bank is taking on in the process.

This is why it is important to track covenants closely and set them conservatively at the outset. Still, given the uncertainty of buyouts, it is not uncommon in these deals to break a covenant. It happens in roughly half the deals we work on. When it happens, you swallow hard and pay the extra interest and penalties. More often than not, if the fundamental business is solid, you go on to earn it back and then some. Looking back at that point, you have much less regret about the extra money you paid to the bank.

You should also recognize that banks in leveraged transactions have a first lien on all of assets and a first lien on your stock. If things go badly, the bank has every ability to take over the company and own everything. If you are way off your performance targets, and don't have a good relationship, they can send you into pure banking hell. Actually, they send your loan into the workout group, which is where all the banking knuckle-breakers work. Your flexible days are over. You only have to have one experience with the workout group to know you never want to be there again.

Asset-Based Deals vs. Cash-Flow Deals
In seeking bank financing, it is important to note that lenders make their loans based on either assets or cash flow. Which type of lender you choose depends on your type of business. A manufacturing business with many assets may prefer an asset-based lender. A service business with few fixed assets has no choice but to go to a cash-flow-based lender. In large banks, these two types of lending operations are usually present in a single organization, but there are

banks such as Foothill Financial or CIT Credit that are well known for lending against assets. A list of prospective lenders and their particular interests is provided in Appendix J.

For the asset-based lender, earnings are beside the point. A company with assets sufficient to cover the loan can get a loan, even with poor earnings. Banks normally lend to 50 percent of the liquidation value of the assets. These banks have experience in liquidating assets and are often comfortable lending with limited cash flow.

For the cash flow-based lender, there are few assets to sell. If all Techway's employees walked and contracts were withdrawn, there wouldn't be much for the banks to grab on to. In these cases banks will still lend money, but they have to be able to see that the enterprise is making money and has the ability to do so in the future. And if cash flow starts to flag, they have to pull the plug as quickly as possible because it could be a sign that the investment is going south. A service business that is not making any money today will not be able to borrow anything.

These distinctions are important to know, so you can understand how banks are evaluating the loan. It also helps to make sure you are talking to the right department of the bank.

Better Living Through Chemistry

While much of the focus of negotiations with buyout partners and banks is necessarily focused on the money, don't lose sight of the importance of chemistry. This is not a one-time transaction but rather a long-term relationship. You will be together through better or worse, up years and down, profits and losses. Personal chemistry is important in any transaction.

While many things may be uncertain, it is a sure bet that your deal will hit hard spots along the way. Every deal has them. Revenue falls short for a quarter. A key acquisition drops dead at the eleventh hour. The market gets the jitters and sends the stock into a tailspin. Whatever the cause, you will be making an uncomfortable late-night call to your investment partners one day. And when you pull them out of a deep sleep, you sure as heck want them to be glad to talk to you, even if they know they are not going to like the news you give them.

And it is not just the bad times that require good chemistry. The more this feeling of partnership can be developed, the more constructive the overall relationship becomes. It builds the kind of trust that leads to greater flexibility in developing new strategies to seize new opportunities. Your life will be better, and it will have a positive effect on the business.

Be Conservative with Leverage

One obvious item to watch for is that you don't overleverage your company. The firm will inevitably hit a bump in the road, and then the financial structure of bank debt can come crashing down on you. You don't want the financial structure to break you, and you should run many downside models to be sure your capital structure is appropriate for the type of business you are acquiring.

To state it simply, if the business has large operating risks, you can only layer on very limited financial risk through leverage. If the business is extremely stable and predictable from an operating perspective, you can be much more aggressive on the financial leverage. Remember the mantra that operating risk plus financial risk equals total risk, and you need to get the equation right.

Some managers are tempted to substitute cheaper bank debt for equity investments so they can achieve a higher level of return. It may look good on the upside, but the financial risk is so great it is often not worth doing. As Michael Milken's bondholders found out at the end of 1990, leverage is a good thing until it tilts against you. Then watch out. So go into deals with a conservative mix of capital, watch your covenants, and keep an eye on the business.

My primary advice is to be very conservative on your debt structure. If you underleverage the deal, you may take your IRRs down a few points, but no management team has ever lost all their money by *underleveraging* a buyout.

At the center of all these considerations of leverage and deals with equity partners and banks is the question of what it really means to you personally. The bank debt and agreement with equity partners affect the returns that managers will take away from the deal. But how do these deals translate into your own bottom line?

What could a 15 percent stake mean to you in cold hard cash? How do the price and other terms you agree upon with the seller affect what you walk away with from the deal? Chapter 8 takes a more detailed look—using a simple computer model—at analyzing the risk and returns of the deal for managers and investors.

CHAPTER 8

What's in It for You?

"It is better to have a permanent income than to be fascinating."

—OSCAR WILDE

Although the adrenaline rush of leading a buyout may be enough of a reward for some managers, most want to see that they have a reasonable chance of achieving higher tangible returns by sticking their necks out and leading a management buyout (MBO) than by keeping their heads tucked into their comfortable corporate shells. Certainly, investors need to see that they have a reasonable chance of earning high returns for the risks they assume in a leveraged transaction. But the returns for managers and investors depend upon a complex mix of purchase price, the revenue and margins you can deliver, and the deals you strike with equity partners and your management team. How do you make sure you don't walk away from a sweet deal that has a high probability of making you comfortable for life? How do you know when you've reached the point where the deal is no longer worthwhile and you should walk away?

This chapter explores the process of assessing the returns from the deal. This is a fluid assessment because all the factors that contribute to these returns evolve as the deal progresses. Many of them depend on the strength of your own projections of the potential for reducing costs or growing the business. The return analysis of a buyout requires defining the key metrics that drive your business, making assumptions, and then experimenting to test these hypotheses. The outcomes of these analyses will either reward you with lots of money or cost you big time. So it helps to do a few calculations as you enter into the process and at every step along the way.

You might imagine the buyout process as a kind of low-altitude manned space mission. Before you leave the ground, you figure out the right trajectory and thrust you need to get on your way. But when you are on the launch pad, you keep reworking the numbers and if they don't look right, you abort or adjust. Then, even as you are headed out into the great unknown, you continue to assess all the factors that will lead to a successful mission. Do you have the water, oxygen, and food needed to survive? Are you still on course? And if you suddenly find an explosion has blown an Apollo 13–size hole in the side of the deal and you are leaking oxygen, you want to know about it sooner rather than later, so you can respond to it quickly. You can make midcourse corrections only if you have been paying attention.

While a slight deviation may initially appear to be insignificant, once you run the analysis you may find that it will take you thousands of miles off course. Similarly, some fairly innocuous-sounding concessions you make on the way to your deal may actually have very significant consequences in the returns you achieve on reentry.

Fortunately, analyzing deals is not rocket science. As we'll explore below, some fairly simple metrics can tell you where you stand. This ongoing analysis is extremely valuable when you reach the go, no-go points, often with limited time to make decisions that will affect your future career and fortunes. At certain points in every deal, you need to make the difficult assessment of whether the returns are worth the risks you are taking. This is not a straightforward equation since we all have different tolerances for risk. But with fairly accurate numbers, you will have a clearer understanding of the true potential returns and risks and can make a better decision when you arrive at these moments of truth.

Fish or Cut Bait

Bill Hoover had put the question to his team. They either had to fish or cut bait, move forward with the business plan they had contemplated for weeks or get on with their lives. Hoover, a compact, soft-spoken fifty-year-old man, was about a decade older than the partners he had invited to start the new information technology business. He had worked with all three men during his career as a senior executive at Fortune 1000 information technology (IT) firms. When they would get together in the evenings, they would talk about striking out on their own. They wanted to lead their own company, to build something.

With a long record of success, Hoover had developed a strategy for a consolidation of government information technology services companies. The federal IT services market was very fragmented with a large number of small to midsize competitors in the $25 million to $50 million range. Companies at this level often reached the maximum capability of their management team at the $50 million point and couldn't seem to grow beyond that level. However, with his excellent record managing much larger enterprises, Hoover could bring several of these companies together to build a substantial competitor. His goal was to build a $1 billion revenue company, and it was achievable. He pitched our firm on the idea. We thought the idea was terrific and Hoover was even better. The reference checks on Hoover were some of the finest we'd ever seen.

We committed to back him with $50 million of equity to start the project. But for Hoover, having his A-team with him in this effort was essential. He had accomplished all the heavy lifting: He had an approved plan and a bunch of cash. The train was ready to leave the station, but he still didn't quite have his team on board. All his partners had to do was walk out of their relatively secure corporate jobs into the great unknown. The discussions dragged on. Hoover finally forced the question. Fish or cut bait. Yes or no.

They said no.

"At some point, you have to put up or shut up," Hoover said the day after he received their reply. "I can understand. They are not in my position. If it failed, it would have hurt me, but not as much. They are about ten years younger than I am. They would have to go out and put their houses up. They don't have a cushion."

Two Decades Postponed

Hoover had carried the dream of starting a business with him since he left the navy in 1978. A Naval Academy graduate with an aerospace engineering degree, Hoover had planned to make a career of the military. After seven years in uniform, however, this self-described "change agent" left when he found the bureaucracy stifling. It might have been the ideal time to start a business if not for his personal circumstances.

His first child, Leslie Anne, was diagnosed with cancer and died in April 1979, before her fourth birthday. "I had enough chaos in my life at that time," Hoover said. "I didn't need to introduce professional chaos." He went to work as an engineer in Ford Motor Company's light truck division. The twilight era of the Big Three made even military organizations look streamlined. "I had never seen such lethargy as I saw in Dearborn at that time," he said. Two years later, he left to join a growing high-tech company, Advanced Technology, Inc., walking away from a more lucrative offer from Booz Allen to join the $13 million technology firm. He found the kind of excitement he was looking for.

Hoover helped build the company to more than $200 million in revenue and led its merger with Planning Research Corporation (PRC), a large federal government IT contractor. At PRC, he led the team that carried the company through a major turnaround. During sixteen years in the organization, he rose to become president and COO of PRC. When parent company Black & Decker put PRC on the block, Hoover and other managers organized a bid for an employee stock ownership plan. Again, he came within inches of owning the company with other employees, but they lost out to Litton by a few thousand dollars. Because of how quickly the deal came together, Hoover didn't have time to shop it around to different buyout shops. They settled on one New York firm, which was a solid company, but didn't understand the market well. "In retrospect, if we'd had more time, we could have done a better job with the deal," he said. "It really can be a partnership."

After the merger and a transition period, Hoover moved to BDM, another large and prominent federal IT firm, where he spent two years as executive vice president and president of their federal systems division, helping to lead a strategic restructuring. He was a member of the three-person executive leadership team that was instrumental in selling BDM to TRW in December 1997. He left TRW to start his own consulting company in 1998—and to begin laying the foundation for his new business. But now, when his partners had dropped out of the race, he suddenly found himself running alone.

Hoover still held out hope that his team members might change their minds. "With some passage of time they might wish to try to resurrect this again. I'm not going to do anything that forecloses that. To some degree, I feel like I've been released from the personal commitment I had for these guys. They helped me get to where I am today and I have helped them get to where they are today. There was a commitment I felt very strongly about. That was part of what was very enchanting, to create an opportunity for them. I presented them with that opportunity and now I am kind of released from it."

The strategy is still compelling and the dream of creating a business lives on. "It is still a personal ambition," Hoover said with a broad smile. "I know that their choice was not personal; they made a business judgment. There was a risk that they presumed in the deal that was greater than they were willing to accept. I have always been somewhat of a risk taker myself. Not an entrepreneur, but I like to do things that are a little more challenging that not everyone would want to do. I've been told I'm crazy, but risk takers don't take crazy risks. There are a lot of people out there like me. They really are willing to take risks to make a dream come true."

Analyzing the Deal

The choice to jump out and put together a management deal takes a lot of courage. Hoover had a dynamite strategy and almost had a lock on the management team to pull it off, but they got cold feet. A buyout does involve substantial risks. But what's the upside? How high does management have to jump to achieve it? What are the downside risks? Who needs to be cut into the deal and for how much? How could Hoover and his team assess the potential upside and downside of the deal so they could accurately respond to the risks? These are the major questions that loom at the beginning of every deal and recur throughout the process as offers and counter-offers are passed like cards at a poker table.

Deals rarely offer neat answers to the simple question: What's in it for me? Equity partners and banks are contributing the lion's share of the financing and rightfully expect a solid return on their investments. The seller wants the highest price possible. Various managers on the team may have different expectations of what is fair. There is a lot of uncertainty in the business plan and the environment. No one can predict how the future will turn out. The key terms of the deal—from selling price to financing—are subject to negotiations. This creates a moving target throughout the process, so knowing where you are at any given point in time is crucial.

As discussed in preceding chapters, there are many tools used for tracking the intricacies of a transaction. No tool is more central at every stage of the deal than the financial model that assembles all of the key metrics of a transaction in one place and gives you the opportunity to manipulate the data to see if the deal works. You'll begin working with this model—with crude inputs—at the start of your analysis and structuring of the deal. And you'll still be working with it as you fine-tune the documents leading up to closing. It is a touchstone throughout the deal process.

The Financial Model
The financial model is a core tool used to monitor the movement in the economics of a deal. It delineates, in a relatively complete way, the foundations of the deal. A few of the items the financial model covers are:

- Total purchase price for the asset
- Financing split between debt and equity
- Management interest in the deal and its projected value
- Projected returns to equity investors
- Projected income statement and balance sheet for the target company
- All major income statement assumptions, such as margins and growth rates
- All major balance sheet assumptions, such as inventory turns and receivables days outstanding

This model becomes the basis upon which all of the economics of the deal are analyzed, and it sets the required level of income that must be generated by the company to yield the returns necessary for all parties in the deal. If you need to invest more equity, you put that assumption into the model and run it to see how returns are affected. If you need to spend $2 million in capital expenditures in the second year after buying the company to build a new plant, you put it in the model. The model is the central, governing tool of the management buyout. If the model doesn't work financially, the deal doesn't work. It's as simple as that.

Building Your Model
There are many varieties of financial models on which to build transaction analysis. Some investors use a short two- or three-page model with the basic assumptions to analyze a deal. Other investors, particularly on a complex deal, will build a model with seventy-five pages of computer output analyzing myriad assumptions.

Several software companies offer financial analysis or merger models on which to base your transaction. And many teams simply build their own model in Excel or Lotus. These models are not overly complicated, but they must be accurate and useful in evaluating the key metrics of any business. You and your financial partner must understand the workings of the model intimately.

The model we use to explore the Techway deal is a traditional MBO model that has about ten pages of output and is useful in analyzing most deals. If you're not used to working with these models, they look intimidating at first, with tiny numbers all over the place. But they're very straightforward and you'll become facile with them quickly. To try to make this chapter somewhat user-friendly, we've focused on only the first page of the model, which is a one-page executive summary of all the major assumptions that make the deal go. You can look at the complete model and all the assumptions in Appendix K.

This model is frequently updated as the process moves forward to give managers and other investors a snapshot of their expected returns at any given moment. It also shows managers performance goals they need to achieve to get there and the costs of falling short. Initially, this type of analysis can help managers identify some key cutoffs that make the deal possible—in both the results they need to achieve in their business plans and the offers they can accept from sellers and financial partners.

Typically, we run one sheet for the base case—the expected outcome—and a second for a downside case and a third, very optimistic upside case. With the model, you can run many cases testing many assumptions. This gives managers and investors a sense of the lay of the land. The model helps answer questions such as:

- How much can we reasonably offer for the business?
- What percentage of the deal do we need to make it worthwhile?
- How sensitive is our return to meeting our performance targets?
- What level of negative performance will hurt our deal with the banks?
- If the business is flat for two years, how will that affect returns?

As new information comes in, the model is updated and offers further guidance on how each emerging piece of the puzzle affects the bottom line for managers and other investors. This is crucial information. It helps keep you from getting swept away in the passion of the deal so you fail to see that you are headed past the point of diminishing returns.

Background on the Techway Deal

The Techway senior management team had met extensively and the CEO and CFO both believed that the company was worth between $100 million and $120 million. At the low end of the range, they felt they would be getting a good deal and were excited to pursue it on their own. At $120 million, they felt less well about the deal. Their gut feeling was based upon simple but accurate and often used financial metrics. They were comfortable that the company would generate $17.5 million of earnings before interest, taxes, depreciation, and amortization (the famous EBITDA, which essentially represents pretax cash flow before capital expenditures). They had done some summary industry research that told them that businesses of this type should be valued at six to seven times EBITDA (the purchase multiple). This would value Techway at between $105 million and $122.5 million. But now that they had this range, how did they know they could actually pull off a deal at this level?

I had met them at their sale presentation for the company and suggested that they should lead an MBO. An MBO was a perfect vehicle because in a business only made up of people, management continuity was key. A management-led deal would ensure continuity and would push equity in the company down to the mid- and low-level managers, increasing motivation. They liked my pitch and our team visited their office to talk them through the basics of making a deal. They started getting excited (and scared at the same time, particularly about floating free out from under the $50 billion mother ship) and asked us to put a model together for the deal.

It is typical that your buyout partners will put together a first run of the model. This is simply because they have easy access to that model and can create it through basic inputs in a couple of hours. At some point, management must also have an operative model and know how to run it. Of course, if you're working to add the most value up-front, you'll want to have your own model at the outset with any deal you're pursuing seriously. In this book we give you the basics of the model and tell you where to access an off-the-shelf version on which to model your deals.

In preparing the Techway model, we used the managers' price of $100 million as the target for the model to see if the deal "penciled" at that level. The key assumptions and their rationale are delineated below:

Key Assumptions

- *Purchase Price.* $103.3 million

As discussed previously, $100 million was a number that made sense and a number the team was comfortable with. Also, to close a deal such as this, it normally costs approximately 3–5 percent of the total purchase price in legal, accounting, advisory, and investment banking fees, so we assumed $3.3 million of fees that would need to be financed at closing. These closing fees should never be overlooked and do not represent additions to the purchase price.

- *Financing.* 50 percent debt/50 percent equity

Here, to maximize equity returns, you normally borrow as much as you can from the banks to finance the deal. As discussed earlier, for a service business of this type, one can usually borrow about three times EBITDA, or in this case a little over $50 million. So we used $50 million in borrowings and therefore would need $50 million in equity to complete the deal.

- *Structure.* "Recapitalization" with Techway Shareholders retaining 10 percent before management options

This recapitalization allows the buyers to avoid adding "goodwill" to their balance sheet, which is very helpful from an earnings perspective after closing.

- *Management Ownership.* Equity coinvest worth 15 percent of the common equity

This piece is the management Holy Grail. On any model, a buyout investor's eyes go to the equity internal rate of return (IRR) box first, and management's eyes go immediately to the management return box.

- *Techway Value.* $95 million in cash and 10 percent ($5 million) of the equity, valued at approximately $15 million to $20 million in year four

The parent company will receive $95 million in cash and a piece of stock in the new company initially valued at $5 million. This is their "rollover" interest, which facilitates the recapitalization discussed earlier.

- *Management Coinvestment.* Management coinvestment is only in the common equity, allowing management to invest a relatively small amount while retaining 15 percent of the upside opportunity. The return is the same as if they were provided options but can benefit from capital gains treatment in this scenario.

This is a critical structure from a manager's viewpoint because of the large gap between ordinary income taxes and capital gains taxes. This is accomplished by splitting the equity into preferred and common stock and having all of the management interest in the common stock.

- *Future Operating Assumptions.* Based entirely on normal business performance and providing no assumption for extraordinary performance or the sale of real assets such as real estate

The model assumes no extraneous or out-of-the-ordinary events. In the case of the Techway managers, they also controlled substantial real estate but this was not factored into the model. It simply was there as an asset to protect all investors in case the deal did not go well.

The Techway managers also knew they could cut overhead by restructuring benefits. The parent company forced them to use a bloated and overly expensive benefits package. They further expected they could boost revenues by going to a commission sales system. Commissions, which had been blocked by policies of the parent, were crucial to attracting top sales talent in the industry. The projections that managers made in their business plan became the inputs for the model.

For Techway, as is very traditional, we started with a base case, which is the expected outcome. The base case represents your highly confident plan. From there, you always look at sensitivities on the upside *and* the downside. Where can margins slip? What if interest rates go way up? What's the recession case? One of the greatest things about the computer model is the number of sensitivities you can run relatively painlessly. For Techway, we considered three cases (see Figures 8-1, 8-2, and 8-3) each driven by one key metric—the annual revenue growth assumption used in the projections. It is usually revenue growth and margin assumptions that are the primary drivers for the performance of the model. Our Techway scenarios were as follows:

• *Base Case.* We projected 7.7 percent to 8.3 percent annual revenue growth through 2001 and then assumed a 7 percent growth rate going forward while maintaining all other expenses at the 2001 levels as a percentage of revenue. The 2003 projected EBITDA in this case is $33.4 million.

• *Investor Upside.* Here we made the same revenue assumptions as in the base case with the exception of an increase of 20 percent in EBITDA in 2000 and going forward, which is affected by an increase in the gross margin of 1.2 percent in 2000 and maintaining that margin going forward. Note that the 2003 EBITDA projection in this case is $37.5 million. Ask yourself a simple question for this case: What can go right? At business school, this was the WCGR (what can go right?) scenario. It's a helpful but simple exercise.

• *Investor Downside.* This scenario assumes all of management assumptions except that operating expenses are maintained at 1998 levels as a percentage of revenues (rather than decreased). Note that 2003 EBITDA projection in this case is $23.7 million. This is the case that looks at WCGW (what can go wrong?). This is actually much more important than WCGR. On the upside, everybody's happy. On the downside, it's tough sledding, and you should carefully consider every element of WCGW and think about how these scenarios will impact your numbers. You need to recognize that you'll have a natural tendency to want to avoid looking at this scenario, but you need to take an unflinching view of it.

The Model Summary Sheet

Based on some of these assumptions, let's take a look at the model summary sheet. This one-page sheet distills all of the analysis in the back of the model and, in one page, lets you know whether or not the deal will fly. Please be patient with this section of the book; it's highly detailed but very important from an analytical perspective. Figure 8-1, which is the Techway base case model, highlights each of the different sections (the boxes labeled A through E) of the summary sheet we'll discuss. Let's take a quick swing through the sections to orient ourselves.

Section A: Sources and Uses of Funds. This is a fundamental section that lays out your sources of capital for the transaction, such as how much debt and equity you will need to finance your purchase. You can see in Figure 8-1A that there is room for various layers of debt financing (i.e., sources of funds) that may have different interest rates. In most deals, the debt pieces are pretty simple, but at least the model makes room for a more complex structure.

The "uses" side of the ledger shows you where cash will go in the deal: the payments to the sellers, the rolled equity, and all the fees you'll pay. One small item is that, obviously, the sources and uses side of the ledger must balance. Here we have a $103.3 million deal for Techway.

Section B: Pro Forma Capital Structure. This section repeats your sources and uses of funds information but also gives you additional, important information such as what percentage of the capital struc-

Figure 8-1. Techway base case analysis.

A: Sources and Uses of Funds

Sources of Funds	Amount ($)	Interest Rate
Cash From Balance Sheet	0	
New Revolver	13.25	0.09
New Senior Term A	40	0.09
New Senior Term B	0	0
New Senior Term C	0	0
New Sub Debt	0	0.12
Note to Sellers	0	0.12
New Preferred Equity (PIK)	46	0.15
Rollover of Equity--Seller's (a)	0.4	0
New Common Stock	3.6	
	$ 103.3	

Uses of Funds	Amount ($)
Cash to Owners	95
Equity Ownership	5
Note to Owners	0
Excess Cash	0
Value to Owners	100
Repay Debt	0
New Cash Infusion	0
Buyer Expenses	3.25
	$103.3

(a) Some portion rollover equity rolled into preferred.

B: Pro Forma Capital Structure

PF Capital Structure	Based on Market Value		Cal 1998 xEBITDA	Fisc 1999 xEBITDA
Revolver	13.25	12.8%	0.8	0.8
New Senior Term A	40	38.7%	2.3	2.3
New Senior Term B	0	0.0%	0.0	0.0
New Senior Term C	0	0.0%	0.0	0.0
New Sub Debt	0	0.0%	0.0	0.0
Total Debt	53.25	51.0%	3.1	3.1
Note to Sellers	0	0.0%	0.0	0.0
PIK Preferred	46	44.6%	2.7	2.7
Rollover Equity	0.4	0.4%	0.0	0.0
Common Stock	3.6	3.5%	0.2	0.2
Total Equity	50	48.4%	2.9	2.9
Total Cap (incl. Cash)	103.25	100.0%	6.1	6.0

C: Equity Ownership

Equity Ownership	Equity Common	Equity Preferred	Total	% of Investment Common	% of Investment Preferred
Rollover Equity--Parent	0.4	4.6	5	8.5%	10.0%
Equity Investor	3.6	41.4	45	76.5%	90.0%
Management Ownership*	0.7	0	0.7	15.0%	0.0%
Sub Debt	0	0	0	0.0%	0.0%
PIK Warrants	0	0	0	0.0%	0.0%
Total Ownership	$4.7	$46.0	$50.7	100.0%	100.0%

Ownership

	Common	Warrants	PreOption Ownership	Perform Options	Fully Dil. Ownership
	8.5%	0.0%	8.5%	0.0%	8.5%
	76.5%	0.0%	76.5%	0.0%	76.5%
	15.0%	0.0%	15.0%	0.0%	15.0%
	0.0%	0.0%	0.0%	0.0%	0.0%
	0.0%	0.0%	0.0%	0.0%	0.0%
	100.0%	0.0%	100.0%	0.0%	100.0%

D: Internal Rate of Return

Internal Rate of Return

	Total Investor Return				Investor Investment Gain				Management Coinvest Equity Value		
Multiple of EBITDA	Year 3	Year 4	Year 5		Year 3	Year 4	Year 5		Year 3	Year 4	Year 5
6.00	36.9%	31.3%	28.4%		$70.5	$88.8	$111.9		$10.3	$12.0	$14.4
7.00	45.2%	36.7%	32.3%		$92.7	$112.3	$137.3		$14.7	$16.7	$19.4
8.00	52.6%	41.6%	35.8%		$115.0	$135.9	$162.7		$19.0	$21.3	$24.4

E: Income Statement Projections

	Fiscal Year Ending December,				Calendar		Projected twelve months ended December,					
	1996	1997	1998	1999	2000	2001	2002	2003	2004	2005	2006	2007
Net Revenues	$270.5	$256.5	$278.0	$300.0	$325.0	$350.0	$374.5	$400.7	$426.8	$458.8	$490.9	$525.3
% Growth		-5.2%	8.4%	7.9%	8.3%	7.7%	7.0%	7.0%	7.0%	7.0%	7.0%	7.0%
EBITDA (before management fee)	3.1	0.0	17.1	17.5	24.0	29.3	31.0	33.4	36.1	39.2	43.1	45.6
% of Net Revenue	1.1%	0.0%	6.1%	5.8%	7.4%	8.4%	8.3%	8.3%	8.4%	8.5%	8.6%	8.7%
EBITA (before management fee)	0.5	-2.8	14.8	14.3	20.6	25.7	27.5	29.4	31.5	33.7	36.0	38.6
% of Net Revenue	0.2%	-1.1%	5.3%	4.8%	6.3%	7.3%	7.3%	7.3%	7.3%	7.3%	7.3%	7.3%
Capital Expenditures	0.0	1.6	2.3	4.5	4.5	2.2	2.3	2.5	2.6	2.8	3.0	3.2
Net Debt			53.3	50.8	46.3	36.0	24.2	10.6	-5.0	-22.8	-43.5	-65.6
Total Debt Outstanding			53.3	50.8	46.3	36.0	24.2	10.6	0.0	0.0	0.0	0.0
EBITDA/Total Interest			3.6	3.6	5.2	7.0	9.5	15.3	37.8			
EBITDA--Capex/Total Interest			3.1	2.7	4.2	6.5	8.8	14.1	35.0			
Total Debt/EBITDA			3.1	2.9	1.9	1.2	0.8	0.3	0.0	0.0	0.0	0.0

*Management equity to be funded in some combination of cash from management and loans from the company. For simplicity, not included in sources of funds.

ture is debt (in this case 51.6 percent) and how many multiple points of EBITDA the debt capital represents (in this case 3.1 times). Service deals such as the Techway deal can normally borrow about three times EBITDA. If your model showed you that debt was fives times EBITDA, you'd have too much debt. At the bottom right of this section it shows that you're paying six times EBITDA in total for the business, which is our goal.

Section C: Equity Ownership. Now we're getting into the good stuff! This is an important box that shows you who owns which piece of the company and how much they're paying for it. In this case you can see that the equity investor is putting up $45 million to ultimately own 76.5 percent of the company, while management is putting up $700,000 to own 15 percent of the company (now that's leverage!).

Section D: IRR. This is the bottom line: rates of return on dollars invested. This is the equity investor's most important section of the model and should be yours, too. There are many important elements in this section of the model. First, just a brief comment on IRR. The IRR simply measures the compounded annual return on cash invested in the deal. It looks at your first investment as a cash outflow, then looks at the imputed return you receive on all subsequent annual cash inflows *plus* the residual value, or exit value, of your investment. Two more comments on IRRs: First of all, as you will see when you run different scenarios, IRRs are very sensitive to exit multiples and, particularly, the amount of time measured. It's much easier to achieve a 40 percent projected two-year IRR than a five-year IRR. The effects of compounding are powerful, and it's hard to compound dollars at a high rate over a prolonged period. Second, some investors feel that IRR is less important than absolute dollar gains. As they say, IRR doesn't buy groceries. An investment may have a huge short-term IRR but have meager dollar gains. You should look at both, because in the end it'll be the dollars returned that make the deal swing for you. So in this box (Figure 8-1D) there are many critical elements. First, it shows the range of exit multiples. One important rule of thumb is, do not assume an exit multiple that is higher than your buy-in multiple. If you're buying a company for five times EBITDA, assume you'll exit at five times

EBITDA. *Do not* assume future multiple expansion. If it happens, great; that's a windfall. But don't count on it in your analysis. In this case, we were buying in at six and looked (optimistically) at six, seven, and eight times EBITDA for exit scenarios.

Next you'll see that the model looks at a time to exit. As we've discussed, and you can see in the numbers, time has a huge impact on IRR, and the IRRs are always higher on a shorter exit. Three- to five-year hold periods are typical. The next section of the IRR box shows the total dollars the investors will make under these scenarios. Big numbers, of course, but also big risks on big dollars for them if the deal doesn't work.

Last is the key section on the page for management: If the deal works, how much will the team make? Figure 8-1D shows a huge range of more than $10 million in three years at a six times exit, and more than $24 million in year five at an eight times exit. It's a big range and illustrates the sensitivity to hold periods and exit multiples. Divide those dollars among your team of five senior managers and it starts to look pretty compelling. Now all you have to do is the hardest part—execute.

Section E: Income Statement Projections. This last section of the model is obviously critical and requires great thought on management's part. What will the company make in the future? How quickly will revenues grow and margins expand or contract, and how much debt will we pay down in the future? No one can predict the future perfectly, but here you must generate your best, educated plan. To build the plan, pull the business apart unit by unit and customer by customer, then rebuild it into your base case plan. Be relatively conservative; do not plan or anticipate events that have a limited likelihood of occurring. Also, be careful to look at your projected capital expenditures and working capital utilization. These things cost cash, which otherwise could be used to pay down debt and enhance your equity returns. This section of the model is the final distillation of all your planning and all of the pages behind the model, which analyze these metrics in detail.

Specifically, here you should see revenues growing at about 7–7.5 percent annually (or a little more slowly to be conservative), which is consistent with the company's marketplace. Also, they show EBITDA margins *increasing*, which is not easy to do but in this case is documented through projected cost savings. Also, increased capital expenditures of $4.5 million per annum (versus $2.3 million in the prior year) are projected to put in place systems that are currently being funded by the parent company. Then, at the bottom of Figure 8-1E the model looks at basic debt ratios, such as EBITDA divided by total interest, to test the company's leverage. In this case an EBITDA coverage ratio of 3.6 is high (good), which reflects the relatively large amount of equity (and modest debt) on the deal.

In all, this one-page model summary gives you a snapshot of everything you need to know about the deal. In this case, the projections are not overly aggressive given the company's market and the ratios of return are fine given the risks in the deal. From an investor's perspective, this is a deal that should get done. From here, it is important to look at three different cases (base, upscale, and downside) to see how those cases impact management dollars. You will find the full upside and downside models in Appendix K.

Returns to the Team under Different Scenarios
By examining the base, upside, and downside cases, we can see how investor and management returns are significantly affected by varying sets of performance assumptions. In the base case, Techway's CEO and his team have the potential to earn equity of $19.4 million in year five (assuming the company is valued at seven times EBITDA at the time of exit). On the upside, they could go as high as $25 million and, on the downside, could end up with only $5.8 million as a team (see Figures 8-2 and 8-3 after this page).

As we discussed, the multiples used are based on prevailing multiples for the industry and are usually taken as a range. For Techway, the overall range used in the model was six to eight times EBITDA. As referenced, the prevailing multiple times the revenue (EBITDA) equals the total enterprise value. To look at the exit, you then take this total enterprise value and deduct the total debt (which yields the equity value), and the managers receive 15 percent of the equity value.

These analyses also show the returns to investors: The base

case offers a respectable 32 percent return to investors or a gain of $137 million. The upside is even better, but the downside is only 20 percent. Private equity investors require annual returns over a three- to five-year period of 30 percent per annum, so if the downside case were the base case, then the deal would be unattractive to outside investors. If this is the case when you run your model, the model is sending you a message loud and clear: You are paying too much and must lower your price.

The numbers managers put into their plans are absolutely crucial to assessing the deal. If the equity partners believe the numbers and they offer good returns, the deal is a go. If not, it may be difficult to find anyone who is interested. That is why having a solid business strategy, discussed in Chapter 5, is fundamental to attracting money and making the deal a success.

There is no point in pushing for overly aggressive upside numbers early on. Many managers get to this analysis, or get to the point where they have to commit to a plan with investors, and they back off from their aggressive numbers, thereby dinging their credibility. Whatever plans you present, you will live and die by them for many years. It is best to make them honest and achievable, or it will be your tail in the wringer later on.

Watch the Fees

Under "uses of funds" in Figure 8-1A, nearly $3.3 million goes to buyer's expenses. This is not unusual as fees go, but it is something to watch as the deal progresses. These fees come directly out of the company and are essentially funded by the banks at closing. It is important, however, to discuss up front with your equity partner how deal expenses will be handled if the deal breaks. It is customary for each side to bear their own expenses and for the private equity firm to choose all lawyers and accountants *and* to bear those large expenses if the deal breaks. Private equity firms are normally reimbursed for these costs by their partners and also usually have special deals with legal and accounting firms to get cut rates if the deals break.

The sheets in Appendix K offer a more detailed look at the base case to show how the top-sheet numbers were generated.

Figure 8-2. Techway upside case.

Sources of Funds	Amount ($)	Interest Rate
Cash From Balance Sheet	$0.0	
New Revolver	13.3	9.0%
New Senior Term A	40.0	9.0%
New Senior Term B	0.0	0.0%
New Senior Term C	0.0	0.0%
New Sub Debt	0.0	12.0%
Note to Sellers	0.0	12.0%
New Preferred Equity (PIK)	46.0	15.0%
Rollover of Equity - Seller's (a)	0.4	0.0%
New Common Stock	3.6	
	$103.3	

Uses of Funds	Amount ($)
Cash to Owners	$95.0
Equity Ownership	5.0
Note to Owners	0.0
Excess Cash	0.0
Value to Owners	$100.0
Repay Debt	0.0
New Cash Infusion	0.0
Buyer Expenses	3.3
	$103.3

(a) Some portion rollover equity rolled into preferred.

PF Capital Structure	Based on Market Value		Cal 1998 xEBITDA	Fisc 1999 xEBITDA
Revolver	$13.3	12.8%	0.8 x	0.8 x
New Senior Term A	40.0	38.7%	2.3 x	2.3 x
New Senior Term B	0.0	0.0%	0.0 x	0.0 x
New Senior Term C	0.0	0.0%	0.0 x	0.0 x
New Sub Debt	0.0	0.0%	0.0 x	0.0 x
Total Debt	53.3	51.6%	3.1 x	3.1 x
Note to Sellers	0.0	0.0%	0.0 x	0.0 x
PIK Preferred	46.0	44.6%	2.7 x	2.7 x
Rollover Equity	0.4	0.4%	0.0 x	0.0 x
Common Stock	3.6	3.5%	0.2 x	0.2 x
Total Equity	50.0	48.4%	2.9 x	2.9 x
Total Cap (incl. Cash)	$103.3	100.0%	6.1 x	6.0 x

Equity Ownership	Equity			% of Investment		Ownership				
	Common	Preferred	Total	Common	Preferred	Common	Warrants	PreOption Ownership	Perform Options	Fully Dil. Ownership
Rollover Equity - Parent	0.400	4.6	$5.0	8.5%	10.0%	8.5%	0.0%	8.5%	0.0%	8.5%
Equity Investor	3.600	41.4	45.0	76.5%	90.0%	76.5%	0.0%	76.5%	0.0%	76.5%
Management Ownership*	0.706	0.0	0.7	15.0%	0.0%	15.0%	0.0%	15.0%	0.0%	15.0%
Sub Debt	0.0	0.0	0.0	0.0%	0.0%	0.0%	0.0%	0.0%	0.0%	0.0%
PIK Warrants	0.0	0.0	0.0	0.0%	0.0%	0.0%	0.0%	0.0%	0.0%	0.0%
Total Ownership	$4,706	$46.0	$50.7	100.0%	100.0%	100.0%	0.0%	100.0%	0.0%	100.0%

Internal Rate of Return

Total Investor Return

Multiple of EBITDA	Year 3	Year 4	Year 5
6.00 x	44.4%	36.7%	32.5%
7.00 x	52.8%	42.1%	36.4%
8.00 x	60.4%	47.0%	39.9%

Investor Investment Gain

	Year 3	Year 4	Year 5
	$90.6	$112.0	$138.6
	$115.6	$138.6	$167.2
	$140.6	$165.1	$195.8

Management Coinvest Equity Value

	Year 3	Year 4	Year 5
	$14.2	$16.6	$19.7
	$19.1	$21.8	$25.3
	$24.1	$27.0	$30.9

	Fiscal Year Ending December,			Calendar	Projected twelve months ended December,								
	1996	1997	1998	1998	1999	2000	2001	2002	2003	2004	2005	2006	2007
Net Revenues	$270.5	$256.5	$278.0	$278.0	$300.0	$325.0	$350.0	$374.5	$400.7	$428.8	$458.8	$490.9	$525.3
% Growth		-5.2%	8.4%		7.9%	8.3%	7.7%	7.0%	7.0%	7.0%	7.0%	7.0%	7.0%
EBITDA													
(before management fee)	3.1	0.0	17.1	17.1	17.5	27.9	32.9	34.9	37.5	40.5	43.9	48.1	51.0
% of Net Revenue	1.1%	0.0%	6.1%	6.1%	5.8%	8.6%	9.4%	9.3%	9.4%	9.5%	9.6%	9.8%	9.7%
EBITA													
(before management fee)	0.5	(2.8)	14.8	14.8	14.3	24.5	29.3	31.3	33.5	35.9	38.4	41.1	44.0
% of Net Revenue	0.2%	-1.1%	5.3%	5.3%	4.8%	7.5%	8.4%	8.4%	8.4%	8.4%	8.4%	8.4%	8.4%
Capital Expenditures	0.0	1.6	2.3	2.3	4.5	4.5	2.2	2.3	2.5	2.6	2.8	3.0	3.2
Net Debt			53.3	53.3	50.8	43.8	31.2	16.8	0.3	(18.4)	(39.5)	(63.6)	(89.4)
Total Debt Outstanding			53.3	53.3	50.8	43.8	31.2	16.8	0.3	0.0	0.0	0.0	0.0
EBITDA / Total Interest			3.6 x		3.6 x	6.1 x	8.3 x	12.3 x	24.7 x	1390.3 x	#DIV/0!	#DIV/0!	#DIV/0!
EBITDA - Capex / Total Interest			3.1 x		2.7 x	5.1 x	7.7 x	11.5 x	23.0 x	1299.4 x	#DIV/0!	#DIV/0!	#DIV/0!
Total Debt / EBITDA			3.1 x		2.9 x	1.6 x	1.0 x	0.5 x	0.0 x	0.0 x	0.0 x	0.0 x	0.0 x

*Management equity to be funded in some combination of cash from management and loans from the company. For simplicity, not included in sources of funds.

Figure 8-3. Investor downside case.

Sources of Funds	Amount ($)	Interest Rate
Cash From Balance Sheet	$0.0	
New Revolver	13.3	9.0%
New Senior Term A	40.0	9.0%
New Senior Term B	0.0	0.0%
New Senior Term C	0.0	0.0%
New Sub Debt	0.0	0.0%
Note to Sellers	0.0	12.0%
New Preferred Equity (PIK)	46.0	12.0%
Rollover of Equity - Seller's (a)	0.4	15.0%
New Common Stock	3.6	0.0%
	$103.3	

Uses of Funds	Amount ($)
Cash to Owners	$95.0
Equity Ownership	5.0
Note to Owners	0.0
Excess Cash	0.0
Value to Owners	$100.0
Repay Debt	0.0
New Cash Infusion	0.0
Buyer Expenses	3.3
	$103.3

PF Capital Structure	Based on Market Value		Cal 1998 xEBITDA	Fisc 1999 xEBITDA
Revolver	$13.3	12.8%	0.8 x	0.9 x
New Senior Term A	40.0	38.7%	2.3 x	2.6 x
New Senior Term B	0.0	0.0%	0.0 x	0.0 x
New Senior Term C	0.0	0.0%	0.0 x	0.0 x
New Sub Debt	0.0	0.0%	0.0 x	0.0 x
Total Debt	53.3	51.6%	3.1 x	3.5 x
Note to Sellers	0.0	0.0%	0.0 x	0.0 x
PIK Preferred	46.0	44.6%	2.7 x	3.0 x
Rollover Equity	0.4	0.4%	0.0 x	0.0 x
Common Stock	3.6	3.5%	0.2 x	0.2 x
Total Equity	50.0	48.4%	2.9 x	3.3 x
Total Cap (incl. Cash)	$103.3	100.0%	6.1 x	6.7 x

(a) Some portion rollover equity rolled into preferred.

Equity Ownership	Equity			% of Investment	
	Common	Preferred	Total	Common	Preferred
Rollover Equity - Parent	0.400	4.6	$5.0	8.5%	10.0%
Equity Investor	3.600	41.4	45.0	76.5%	90.0%
Management Ownership*	0.706	0.0	0.7	15.0%	0.0%
Sub Debt	0.0	0.0	0.0	0.0%	0.0%
PIK Warrants	0.0	0.0	0.0	0.0%	0.0%
Total Ownership	$4,706	$46.0	$50.7	100.0%	100.0%

	Ownership				
	Common	Warrants	PreOption Ownership	Perform Options	Fully Dil. Ownership
Rollover Equity - Parent	8.5%	0.0%	8.5%	0.0%	8.5%
Equity Investor	76.5%	0.0%	76.5%	0.0%	76.5%
Management Ownership*	15.0%	0.0%	15.0%	0.0%	15.0%
Sub Debt	0.0%	0.0%	0.0%	0.0%	0.0%
PIK Warrants	0.0%	0.0%	0.0%	0.0%	0.0%
Total Ownership	100.0%	0.0%	100.0%	0.0%	100.0%

Internal Rate of Return

	Total Investor Return		
Multiple of EBITDA	Year 3	Year 4	Year 5
6.00 x	15.3%	15.4%	16.1%
7.00 x	23.5%	21.0%	20.2%
8.00 x	30.7%	25.9%	23.8%

Investor Investment Gain

Year 3	Year 4	Year 5
$23.9	$34.9	$50.0
$39.7	$51.5	$68.0
$55.4	$68.1	$85.9

Management Coinvest Equity Value

Year 3	Year 4	Year 5
$1.2	$1.5	$2.3
$4.3	$4.7	$5.8
$7.3	$8.0	$9.3

	Fiscal Year Ending December,			Calendar 1998	Projected twelve months ended December,								
	1996	1997	1998	1998	1999	2000	2001	2002	2003	2004	2005	2006	2007
Net Revenues	$270.5	$256.5	$278.0	$278.0	$300.0	$325.0	$350.0	$374.5	$400.7	$428.8	$458.8	$490.9	$525.3
% Growth		-5.2%	8.4%		7.9%	8.3%	7.7%	7.0%	7.0%	7.0%	7.0%	7.0%	7.0%
EBITDA													
(before management fee)	3.1	0.0	17.1	17.1	15.5	18.8	20.8	21.9	23.7	25.7	28.1	31.2	32.8
% of Net Revenue	1.1%	0.0%	6.1%	6.1%	5.2%	5.8%	5.9%	5.8%	5.9%	6.0%	6.1%	6.3%	6.3%
EBITA													
(before management fee)	0.5	(2.8)	14.8	14.8	12.3	15.4	17.2	18.4	19.7	21.0	22.5	24.1	25.8
% of Net Revenue	0.2%	-1.1%	5.3%	5.3%	4.1%	4.7%	4.9%	4.9%	4.9%	4.9%	4.9%	4.9%	4.9%
Capital Expenditures	0.0	1.6	2.3	2.3	4.5	4.5	2.2	2.3	2.5	2.6	2.8	3.0	3.2
Net Debt			53.3	53.3	52.0	50.7	45.7	39.9	33.0	24.9	15.2	3.0	(10.2)
Total Debt Outstanding			53.3	53.3	52.0	50.7	45.7	39.9	33.0	24.9	15.2	3.0	0.0
EBITDA / Total Interest			3.6 x	3.6 x	3.2 x	4.0 x	4.5 x	5.3 x	6.5 x	8.6 x	12.4 x	22.6 x	119.9 x
EBITDA - Capex / Total Interest			3.1 x	3.1 x	2.3 x	3.0 x	4.0 x	4.7 x	5.9 x	7.7 x	11.2 x	20.4 x	108.0 x
Total Debt / EBITDA			3.1 x	3.1 x	3.4 x	2.7 x	2.2 x	1.8 x	1.4 x	1.0 x	0.5 x	0.1 x	0.0 x

* Management equity to be funded in some combination of cash from management and loans from the company. For simplicity, not included in sources of funds.

Dividing the Spoils

Another key issue in analyzing the deal is selecting the central management team and deciding how to divide the returns among them. In an internal buyout, the team is fairly self-evident. It is usually the top four to five managers at the company, and the only challenge is where to draw the line. This senior team usually includes the CEO, CFO, and the heads of sales, manufacturing, and marketing. In some businesses, such as technology companies, you may include the chief information officer and the head of human resources. Managers a bit farther down in the organization can be given equity stakes as well, which can be done at closing or after the buyout has been completed.

You need to ensure you have the right portfolio of skills. Even with the existing management team, you may need to bring in other partners at the outset or add skills along the way. You may need someone with entrepreneurial experience or skills in investor relations, marketing, or technology. If a lawyer isn't on the core management team, you may need to bring in someone with a legal background to act as general counsel. These people can either be added as core partners or brought in as employees, depending on how essential these skills and perspectives are to making the business a success.

With an external buyout or roll-up, the creation of the team is a much more directed process. As Bill Hoover and Stu Johnson did, you can assemble the "dream team" from your past career, though getting them to come on board may be more difficult. People within the team may actually question the value of other members, knowing that they are taking up a share of the returns. This can become a source of conflict. "We had some very interesting conversations," Hoover said. "Some were questioning the value of other members of the team. What is the value-added that you provide?"

What do you do if someone you target for the team balks? This is rarely the case with internal deals. People do not want to be left behind and they know if they don't join in the deal, the best they can hope for is to maintain their position in the new firm, without the huge upside offered by the buyout. While managers may be reluctant to initiate a buyout, very few are willing to let it leave the station without climbing aboard.

For external teams, it is a much harder sell to get people to leave their jobs and take on this new venture, as Bill Hoover found out. Selling the upside, ensuring they have good terms, and bringing in a strong partner can help. You need to give them a sense of the potential while being realistic about the risks. Even worse than having people back down before the deal is to have them suddenly get cold feet at the first sign of trouble. Ultimately, the decision depends on individual perspectives, and it takes a lot to get people to jump out into the unknown.

Since there is much work to do to make the deal happen, and all of it is crucial to the success of the venture, the team has to work well together, so chemistry is crucial. The core team has to be in "mind lock." Hoover knew this, which was why he didn't want to proceed if he didn't have the team behind him. "There better not be any disagreement from the perspective of what they want to do," Hoover said. "There better not be any coercion. Some people you can manipulate to say yes. You have to have absolute commitment to that group." There also has to be this same type of synchronicity with the external capital partner.

The leader of the buyout has to be careful to manage the pre-deal to post-deal relationships. Before the deal, they are partners working together to make the deal happen. After the deal, the CEO is still the CEO, whatever the financial arrangements. The more clearly the post-deal working relationships can be worked out, the easier the transition.

Dividing Equity among Top Managers

Agreements with equity partners generally only specify the total pool of management equity. It is largely up to managers to decide how this equity is ultimately divided up among themselves. This can be a tricky challenge. While the buyout firm won't negotiate individual contracts with management, it will have an interest in knowing how you plan to divide it to motivate employees in the organization. Normally the majority—70–80 percent—is taken by the top five or ten people in the company. The CEO generally gets one-third to one-half of this total top management share. In other words, if managers negotiate 15 percent equity, senior management receives the pool of about 12 percent of that, with the CEO typically receiving 4–6 points. The CFO usually will receive half of what the CEO gets, in this case 2 to 3 points.

To motivate a broader group of managers, often the balance of 20 percent or so is divided among managers farther down in the organization. For example, Software AG pushed equity to the top seventy or eighty people in the 900-person firm. Managers should also negotiate up front with investors to have an additional 2 to 3 percent pool for subsequent hires.

How this equity stake is communicated is as important as the actual percentages. No managers are going to be excited about receiving one-half of 1 percent of the business for all their services. On the surface, though it just sounds like chicken feed, it actually translates to lots of potential equity gains. It is much better, from an internal communications perspective, to express their position in total numbers of shares. For example, in the case of Techway, there was $50 million invested. If management has options on 15 percent, other investors are putting up $50 million for 85 percent of the company. So the value of the total equity is about $59 million (50 million/0.85). If shares are set at $1 per share, then 50 million are owned by the investors and 9 million are passed around among managers. Now, if you give a manager in your organization 1 point here, that represents 590,000 shares. The manager who receives a smaller slice of the company doesn't receive a puny .03 percent but rather 20,000 shares. That sounds a whole lot more impressive, doesn't it? (And if you make your plan, it really will be.) To make your plan, however, you still need to navigate through the delicate minefield that leads from agreements with sellers and equity partners to closing. This is the "ground war" examined in Chapter 9.

Preparing for the Ground War

"Show me a man who cannot bother to do little things and I'll show you a man who cannot be trusted to do big things."
—Lawrence D. Bell, American helicopter manufacturer

You've signed the letter of intent with the seller and buyout partner. Your bank financing is lined up and your computer model for the deal is telling you it will generate a huge internal rate of return and put you on the Côte d'Azur. You've surveyed the terrain at 30,000 feet and everything looks pretty simple, perhaps even tranquil. This deal process may be easier than you had expected. But then you descend through the clouds into the fray of due diligence.

You no longer have the luxury of broad perspective. While you worked fairly autonomously up until now, at this point you move forward trench by trench with a huge platoon of lawyers, accountants, industry consultants, bankers, investors, and casts of thousands. Sometimes it can be a relatively smooth and orderly march to victory (although still exhausting). Other times it can be like landing on the beach at Normandy.

This is the ground war. Accountants and lawyers will be marching in and out of the firm. The CEO and senior managers will have to make presentations to everybody involved in the deal. Three banks that can make or break the deal will be calling with questions. Lawyers, accountants, and nervous partners will be calling with myriad questions—good, bad, and wildly off-point. You have to answer them all. You'll spend hours in conference calls and put yourself to sleep at night reviewing reams of legal documents. Like any ground war, the deal process never sleeps. It doesn't take vacations, doesn't break for nights and weekends. Day after day, the march forward continues.

And while all this excitement is swirling around you, you may still have to run the business. This is the worst time to make a strategic misstep with the company, so you have to do the best ever with your day job at the same time you "moonlight" as a management buyout guru. Most of the challenges of the deal are totally new.

You can't tell anyone except a few close confidants. You have to make up cover stories for all the "suits" suddenly swarming into every open door of the business because only a handful of top managers and insiders know what is going down before the formal announcement.

Then, there is the uncertainty. There is no guarantee after all this work that the deal will go through. That shaky agreement you signed five years ago with your suppliers or an old lawsuit may come back and blow the whole buyout out of the water. If you didn't know how much a successful deal could change your life professionally and financially, you would never put yourself through this process.

With your eye on the prize, you need to clear your calendar for several months. Put vacations on hold. Cancel weekend plans. Accept that everyone will be in your pants for three months while you try to run the company. If you can win this ground war, victory—and equity—will be yours.

You Cannot Be Too Careful

Preparation is the best way to pave the way for a smooth diligence process. The more issues you address when you craft the management term sheet and letter of intent with the seller, the better your life will be during the ground war. If you anticipate the dangers you will meet during the ground war and get them on the table, you might actually forestall some of the problems. If you see the bridge is out, you can change your plans before you invest in putting troops there.

The one guarantee is that there will be many surprises during the diligence process and few of them will be pleasant ones. More unexpected troubles come out of the woodwork than relatives at a millionaire's funeral. Diligence is where the bad news is excavated, where the warts and moles that were invisible from a distance become glaringly obvious, and buyers have to decide whether they intend to buy the company "warts and all."

Managers might remember the underfunded pension plan they never thought would enter into the deal. Or maybe there is a nasty piece of litigation out there that they had been ignoring. Or they might wish they had never dumped those PCBs behind the building for the past few years. The dark secrets will come out in the diligence process.

The diligence process is guaranteed to make you humble, because all the diligence in the world cannot save you from all the deal pitfalls that exist in front of you. I learned this lesson well with my descent into deal hell with Ceramic City, as described in gory detail in Chapter 3. This is why careful diligence is important. Here are two more examples:

• A large consumer-products direct-marketing firm showed thirty-five years of growth when buyers were analyzing a purchase. They had no reason to suspect there might be a problem, but there was. The buyers conducted months of due diligence, but after the sale there was a mysterious drop in earnings. It turned out that a year before the sale, the company had made a subtle change in its credit policies, extending more generous financing terms to customers. The better terms made it easier to attract new customers but harder to get them to pay up. The customers grew, but receivables fell. Earnings pegged at $23 million came in at closer to $15 million. The sellers of the company gave representations and warranties that existed for only a year, and it wasn't until after that the problems emerged. The buyers then owned the problems and would likely lose all their equity.

• In another deal, before its sale to unsuspecting buyers, a telemarketing business had subtly overbilled its clients by failing to adjust for very small work breaks by its operators. These tiny minutes of overbilling added up to a huge annual bill when they were discovered, an adjustment of $2 million per year on a company making only $8 million. If they had been known in advance, they certainly would have killed the deal. As it is, they nearly killed the investors.

All the due diligence in the world cannot find these problems. If you are a manager leading the buyout of your own firm, you have a great advantage in this process. Managers generally know where the skeletons are buried. But any skeletons missed in diligence will come back to haunt you. The direct marketing and telemarketing companies were picked over by an experienced auditor, looking for trouble.

I've done more than fifty deals and three of them went bad afterward. All were cases where we missed something in due diligence. We were saved from many other disastrous near-deals only because a thorough due diligence process pulled our feet out of the boiling cauldron of hot oil just before we were cooked and eaten. The moral is, you cannot be too careful in the diligence process.

Forensic Research

Even if you are the one diligence is being done to, it can be a challenge. For managers, it means a lot of people will be crawling all over your firm as if their careers and fortunes depend upon it (they often do). You can be guaranteed that there will be teams of experts sweeping for these mines, and more often than not they will find them. You will have to assemble documents and answer many questions, often uncomfortable ones. Any of these details could sink the deal or even the company.

What is usually most shocking and uncomfortable about the diligence process for managers is its "forensic nature." Teams of three or four accountants go over work papers. Lawyers go through all agreements. The buyout firm calls ten references and then asks those ten for less favorable references. The firm does personal credit checks and background checks on management. Just about everything short of a body cavity search.

Companies routinely hire consultants to do a criminal investigation of managers (with their knowledge, of course). This investigation shows outstanding credit card balances and felony or misdemeanor criminal charges. It also confirms job history, which should match with the resumes that were submitted earlier in the process. There are no secrets. If there is any dirt out there, it is going to be found. Buyout firms know more about the managers they work with than most people know about their spouses. There will also be site visits to company offices and plants, personal reference checks, and customer background checks.

There are general areas of diligence and then there are also ones that are specific to the industry. A steel manufacturer will have to sweat environmental issues. A retailer will need to detail when leases expire. In information technology services, professional turnover will be a central concern. Most of the major accounting firms have dedicated M&A divisions that are skilled at finding problems.

Be Patient, Something Will Go Wrong

There are many issues to consider in the due diligence process. And even if you have excellent advisers, it pays to keep your eye on the ball. Appendix H contains a fairly thorough due diligence checklist, which you can use to think through the issues you need to consider. As you can see, the list of issues seems to never stop. But it is also important not to get lost in this forest of issues and to find some of the key issues that are often lost in the shadows.

In this section we explore some of the critical areas I've identified from my own experience in the due diligence process. I also asked an experienced accounting partner and a law partner I've worked with for their input. I am grateful to Dan Tiemann of Arthur Andersen in Chicago and Chris Hagan of Hogan & Hartson in Washington, D.C. for contributing their insights to the following lessons on due diligence. Our advice on key issues to watch for in the diligence process:

• *Focus on the human issues, not just numbers.* Most buyers are focused so intently on the financial side of the deal that they don't analyze the employee issues sufficiently. If the owner sells the business and takes $40 million off the table without giving anything to employees, they may look at the deal bitterly. After all, they helped build the business and the owner didn't share anything with them. They feel betrayed. This is not a problem for sellers, because they usually don't have to see employees again. It's now your problem. You own a wonderful business full of angry employees. Often after a deal is completed, key employees walk out. Many employees start floating their resumes when they hear the company is up for sale.

If you bring up this issue at the outset, the owner may be willing to give up a meaningful piece of the purchase price to employees in the form of options. Owners usually feel some loyalty toward former employees (more at the beginning of the deal than the end) and don't mind giving up a little of their own windfall for them. But it won't happen if you don't ask for it and keep an eye on the human issues.

In addition to compensation, a lot of due diligence should be spent on employee issues and communicating with employees. You should look at all major employment agreements to see whether employees are committed to the firm for the long haul. If you are making follow-on acquisitions, you need to be sure you have a clear integration plan that you can roll out quickly. If you do it on the fly, the employees and the business may disappear while you are working out the details.

• *Look to the future.* Most managers entering into deals have their eye on the past. They are looking at past performance, past problems, trying to rout out every possible old skeleton in the closet. The accountants are going over every book and contract with a fine-tooth comb. This is important, but while looking for the pothole in the past, they often walk into a cavern waiting for them in the future. How strong are the business opportunities? Will old customers continue on after the deal? Will there be changes in employment rules? Will regulations change or new entrants appear? Chris Hagan says, as a rule of thumb, buyers should spend two hours on "going forward" issues for every one hour looking back.

• *Don't just take a report.* Debrief with your accountants and lawyers. They spend endless hours working in the company before issuing their reports. They typically spend a week or two in the field, not only gathering numbers and papers but also talking with people in the organization. Like buying a house, when the buyers come in everyone has on their best face. But you can't keep that up for weeks at a time. So these professionals get more of a glimpse of the dirty laundry. The reports are thorough, but they often leave out key insights that are outside the scope of the document. You can benefit from their on-the-ground experience if you make it a point to sit down with these professionals after the review. There may be a small issue buried on the last paragraph of a fifteen-page legal diligence memo. Or deep into a forty-page accounting report, there is a red flag that accounts payable is running at 120 days. If you are not paying suppliers promptly, are they ready to walk? Often the lawyer or accountant will flag such issues in a cover memo, but you still do better talking to them after you read the report.

• *Know thy business.* As a manager, you understand the key strategic issues that can make or break your business. These are the things to watch in diligence. For a knowledge-based company, keep an eye on intellectual property (IP). Do you really own all the IP? Will someone come in after the deal and try to renegotiate? For an industrial company, environmental or Occupational Safety and Health Act issues can be critical. Do you know what's under the ground at your plants? How has waste been dealt with? In an information technology firm, key employees are the critical asset, so look closely at your employment agreements and compensation. If it is a communications firm, how firm are your Federal Communications Commission licenses? Are there regulatory changes on the horizon? Blanket checklists won't identify the issues. Professionals will get at some of these issues, particularly if they have experience in your industry, but managers have much to contribute. Make sure you ask the right questions.

• *Look for the tip of the iceberg.* Don't give in to the temptation to overlook small discrepancies. On the fraud side, often the initial indications are rather small, but they ultimately could point to more serious problems down the road. You need to look for holes in the integrity of management. You also need to talk with managers lower in the ranks directly to find out what is going on. The CFO may not tell you but the accounts payable person will. Even if you don't talk to these people directly, your accountant may and can give you indications that there are problems. The industry may also raise red flags. For example, you'd want to look much more closely for kickbacks in the trucking industry. If you find one piece of evidence of a kickback, Tiemann recommends that you "run, don't walk away from this deal. If one thing is bad, usually it is just the tip of the iceberg." Buyers that go ahead with these deals usually end up regretting it. "Consider yourself lucky you found it," Tiemann said.

• *Watch for window dressing.* Without any outright fraud, buyers often dress up the company for sale. The most common practices are to spend reserves, to make financials look strong, and to defer maintenance and capital expenditures, looking to the next owner to spend the money. To find clues, look at trends over a period of years. These trends don't always keep you out of trouble (e.g., if there is a dip in the trend at the same time managers are spending more), but you should flag any clear breaks with history. Either there is a good explanation or it just makes the numbers look better. In addition to past history, industry norms can also flag areas where the company is either doing much better or worse—or just accounting differently. A health care company, for example, that depended heavily on Medicare receivables had aged its receivables only ninety days. These payments often take a year or more to collect, so this was a red flag. Also look for any recent changes in accounting policies or methodologies.

• *Protect intellectual property.* Licensing and patent protections are an area where problems often crop up. If the intellectual licenses are not clearly assigned, you may find yourself renegotiating intellectual property rights that you assumed were part of the business. If the business depends heavily on intellectual property, look closely at this issue to identify potential problems and people who might have a claim to your key knowledge.

• *Watch for change of control.* Many agreements (e.g., those with customers, suppliers, key employees, and landlords) will have change-of-control provisions that go unnoticed until the deal is moving through diligence. Managers often don't give these provisions a second thought when the contracts are signed; then some lawyer will be reviewing documents four days before closing and find a change-of-control provision in a lease signed five years ago.

It says the lease cannot change hands without approval by the land-lord. At the eleventh hour, you have to go groveling to this landlord who, more often than not, makes banker Henry Potter from *It's a Wonderful Life* look like Mother Theresa.

Of course, you never let on how desperately you need this sig-nature that could derail the whole deal, but astute landlords know something is up and will often extract a hefty premium for every letter of their name on the contract.

In one deal for a $275 million company, we found one Euro-pean investor who had bought only $160,000 in preferred stock more than six years earlier, but had a change-of-control provision in the contract. No one in the firm knew they had this obligation until the lawyers turned over the rock, and there it was. When the issue arose, we didn't even know exactly where in the world this investor lived. After hiring a private investigation firm, we tracked him down in Switzerland and had to fly over to see him. We told him we had excellent news, that we were cleaning up these little financial matters and could pay this provision off with a $10,000 premium. In this case, the proposal worked, but we were sweating it to the end.

The earlier you can see these change-of-control issues, the eas-ier they are to clean up. If you go to the landlord or the investor early in the process, they have much less leverage and you have much longer to wait them out. At the last minute, you are at their mercy.

Handling the Bad News

There will be some bad news. Every woodpile has its snakes. There are no pristine situations. What separates a successful deal from an unsuccessful one is how managers react to it. If bad news is revealed to the managers first, they need to share it with partners right away. If a management team tries to sweep something under the rug, it will end up being a bigger problem later. Get the bad news on the table as early as possible and deal with it as quickly and cleanly as possible. If there is a complaint that comes up during the diligence process, don't become defensive. Take it calmly and put together a strategy to deal with it.

One management team in an early meeting with buyout inves-tors revealed that one of the managers had once been indicted for a felony. It didn't derail the deal at that point. In fact, instead of being a ding to their trust, this revelation helped establish open communications and allowed the buyout partner to deal with the issue openly with other investors. If managers hadn't put it on the table and it came out in later diligence, it could very well have been a deal breaker.

Making the Place Presentable

Can you spruce up the place in advance of the deal? If you have a few years' head start, there are certainly things that you can do to put the house in order. Getting strong financial systems, clear accounting, and three years of Big Five audits in place will save you headaches during the diligence process. Installing that new inventory management software program can make life easier. Dealing with outstanding legal issues cleanly and clearly can save you lengthy go-rounds with lawyers. You should give yourself a few years to get these systems in place. You don't want to be working out the bugs while you are doing diligence. You also don't want to plaster over serious problems, because a good due diligence process will usually penetrate any strictly cosmetic improvements to get to the underlying problems.

If the records are not in good shape, it usually won't scuttle the deal, but it may add a level of risk to it in the eyes of the investors. This risk will be assessed in the context of the deal. If the industry has 10 percent margins and the company is reporting 20 percent margins, shoddy accounting will make the deal more suspect. The company may be underaccruing bonus and vacation expenses, for example. On the other hand, if the company is running 6 percent margins and has bad accounting systems, the investor may think that with a better system the company could come up to industry standards.

Usually, if management is continuing to run the business and is putting equity into it, there is less suspicion that bad records are meant to hide something. If the management or owners are just turning over the business, there is a very good chance that they have underinvested in some important capital expenditures in the year before the deal. They want the figures to look as good as possible going into the deal, and they won't be around to pick up the pieces.

Keeping It Secret

Most buyouts are covert operations until they are announced to employees, customers, suppliers, and the world. Unless the company has publicly put itself up on the auction block, an announcement that a deal is in the works will just unsettle the organization. Employees either will go into a holding pattern, waiting to see what happens, or they will preemptively jump ship. Customers will worry about signing contracts or put off purchases to see what happens. If the deal is an exclusive one, publicity only attracts other suitors.

The deal is pretty easy to keep quiet when it is just a few small discussions over lunch or dinner to create term sheets and letters of intent. Keeping high-level discussions quiet is not a big problem. But hiding the ground war takes a little more ingenuity. Managers can use the following approaches:

• *Craft a cover story.* Any employee with a pulse will know something is happening when all these suits show up at once. The e-mail and the rumors will fly. You can't ignore them, but you can explain them. Management usually creates a cover story. Most often, the story is that the company is working on getting some new financing, a fresh infusion of capital. This is true but, of course, doesn't tell the whole story. Customers and suppliers also may get nervous about dealing with a company in which a change-of-control transaction appears to be happening. In particular, when the buyout partner or other investors do customer reference checks, it is likely to arouse suspicion. These customer calls are usually done by an outside consultant under the cover of a customer satisfaction survey. This is also true but just doesn't reveal *why* the company is suddenly interested in customer satisfaction. Even with the cover story, customers may be suspicious about why the company is suddenly interested. Does it have customer problems? Is something else afoot? That is why these external reference checks should be done as close as possible to the consummation of the deal.

• *Set up the war room.* No ground war can proceed without a war room. To keep the diligence process a secret, you need to contain it. Companies usually set up a war room or data room (for those who prefer less militaristic images). Sometimes companies rent a room at a hotel or an off-site office where they bring copies of all the key company documents. Other times, they will find an out-of-the-way internal conference room.

Into this room go copies of every relevant document needed to review the deal. More documents are pulled in by the barrelful during the process. There are primary customer contracts, primary supply contracts, leases, environmental insurance, 401(k) plans, all audits for the last four years, primary management reports, employment contracts, and recent industry analyses. This room becomes the center of the deal, with auditors, lawyers, investment partners, and others coming in to pick over the documents they need.

• *Choose a few insiders.* The war room documents are usually assembled by a small group of insiders from the finance department, maybe the CFO and two controllers. While all the troops may not know the details of the operation, you need a few insiders who are not partners in the deal. Usually a few people from the finance department are brought in under nondisclosure to help in doing financial analysis and answering questions about the company. They know if they talk about the deal, they are history.

• *Guard sensitive information as long as you can.* As in any situation in which the company is disclosing very sensitive information, save the most sensitive stuff for last. As noted previously, customer calls are often held until late in the process because they arouse suspicion. Strategic pricing information is often not revealed until everything else is in place.

• *Be prepared for the leak.* Despite your best efforts, it's still possible that there will be a leak and that employees and customers will learn about the deal. All you can do in this case is think carefully about these issues in advance and make plans to address leaks as they occur. Most important, be prepared for your employee communications with an internal memo written *before* the news breaks. Also, be prepared with fact sheets on the deal and key talking points so your employees, customers, and suppliers understand the rationale for the transaction and its inherent selling points. In the best of all worlds, you won't need these until you are ready to break the news. But if there is a leak, you will be able to move quickly and coherently. Many missteps are made because of hastily assembled communications or long delays that create anxiety and uncertainty among employees and customers.

• *Pull together working group lists.* The team working on the deal is generally pulled together on a working group list with names, e-mail, fax, and work or home phones. This ensures that communication can flow constantly, without interruption. For a sample of this working group list, see Appendix F.

Timeline for the Process

Like any campaign, this ground war moves on several fronts at the same time. Keeping track of time and responsibilities is crucial to making sure the whole platoon makes steady progress toward its goal. The major thrusts of the campaign are:

• *Legal.* Are there legal issues that could create problems later? Lawyers will be scanning supply contracts, real estate, environmental, and other agreements. They will also be developing and refining the key documents for the deal. In the Software AG deal, for example, lawyers cranked out several hundred pages of documents related to the deal.

• *Accounting.* Are numbers what they say they are? Do they have odd reserves that have been built into the numbers or unsound results recently? Accountants will be picking over the numbers to look for problems. Do we need audits for the banks or other investors? What is the timeline for those audits?

• *Business.* What is happening in the industry? What are the competitors doing? Usually the buyout partner or a consultant analyzes the industry and the firm's performance relative to industry benchmarks.

• *Management Team.* Extensive background checks and references will be done on the management team.

• *Insurance/Benefits.* Often the buyout firm will hire a third-party insurance review firm to look at pension plans, 401(k), workers' compensation reserves, directors and officers insurance, and other issues that can create risks. Are there insurance risks that could create problems later, or are there opportunities to improve the insurance costs? All the large insurers such as AON and Marsh & McLennan have groups that specifically analyze transactional insurance risks.

Sample Timeline

In the sidebar example that follows, the timeline from a recent deal is extremely tight at ten weeks. (Software AG actually moved even faster, given the small window of opportunity, but this was a speed record. Typically the process will stretch out to twelve to sixteen weeks.) The legal work and banks are the slowest part of the process because the documents and approvals are so complex. Usually by the time the seller has signed the purchase agreement and the bank has signed a commitment letter, the financing is certain enough that the company then makes the public announcement. In this case, it was targeted for Week 6. After the announcement there is a government antitrust filing (Hart-Scott-Rodino) that, unless there is a significant business overlap or you happen to be Microsoft, is usually a formality. After all the final deals are made, the buyout investor calls capital to obtain funds based on commitments from its own investors and then wires the cash to the seller. Invariably, there is some glitch in the wiring and it is lost and then shows up eight hours later, while the seller paces the floor.

Sample Timeline

Week 1
❑ Sign the letter of intent and commence due diligence.
❑ Start general business, financial, accounting, and strategic analysis.
❑ Set up war room.
❑ Begin negotiations on the management team sheet.

Week 2
❑ Hold kickoff meeting with accountants, lawyers, industry consultants, and investors, during which management provides an overview of the business and the deal.

❑ Have lawyers begin drafting agreements.
❑ Have buyout firm conduct site visits.

Week 3
❑ Continue due diligence by partners, accountants, lawyers, and insurance/benefits consultants.
❑ Make presentation to banks to solicit financing.
❑ Distribute drafts of legal agreements for purchasing agreement and shareholder rights.
❑ Finalize the management term sheet.

Week 4
❑ Negotiate commitment letter from lender.
❑ Receive comments back on legal agreements.

Week 5
❑ Finalize due diligence package.
❑ Negotiate definitive purchase agreements.
❑ Finalize lender commitment letter.

Week 6
❑ Sign bank commitment letter.
❑ Sign purchase agreement.
❑ Announce transaction to employees and key customers first, then to the world.

Weeks 7–10
❑ Make Hart-Scott-Rodino filing.
❑ Obtain shareholder approval (if needed).
❑ Negotiate credit agreement and covenants.
❑ Call equity capital.

Week 10
❑ Receive Hart-Scott-Rodino approval.
❑ Sign credit agreement and receive funding.
❑ Satisfy all conditions to closing.
❑ Close transaction and wire cash.

Reviewing Legal Documents

By the end of most deals there will be files two feet thick and a huge leather-bound book of legal documents that looks as if it could have been written by Leo Tolstoy. (And some of the documents actually read like Russian.) Samples of some of the less detailed versions of these documents appear in the Appendices.

As noted, many of these documents go through an evolution throughout the deal process. They often start out as one-page agreements that are nonbinding, expand to more detailed documents that are more binding, and end up as legal treatises that are completely binding. That one-page management term sheet that you thought you could adjust later has now been enshrined in stone and is about as easy to change as the Ten Commandments. It includes all the vesting, buy-back provisions, employment agreements, severance arrangements, and definitions of firings for cause. Your letter of intent with the seller is now a full purchase agreement. That is why it is almost always a mistake to put off crucial issues of the deal until later.

For a typical deal, these documents might include:

- Management agreement
- Stock or asset purchase agreement
- Recapitalization agreement
- Seller's release of ownership
- Administrative services agreement
- Bank financing commitments
- Promissory notes
- Employment agreements
- Shareholder's agreement with all governance procedures
- Incorporation documents for the new company
- Board resolutions
- Officers and secretary's certificates from the seller and the company
- Tax documents such as 83(b) elections

Some of these agreements will be familiar to most managers, but many will be new. In most cases, the buyout firm and lawyers can guide you through the process. But what should you as a manager be looking for when all these documents come sailing into your hands? The main issue for managers is to make sure all the agreements work from a business perspective. Don't get tied up in the minutia of the legal issues. Instead, focus on their strategic implications. These are the issues that managers can see most easily and are either outside the knowledge or outside the scope of the review of lawyers and partners.

Telegraphing the Victory

At a certain point in the process, the deal needs to become public. The timing of this announcement depends in part on the type of deal and the environment. If the deal needs the approval of a public company's shareholders, it will be impossible to keep it a secret. In most cases, however, you do not want to make the deal public until it is certain it will be completed.

Most of the time, the signing of the purchase agreement is the point at which the company then needs to communicate to customers, suppliers, employees, and the world. When the Software AG managers finally nailed down its agreement to purchase the U.S. division at the end of March, top managers spent most of the next day talking directly to key customers. Such calls help position the deal and show how it will benefit the company and its customers, before they read about it in the papers. Later that afternoon, Software AG managers held a general meeting with employees, as described at the opening of Chapter 1. At the same time, they issued a press release for publication the next day.

Even though the bank agreements will not be finalized at the time of the signing of the purchase agreement, there are rarely problems in translating a credit agreement into final covenants. If you anticipate problems at this time, or with the Hart-Scott-Rodino filing, you may want to wait until the wires have changed hands to make the announcement. This would give employees and customers a few more weeks of nervous anticipation. By the time the purchase agreement has gone through, almost everyone knows something is up, and what they imagine may be pretty bleak. Companies that are not concerned about this kind of turmoil inside and outside the organization sometimes choose to announce that a division of the company is for sale before they have any agreement or even buyers. The announcement itself is used to flush out potential buyers and get a bidding war started.

Choosing the Team

Work with a strong and very experienced team. Hire your accountant and lawyer from the A-list. Don't bring in your spouse's brother at some tiny law firm who always wanted to do M&A work. Find someone with experience in buyouts and preferably in your specific industry. Ideally, they should be close by, because you'll spend a lot of time running back and forth to their offices. Make sure the partner you are comfortable with actually has time to attend meetings and think about the project.

You should interview three or four firms for the work. If you have any influence on the lawyer used by the sellers, don't use it to stack the deck, but make sure they get someone competent and experienced in M&A, not a divorce lawyer. The only thing worse than having a bad attorney on your side is to have one sitting across from you. It is unbelievable how many inexperienced lawyers are hired to run multimillion-dollar deals and the crazy obstacles they can throw in the path of a good deal. They can easily ruin the deal. If the sellers are uncertain about a choice of legal representation, you might give them the names of four or five good firms. It won't look as if you are trying to throw things in your direction. That way they can make their own choice, yet you are assured they will find someone competent.

For the accounting firm, you want one of the Big Five. Make sure the lead partner is going to have time to dedicate to the project and that the firm has experience in your industry. It is extremely important that the firm has conducted similar business and has the metrics with which to compare. Here, the sellers' accountant is not such a significant problem. But if they have a tiny unknown firm, it might be a red flag to look more closely at their financials.

A Few Closing Thoughts

These observations on diligence are not a substitute for thorough evaluation of the deal by qualified professionals. You should always get excellent legal and professional advice for your specific situation. These thoughts are only indications of where to look in the process because many other major issues are bound to come up.

With the advent of the word processor, documents are growing longer. This will drive you totally batty, but try to have a good sense of humor about it and the other bumps you hit on the way to a deal.

Finally, a small piece of common sense advice: Always get important factual agreements in writing, even if it is a deal with your brother (depending on the family, *especially* when it is a deal with your brother). In some cases, the sellers will talk a good line and tell you to trust them on some important point. This is almost always a mistake. If they really believe it, get it in a document. They have no reason to avoid this request unless they have something to hide. Have the hard discussions and put them in writing. Even if the person you are working with is very trustworthy, he or she may be hit by a bus and all you'll be left with is a pile of papers. These papers better say it all, because the seller's replacement could be Jack the Ripper. What is said between partners can be quite satisfying, but what is in print is what you will live or die by.

CHAPTER 10

Riding the Tiger

"[He] who rides a tiger cannot dismount."

—CHINESE PROVERB

After the SAGA initial public offering, Dan Gillis and Harry Mc-Creery found that going public had its price. Along with putting your handsome face on CNN, it also meant every hiccup of your young firm was broadcast to the world through the noisy filter of the stock market. Investors called at all hours with questions or comments. And even family and friends, who may have bought high, are now a bit testy when the stock price rolls down. It is one of the biggest headaches of the post-initial public offering (IPO) world, and one of the reasons some managers find ways other than going public to get cash into the business. Still, as much as Gillis and McCreery might complain about the investor relations migraines, when the question is put point blank—Would you rather deal with the German owners or with the investors?—both of them answer, "The investors," although McCreery adds wryly, "Don't ask us that every day."

The buyout is only the beginning. Now that you have saddled up the tiger, the ride is just getting started. After the buyout, you need to continue to build the company as an independent firm and consider whether to go public. You also need to find the exit strategy, if not for managers, at least for investors. This chapter examines the postbuyout environment where much of the value of the deal is realized.

Living the Dream

At the point that the buyout is over, most managers feel a unique mixture of euphoria and exhaustion. They've talked investors into putting millions of dollars into the deal based on management's vision of where it could take the company. Managers have sunk no small portion of their own net worth and an even larger percentage of their egos into this project. They may have friends and associates whose careers and fortunes are also riding on the deal.

It is at this point that they more fully realize that the buyout is merely prologue. They have managed to pull their car up to the top of the first hill of a huge roller coaster. Now, as they pause before the breathtaking view at the top, there is often a mixture of elation and sheer terror as they stare down the tracks ahead. Much of the success of the deal still lies ahead, as well as much of the excitement. For managers such as Stu Johnson or Dan Gillis who waited all their careers to sit at the top of a public company, now is the moment of truth. They have created the dream. They have sold it to investors. Now they have to make it happen. One thing is certain—from this point on, life will never be dull.

Leveraging the Independence

The first challenge for managers is to leverage the independence of the company and reshape its culture. For leaders like Gillis who are making over an established company, the challenge is to inject an entrepreneurial spirit into an existing large-company culture. For mangers like Ballou at Global Vacation Group, who are building a new firm, the challenge is to establish a culture and bring new acquisitions into it. Companies leverage their newfound independence through new compensation structures, add-on acquisitions, budgeting and planning, communications, and infusion of new skills.

New Compensation Structures

Just as giving top managers more equity aligns their interests more directly with owners, this spirit of ownership needs to be felt at the deepest levels of the organization. Employees need to feel there is a new energy and a new openness to ideas, as well as a new imperative for performance.

The best way to drive this point home is to put money behind it through equity. SAGA quickly extended its equity from the handful of senior managers involved in the deal to more than ninety managers in the firm. The company also used its new ability to grant equity to attract new employees, which was a crucial competitive factor in the software industry.

Among the best ways to create this alignment is through stock options and bonuses linked to company operating profit. In granting stock options to employees, managers need to be careful to communicate the meaning of these options. Many managers, even fairly high-level ones, may not understand exactly how stock options work and how they create value. Also, they need to understand that actions that affect operating profit are multiplied in equity. If they can reduce their operating costs or grow the business, they can benefit directly.

Add-on Acquisitions

The buyout or platform acquisition is often only the beginning. As the company continues to look for opportunities for strategic growth, it will often turn to "tuck-ins" and "add-ons" to the base business. There are two major reasons these deals are a good value. First, it is usually much easier to buy something than to build it from scratch. If you can find firms that already have the types of product lines or distribution you would like to add to the business, buying them will be cheaper and quicker than trying to build them, even if you then have to strip out unwanted parts of the target.

Second, because most follow-on acquisitions are much smaller than platform acquisitions, the purchase price multiples are usually lower. Smaller companies have fewer exit opportunities so they tend to be much more "personality driven" sales. The drawback of smaller deals is that you have to be much more careful how much you invest into them before you know they are going to go forward. Once you get into the deal, there will probably be just as much diligence to do as on a much larger transaction, maybe even more. A $2 million deal can be just as time-consuming as a $200 million deal, and a family firm may have more snakes in the woodshed.

This means the cost of exploring and putting together the deal is going to be a much higher percentage of its price. If the deal is a strong one and there are enough good strategic reasons for doing it, go ahead. But watch your time, money, and other resources.

Where do these opportunities for follow-ons come from? As noted in the discussion of acquisitions in Chapter 4, there is a wide range of sources for potential purchases, such as investment bankers or business brokers. Most of the follow-on deals, however, come through industry contacts. If you are immersed in the industry and other companies know you are looking for acquisitions, the opportunities will present themselves at a pace that I'm sure will surprise you, particularly if you let it be known that you're a buyer.

Budgeting and Planning

Most new buyouts that have been part of larger corporations or new roll-ups don't have solid and extensive internal budgeting and planning processes. The budget process needs to hold people accountable within their units so there is a clear set of unified goals. Managers need to be able to see what they should do to make their numbers and what specifically will happen if they succeed. This often means the budgeting system has to be rebuilt from the ground up. Particularly if the company has plans to go public, it needs a finely tuned budgeting and accounting system by the time managers open the firm to public scrutiny.

The budgeting also needs to be tied to an effective planning process. One way to retool is to hold a management retreat after the deal is done. Taking the top ten or fifteen team members and their spouses for a several-day retreat gives management the opportunity to take another look at their strategy and every aspect of the business. They can then begin rethinking and retooling to ensure the company's success.

Communications

Communications inside and outside the firm become increasingly important after the buyout. The company's new strategy must be clearly understood by employees and potential investors, partners, suppliers, or acquisition targets. This need for clear communication becomes even greater if the company pursues a strategic sale or an IPO. You need to have a great story about the firm and people outside need to hear it, loud and clear.

It is often the first-time managers used to having a large corporate public relations and investor relations office who need to give increased attention to their communications strategy. Many post-buyout firms will hire a public relations firm to ensure the right kind of communication goes out. The goal is to make people aware of the transaction and the benefits of the transaction. Even if you are not actively seeking to attract investors or buyers today, this public communication helps lay the groundwork for future investments. It also lets potential acquisition targets know that you are out there doing deals. This can be a very powerful source of attracting new follow-on acquisition opportunities. If the notice of the acquisition goes into a trade publication, managers might see fifty potential deals as a result.

After an IPO, as discussed later in this chapter, a strong investor relations capability is essential. Companies that are intending to go public may want to build investor relations into their communications strategy so this capability is up and running when it is needed.

Adding New Skills

In addition to communications, the company may need to beef up other skills. It may need to market products for the first time. SAGA created a marketing department and hired executives from Iomega. It also hired its first chief technology officer to lead its new product development. Top leaders need to identify the skills sets needed for the future and build a strong human resources department to find and hire these new employees. As is also noted in the Techway example regarding its sales force compensation, attracting some employees may require a dramatic change in compensation systems.

Making an Exit

You may be happy owning and running the business for the rest of your life, maybe even passing it to your heirs, but investors need to get out sooner. You need to plan an exit within the first five years of owning the company—if not an exit for management, then at least for investors. The first rule is to work out your exit strategy in advance as discussed in Chapter 5. All the potential of a buyout is only vapor or paper until the cash goes on the table. Before the first discussion with the seller or buyout investors, the management team should know how investors and managers can cash out of the deal in the end. Most investors will want to see a return within three to five years; some will want it sooner. If you don't have at least one potential exit, no one will follow you into a cul-de-sac. Roger Ballou's team, for example, had developed three or four exit strategies that included selling out to a larger firm or going to secondary stock offerings on the public market.

The second rule is that the exit that happens to you will likely not be the one you worked out in advance. The exact exit will depend on the opportunities that unfold—sometimes an unexpected avenue opens up. You need to think through the possibilities carefully in advance and be prepared for change when it arrives.

The Most Important Element of the Exit

There are many ways to exit a business, but there is one overriding principle. If your company isn't steaming full-speed ahead, it will be very difficult to find anyone to take the helm. It doesn't matter how good the IPO market is. It doesn't matter how good the industry is. It doesn't matter whether there is money out there burning a hole in investors' pockets. None of it will come to you if you don't have a good product. This is a very simple principle, almost self-evident, but often overlooked as managers get caught up in playing high finance. The best advantage in making a smooth exit is to have a strong company, and the best time to sell is when things are going well.

Whether you are making an IPO presentation or a strategic buyer pitch, if you have a good story to tell about the business, the red carpets will be rolled out in your path. If you've built good relationships with your customers and suppliers and have high employee morale and low turnover, these are signs that the company has value that the new owners can take to the bank. But if your company has just had one of the poorest years in its history, the welcome wagons will be nowhere in sight. The best exit strategy is to build the highest-quality business.

Timing the Exit

Most equity firms are in the deal for at least three to five years. They realize it takes time to build value. There may be unusual "bluebird" deals where investors buy something on the cheap and find a seller willing to double the money in a matter of months. These are the transactions that investment dreams are made of. And unless managers can come up with a convincing argument that the business could be worth four times the price in a year or two, the deal will go through. Managers may have an attachment to the plan for building the business and their position in the firm, but if they shed a tear over the sale, they are crying all the way to the bank.

These bluebirds of happiness don't often fly in. These types of deals, while they are welcome when they arrive, are not the core of the investment business, and most investors spend about as much time looking for them as they do waiting to win the lottery. Investors are primarily looking to get in, build value with the management team, and get their money back in time to provide a solid return to their investors.

But if there is tension in the relationship, it is usually because investors are pushing to go to an IPO or sell the business and managers are not ready yet. Since managers have a big stake in the future of the company, they are almost always on the same side of the issue as the buyout firm. A strong exit benefits everyone. If you have a good working relationship, these discussions shouldn't be adversarial, but there will be some give-and-take.

An IPO and the subsequent investor relations work take an incredible amount of time. This can be at a time when management really needs to devote attention to building the business. Roger Ballou's Global Vacation Group closed its last acquisition on May 8 and needed to submit the next six quarters of financial projections to analysts to support the IPO on May 29. "The fact that we were reasonably accurate given the amount of time we had is pretty amazing," he said. "In retrospect, it was a bit like trying to redecorate your house while you are holding a Christmas party. That part of the process was very, very complicated."

Ballou might have preferred to wait. On the other hand, windows of opportunities in the market have to be considered. Global Vacation Group caught the tail end of a wave in the IPO market that they probably would have missed if they had waited. Having a frank and open relationship with your equity partner at this point is very important.

Four Exit Strategies

While it attracts the most attention, the IPO and secondary offerings are just one way to exit. There are four primary ways to get cash out of the deal:

- An IPO, which paves the way for a stock sale
- A sale to a strategic buyer
- A leveraged recapitalization
- A sale to another buyout firm

For some businesses all four exits might be possible, but for others, only one or two are viable options. For example, a toothbrush company may easily find a strategic buyer or enter a recapitalization with the banks, but investors would laugh the managers out of the office if they suggested they could do an IPO. Unless it is tooth brushes.com, forget it.

Initial Public Offering

Although the IPO is often discussed as an "exit strategy," technically it doesn't represent an exit. It is not a liquidity event. Investors are still up to their necks in the deal after the IPO. It is only after selling the stock that they actually have made their exit and this usually takes two years, if you are lucky. At the time of the IPO, the underwriter requires mangers to hold nearly 100 percent of their position and the equity partner can rarely sell more than 10 percent of its holdings in an IPO. No one can sell any stock at all for the next half year, and at any time in the future someone attempts to, investors will want to know why. You can do a series of secondary offerings, which may allow investors to cash out meaningful pieces of their ownership over time, but this again takes a full road show. The IPO may facilitate an exit later, but it isn't an exit in itself.

To do a successful IPO, you need a very strong story that can be communicated quickly to potential investors. When you are on the road shows, you must differentiate yourself and have a strong plan you can execute. The pitch also has to have a certain pizzazz.

A company making auto supply products or HVAC equipment probably isn't sexy enough unless there is some unique angle. You need a strong story of growth and a lot of differentiation in the marketplace. Management also gets extra points for having strong communications skills. A CEO with some punch can drive the story home.

Timing the IPO is extraordinarily challenging. You have to go when the ducks are quacking, but there is a high price to pay for going to the market prematurely. If you can't accurately predict business income for the next two or three years, you will get crushed by the market. In any event, it takes a lot of management time. There will be $250,000 to $500,000 in expenses just for printing, legal, and accounting. In addition, today's investors and IPO markets are unforgiving. If you miss your numbers, you will get permanently hammered by the market.

You need to look at the strategic issues involved. Don't do an IPO if it runs counter to the strategy of the business. Is it an industry in which business cycles of more than a year create conflicts with the short demands of investors? Will uneven cash flows or business seasonality cause problems? Will going public make it harder to make needed investments that may hurt earnings in the future? How much of management time will be diverted to dealing with shareholders? On the other hand, you should also consider how having a public stock can help the company in funding its further acquisitions and growth or attracting employees. There are no simple answers to these questions, but you should raise the strategic issues as you work with buyout partners to consider an IPO or a sale.

Avoiding IPO Fever. One thing you don't want to do is get caught up in IPO fever. Today, there is so much public interest in the IPO. They seem to have huge sex appeal. Everyone thinks it is sexy to pound the gavel on the New York Stock Exchange and appear on CNN. And all those millions flowing into the business are a bit of a head-turner. That part of the IPO really is pretty sexy. But the dirty little secret is that getting the IPO done is incredibly hard work, and dealing with those investors afterward can be living hell. It looks like Hollywood but ends up being the salt mines. It is a heck of a price to pay just to impress your friends at the country club. Unless there are clear strategic reasons for doing the IPO, look for your fifteen minutes of fame some easier way, maybe joining the first manned mission to Mars.

If you want to sober up quickly, consider the dark side of the IPO that I've lived as an investor in several public companies and as chairman of a public software company. My rule today is to avoid an IPO unless it is absolutely necessary to execute your plan. Let me describe the negatives:

- *Open the kimono.* There is massive public disclosure associated with your IPO and, unless you are by nature an exhibitionist, it will probably be uncomfortable. All your competitors will know exactly what your margins are (or aren't) and worse, all your employees and neighbors will know exactly how much money you make, how much stock you own, how many options you have, and how big your last raise and bonus were. It's a forensic study and you'd better be ready. Have you been in litigation in the last five years? Disclose it. Sold stock on the cheap to your brother? Get it out there. Disclosure rules strip you down to your underwear, and even that is getting skimpier. Now, if you find that prospect sexy, perhaps the IPO will retain its glamorous appeal. Otherwise, it can be a cold and humbling experience.

- *It's your new part-time job.* The large legal, accounting, and underwriting costs of completing an IPO are just the beginning. The two to three months nearly full-time you need to complete a successful offering is a cakewalk compared to what comes after. For the CEO or CFO, you'll probably spend one-third of your post-IPO time talking to or visiting institutional investors. These folks are very high maintenance and they will be living with you. Now you'll spend half your time running the business and half the time schmoozing investors. That's when things are going well. When things go badly, you'll talk to them full-time.

- *Miss your numbers and you're dead.* Quarter to quarter, you will live or die by meeting your numbers. These concerns may quickly undermine your ability to make good long-term decisions for the business. You have to do what it takes to make your numbers. If the analysts have your earnings at 17 cents per share, you better show up with 18 cents or better, or investors will flee your stock like the plague. If you fall short, you've entered the sad twilight zone that analysts kindly call "broken stocks." This means you're probably trading at half your real underlying value, are heavily in the penalty box, and have a year to dig out. Some companies never dig out. They just go into public company hell, and all the great press releases in the world are unlikely to ever get them out.

• *Live with your own special demons to torment you.* While you're down in "broken stock" hell, you will meet up with some creatures who are specially designed to torment the managers of public companies. These are the plaintiff's bar, a group of lawyers that preys on almost any company whose stock goes down precipitously. It's the little added bonus of being public. Not only is your stock down, your shareholders hate you, your employees hate you because their options are underwater, but now you and your company are being sued (personally, I might add). Just hope you have sufficient directors and officers insurance. Here's how it works: These law firms monitor big stock drops and when they see a sharp decline, they'll contact some grandmother who owns a few shares and doesn't know any better. They convince her that she should be outraged by what you've done to her. They tell her they'll bear all the costs and get her some money. She has nothing to lose. Then they go into their word processors, change a few names in their last lawsuit, and hit the print button. Presto, instant litigation. The sad truth is they often win. They allege some garbage that is hard to understand, sue for $30 million in damages, and the company settles for $3 million just to avoid the vicissitudes of court. (How many juries are going to rule in favor of a large corporation against a little grandmother?) The lawyers get a third and when they are done celebrating, they go out and file another one. It's legalized extortion, and going public puts you in the crosshairs.

The challenges are particularly grueling for start-ups and firms moving in new strategic directions. "For me, the degree of time devoted to investor relations and Securities and Exchange Commission requirements in a small firm are a great burden on the firm," said Global Vacation's Roger Ballou. "Investors call up and say they are in it for the long term and then pound away with questions about quarterly results. The travel industry works on eighteen-month cycles, so quarterly results become a distraction from the payoffs that are a year and a half down the road." It means the company will tend to underinvest in strategic moves that do not have an immediate return. Although Global Vacation Group invested heavily in the Internet, it might have put even more money there if the short-term pressures had been less intense.

Relations with investors at a growth company are very different from those at a mature firm. Change is more rapid, as are advances and declines in the company's fortunes. "Watching the quarterly progression of a growth company is like watching quarterly progression of your child," Ballou said. "You get too hung up on the small details. He's only learned three new words this quarter, he's behind plan." The mood swings and hiccups of start-ups or newly reconstituted firms are a burden in the market where investors are buying and selling based on short-term numbers. After its IPO, SAGA's stock almost tripled in value to nearly $30 before sinking to $5. Because of the extraordinary amount of management time involved in going public, it is often more attractive to arrange a private sale, as discussed later.

Benefits of the IPO. With this bleak litany of problems, one may wonder why anyone would consider an IPO. There are still many good strategic reasons to go public other than sex appeal, which explains the continuing popularity of the IPO. These benefits include:

- *Valuation.* There are cases in which the public market is simply paying much more to value companies than anyone else would. Such is the case in today's technology world. If the valuation gap between what is paid in public and private markets is big enough, this premium may make it worthwhile to put up with the hassles of going public.
- *Acquisition Currency.* If you are acquisitive, a public stock currency can be a great acquisition vehicle. This was a big part of the reason why Global Vacation Group decided to do its IPO.
- *Employee Options.* Public stock options are also a great way to attract and retain employees, particularly in the technology sector. They are almost required to interest top talent. You should be

careful not to overrate this benefit, because you can provide stock options in a private company environment to retain good people.

 • *Liquidity Path.* While the IPO doesn't provide instant liquidity, you will over many years be able to sell a meaningful portion of your equity position without leaving the company. This is harder to accomplish in a private company environment unless you sell the whole business.

Selling to a Strategic Buyer

A sale to a strategic buyer usually gives you the best price for the company. Compared with investors who are only looking at the business as a way to earn a return on their dollars, the strategic investor actually knows what to do with the business after the sale. This buyer, often a rival business, may be able to combine the firm with its existing business, making them both more efficient. In addition to a rival firm, the strategic buyer may be a customer who is backward-integrating or a supplier who is forward-integrating. At the end of the day, you will likely get the best price from a competitor because it has the opportunity to take out overhead.

Stripping out overhead usually means employees, so what the investors gain on the financial side may have a high human cost. Some buyers are extremely aggressive in cutting staff, wiping out most of the employees but leaving the customer base standing. Suppliers or customers expanding their businesses would be much less likely to do massive downsizing of the business. If you know there is going to be a lot of breakage, you might pay out a bonus from the sale to employees or extend severance from three to six months as part of the deal.

A strategic sale often means senior managers give up control of the firm. Sometimes they are kept on to run the new entity, but many top jobs are also cut. This can be uncomfortable, and many managers are reluctant to give up the dream of leading the company so soon after achieving it.

Leveraged Recapitalization

Sometimes the banks can offer an opportunity to exit through a leveraged recapitalization that can leave managers in charge of the business. Suppose the buyout began with $15 million in equity and $35 million in debt. Since then, the business has performed well and the debt has been paid down. You may have an opportunity to do a leveraged recapitalization in which the bank lends you $20 million to repurchase stock from shareholders. The original investors can take their money out and the company has more traditional bank financing. This strategy generally results in a lower valuation than you might receive from a strategic buyer, but if there is no strategic buyer, it is a particularly attractive way to cash out. There are no road shows and no investor fallout, just a deal with the banks.

The leveraged recapitalization works particularly well for businesses with a stable cash flow but without a sexy IPO story to tell. (Bankers tend to find stable cash flow a lot sexier than a flashy growth story.) The toothbrush maker that gets the brush-off from public markets may win smiles from the debt financiers. People will always have to brush their teeth, making it very likely that the company will be able to pay off its debt.

Selling the Company to Another Buyout Firm
Sometimes the way out for the original investors is to swap the deal out to another buyout firm. Why would the original investor want to do this? Why would a new firm want to pick up used goods? The original buyout firm may be looking for a way to cash out its investment because the fund may be coming to the end of its life. If there isn't an IPO opportunity or a strategic buyer, investors may turn to another buyout firm to pick up the equity. With the enormous amounts of private equity capital available, many firms are looking for places to put their funds. The original buyout firm probably has a new fund coming on line that it could now use to buy back the company itself, but limited partners tend to look down on these deals because there are too many conflicts inherent in a buyout investor selling to its own funds. It is difficult to tell if you are getting a good price. A sale to a different buyout firm puts cash in the original firm's pockets and gives the management more time to grow the company. It generally results in a higher valuation than a recapitalization through the banks.

To take this route, the company usually goes to an investment bank and shops the company around to several buyout firms. Sometimes management agrees to go forward with the deal; sometimes it makes arrangements to get out itself within a few years. If management isn't making a longer commitment to the project, it will be a ding to the price.

Quite often, management is still enthusiastic about growing the business, so they lead another buyout with the new firm. At this point, they need to renegotiate their management term sheet. Usually, the new buyout firm expects them to roll over at least one-half of the total gains into the new deal. They want management to have more skin in the game going forward than they have had in the past.

Think Exit before You Buy
We've discussed many ways to sell your company and monetize your hard-earned equity gains. The IPO is glamorous but fraught with challenges. Other opportunities such as a recapitalization or a strategic sale are available. The key issue on exit strategy is, like so many other important concepts in this book, knowing where you're going before you get started. As I noted in discussing strategy in Chapter 5, if you don't have a clear view of how you will exit before you buy your company, you probably shouldn't do the deal. After all, buying is only half the fun. It's getting out, and getting liquid— getting that yacht—where you can really celebrate.

Conclusion

I've tried to summarize all I've learned in my fifteen years in the deal business. I hope you've found value in this book. I've enjoyed trying to craft a piece of work that can help managers achieve their entre-preneurial dreams. If this book helps just one manager lead his own management buyout, I will have achieved my goal.

As I've said, this book is for every manager out there who wants to reach for the stars and control his or her own destiny. And let me say this at the top of my lungs:

This is the *manager's decade.*

Capital has never been more plentiful, and it is waiting in every quarter to back you and your vision. This massive war chest, over

$150 billion, is yearning to find a strong leader and team with a well-conceived and credible buyout plan. Can you be that leader? Can you build that team? Yes. Even if you have little capital yourself? Yes. Is it easy? No! It takes guts, determination, stamina, leadership, vision, intelligence, and even, usually, a bit of luck to get it done.

But it's worth it. Just ask Dan Gillis, Harry McCreery, Stu Johnson, Bill Hoover, and Roger Ballou. Some won huge and others struggled. Some made big bucks and others lost money. But I can assure you of this: *None* of them would trade their entrepreneurial company-building experience for some comfortable box in an organization chart in a sprawling bureaucracy.

They had the courage to go for it. They pursued their dreams and, no matter what, tested themselves and learned more about business leadership than they'd ever imagined. You can do it too, and I hope you take your best shot! I've written this book for you. Now, get out there, dream big, and go for it.

APPENDICES: THE BUYOUT TOOLKIT

The following is a set of sample documents from buyout deals. These are generic documents and should not be used without professional legal advice; they are designed to familiarize managers with the guiding documents of the deal. For more information visit our Web site at www.buyoutbook.com.

A. Management Term Sheet, Summary of Understanding, and Employment Agreement
B. Letter of Intent with Seller
C. Bank Commitment Letter
D. Confidentiality Agreement
E. Executive Reference Check Form
F. Working Group List
G. Time and Responsibility Schedule
H. Due Diligence Checklist
I. Directory of Private Equity Investment Firms
J. Directory of Debt-Financing Sources
K. The Financial Model—A More Detailed Look

Appendix A: Management Term Sheet, Summary of Understanding, and Employment Agreement

Sample Short Management Term Sheet

Techway, Inc.
Management Incentive Package
Summary Term Sheet for Discussion Purposes

The following outlines the principal terms of the agreement between Investor and the senior management of Techway (the "Company"):

Equity: Promoted interest of 15 percent of equity, structured as a common stock to preserve capital gains treatment.

Vesting: The equity will vest 20 percent at closing and 20 percent per year thereafter, becoming fully vested at the fourth anniversary of closing.

Investment: Management will invest a total of $750,000 in the transaction on the same terms as the investor.

Current Compensation: Subject to discussion, Investor will preserve the current compensation programs.

Benefits: The nature and issues of the benefits need to be understood more clearly.

Closing Fee: Management will be paid a closing fee equal to 15 percent of Investor's fee; 100 percent of the after-tax portion of this fee will be invested in the transaction in addition to the prementioned personal commitment.

Investor Fees: Investor is to be paid a closing fee of 1 percent on the total transaction size and a $250,000 annual management fee.

Investor's Role: Investor will invest 100 percent of the equity
in the transaction and will arrange the debt
financing with one of its lending partners.

Agreed in
principle: ————————————   ————————————
          Management Signature   Investor Signature

Date: ————————————   ————————————

Sample Management Memorandum of Understanding

Techway Memorandum of Understanding
February 12, 1999

I.   Introduction
     Techway will be recapitalized by a group of investors led by
     Investors and certain other side-by-side investors, Seller, and
     the key executives (each individually, an "Executive" and col-
     lectively, the "Executives") for the purpose of building and op-
     erating a leading information technology services company.
II. Investor's Role
     Investor will provide significant equity capital and support in
     forming and developing Techway. Investor would initially
     commit the necessary equity capital to consummate the re-
     capitalization of Techway (the "Recapitalization"), and Inves-
     tor would provide or arrange for up to 100 percent of the cash
     required to purchase the portion of equity in Techway not pur-
     chased by the Executives or retained by Seller. In addition,
     Investor expects to work closely with the Executives in formu-
     lating a business plan, securing bank and other financing for
     Techway, visiting and analyzing initial acquisition prospects,
     and helping to negotiate and close initial acquisitions.
III. Executives' Role
     The Executives will serve in their current offices of Techway
     except as otherwise agreed by the Executives and Investor.
     Each of the Executives will report to the board of directors of
     Techway. Executives would initially collectively invest not less
     than $750,000 of the equity invested in Techway (including
     the Management Carry described in Section VI below) or such
     greater amount as Executives may wish to commit. All of such
     equity investments by the Executives will be made at the time
     of Recapitalization.
IV. Board of Directors
     The Board of Directors of Techway following the Recapitaliza-
     tion and each subsidiary thereof will consist of one Executive
     and four Investor representatives. A representative of the In-
     vestor will serve as Chair of the Board. The Board may grow in
     size as appropriate as Techway grows and could in the future

include the executive officers of major acquisitions or other strong outside directors, subject to Investor's right to elect a majority of all directors. The Board of Directors shall have the right to approve all material transactions involving Techway, including without limitation, acquisitions and dispositions, material credit facilities, executive employment agreements, budgets, capital expenditures, and major contracts.

V. Funding

    A. *Commitment.* Investor will commit to invest up to $45 million in Techway for the Recapitalization and for acceptable acquisitions. Investor will have the right to assign up to 25 percent of its commitment to an affiliate or any other investor(s) (including Techway and sellers of other acquired business (collectively, the "Selling Shareholders")).

    B. *Future Investments above Commitment.* If Investor invests additional moneys above $45 million, such dollars invested shall be made using the same ratio for preferred and common stock set forth in paragraph C below and all purchased equity and the Management Carry (as defined in Section VI below) will be diluted on a prorated basis.

    C. *Form of Investments.* Except for the Management Carry, all investments by Investor, Seller, and the Executives shall be in a combination of convertible preferred stock (the "Preferred Stock") and common stock (the "Common Stock"). Such investments shall be allocated on the basis of $34 invested in shares of Preferred Stock for each $1 invested in Common Stock. The Preferred Stock will be subject to conversion or redemption upon the earlier of (i) an initial public offering or (ii) a sale of Techway.

VI. Management Carry

    A. *Management Common Equity Carry.* A total of 15 percent of the total common equity of Techway (exclusive of the Executives' purchased equity) will be reserved for the Executives and other members of Techway Management (the "Management Carry"). The Management Carry shall be purchased out of the $750,000 aggregate investment to be made by the Executives. The Management Carry will be subject to "time vesting" (50 percent) and "performance vesting" (50 percent) and will dilute all purchased equity on a pro rata basis. The Management Carry is intended to provide the Executives with a significant upside opportunity at a reduced capital commitment. Because we are issuing the Management Carry up front in shares as opposed to options, it also has the additional benefit of being taxed at capital gains rates as opposed to ordinary income tax rates.

B. *Time Vesting.* Fifty percent of the Management Carry will be subject to time vesting. Generally, the time-vested shares of an Executive will vest over a five-year period from the Recapitalization at the rate of 20 percent per annum on each of the first five anniversaries of the Recapitalization Date as long as such Executive remains employed by the Company as of such dates. All time-vested shares will become 100 percent vested upon either (i) a sale of the Company, (ii) a termination of such Executive without "cause" or "performance cause" within one year following an initial public offering, or (iii) a change of control of Techway.

C. *Performance Vesting.* Fifty percent of the Management Carry will be subject to performance vesting. Performance-vested shares held by an Executive will become fully vested if either (i) Investor receives a specified return on its investment compounded annually (Internal Rate of Return) or (ii) such Executive remains employed by Techway on the tenth anniversary of the Recapitalization. The Performance Vesting Shares shall become vested on the following schedule:

Percentage of Performance Shares Vested	Investor Internal Rate of Return
20%	30% IRR
30%	31% IRR
40%	32% IRR
50%	33% IRR
60%	34% IRR
70%	35% IRR
80%	36% IRR
90%	37% IRR
100%	38% IRR

D. *Sales of Equity to Third Parties.* If in the event Techway sells or issues shares to third parties (i.e., to lenders, in a public offering or if necessary to raise equity to gain compliance with debt agreements), all current equityholders and the Management Carry will share dilution on a pro rata basis.

VII. Ownership

A. *Recapitalization.* At the closing of the Recapitalization, Investor and the Executives will purchase approximately 90 percent of Techway's Common Stock from Seller. This will leave the Techway Common Stock owned as follows:

Investor/Management	90%
Seller	10%

Immediately after such acquisition, Techway will recapitalize into two classes of stock: Preferred Stock and Common Stock. Each existing share of Common Stock of Techway will be exchanged for 10 shares of Common Stock and 90 shares of Preferred Stock. The percentage ownership of all shareholders (including Seller) will be the same in each class as set forth above. Immediately following such acquisition, the Executives will purchase their Management Carry Common Stock. Upon acquisition of their shares, the Executives will make an 83(b) election under the Internal Revenue Code of 1986, as amended.

B. *Ownership.* Fully diluted ownership of the Techway capital stock upon consummation of the recapitalization (including the Management Carry) will be as follows:

	% Acquired Com. Shares	% Acquired Pref. Shares
Investors	76.50%	90.00%
Seller	8.50%	10.00%
Management Carry	15.00%	0.00%
Total	100.00%	100.00%

C. *Repurchase of Stock.* If any other member of management leaves Techway for any reason, Techway has the option to acquire the former employee's unvested Management

Carry Common Stock at its original purchase price. However, the repurchase price shall be the fair market value per share (to be defined, i.e., to be equal to recent acquisition multiples × EBIT + cash − debt − preferred shares or the public market price following an IPO) for the applicable percentage of all time-vested shares and all performance-vested shares (but only to the extent such time-vested shares and performance-vested shares are then vested).

D. *Right of First Refusal.* Techway and the Investor will have a first right of refusal on the sale of any equity shares by the Executives or management.

VIII. Management Team/Compensation

A. *Employment.* Each Executive will enter into a customary employment agreement with the Company mutually acceptable to the Executive, the Investor, and Techway. The terms of each Executive's employment by Techway will begin on the date of closing of the Recapitalization and shall continue for a period of three (3) years thereafter, provided, however, that such employment shall automatically renew for additional one-year terms unless either party gives the other a nonrenewal notice six (6) months prior to the end of any term.

B. *Compensation.* Subject to a detailed review of the existing compensation structure, all current compensation levels will be maintained at current levels or, if appropriate, raised to reflect market compensation for comparable positions at similar firms in the IT industry. Executives will be compensated with a Base Salary and a Bonus Opportunity. The Base Salary for each Executive will be subject to annual review by the Company's Board of Directors. The Bonus Opportunity will be calculated as a range based on a percentage of an Executive's Base Salary commensurate with his or her position. Generally, we would expect that the Bonus Opportunity would range from 50 to 120 percent of an Executive's Base Salary (depending on the position of Executive) with attachment of agreed-upon financial goals being the primary determinant and individual contribution the secondary determinant. The total Pool Available for bonuses will be determined in cooperation with the Board. The Company's CEO will have primary discretion in establishing individual performance goals and bonus awards.

C. *Benefits.* Subject to a detailed review of existing plans, all Executives will be entitled to all standard benefits, including health insurance, retirement/401(k), vacation, and other benefits and perquisites that may be established in consultation with the Board of Directors.

D. *Termination.* If an Executive is terminated after closing of the Recapitalization without "Cause," he or she will receive twelve months of severance pay and benefits allowance. If terminated for "Performance Cause" (to be defined as missing 80 percent of any operating budget for any twelve-month period), then he or she will receive three months of severance pay and benefits. An Executive can be terminated for Cause without payment of any severance.

IX. Expenses and Fees

Techway will pay Investor's reasonable legal expenses in connection with any financing and any later enforcement of the rights of Investor, as well as any out-of-pocket expenses incurred by Investor in attending Board and other company-related meetings. Investor will also receive a transaction fee equal to 1 percent of all funds (debt and equity) raised by Techway. Techway will pay the Executives' reasonable legal expenses related to entering into definitive management agreements upon close of the Recapitalization.

X. Other

A. *Nonbinding Letter.* Except for paragraphs B and C below, which shall be binding, this agreement is not binding until execution of definitive legal agreements by Investor and the Executives. Such agreements will be negotiated and completed in conjunction with the Recapitalization. Notwithstanding the foregoing, in the event that the parties hereto agree, the principal terms of this letter agreement shall govern any such definitive legal agreements between them.

B. *Terms Held in Confidence.* Terms of this letter of understanding will be held in confidence by Investor and the Executives.

C. *No Shop.* In consideration for the Investor's advancing expenses in connection with the Recapitalization, each Executive agrees that following his or her acceptance of this letter and until ninety days from the date hereof, he or she shall not offer to buy, entertain, or discuss an offer to buy, or solicit any proposals regarding the sale of all or any part of Techway, with any party other than Investor (except as contemplated by this letter).

D. *Investment Agreements.* The parties will enter into investment agreements consistent with this understanding and containing customary private equity terms such as information rights and drag-along rights and appropriate non-competition provisions.

The parties to this letter agreement hereby agree to execute and deliver this letter agreement as of the last date set forth below:

By: _____   _____

    Name: _____

    Title: _____

_____   _____

                             Date

_____   _____

                             Date

_____   _____

                             Date

Summary Employment Agreement

Executive:	_____ ("Executive")
Responsibilities:	Executive will serve as CEO and as [a member/chairman] of the Board of Directors of the Company.
Employment Term:	Three year minimum, automatically extended one year at the third anniversary and at each anniversary thereafter unless sixty days written notice is given by either party.
Salary:	The initial salary of Executive will be set at $200,000 once the initial acquisition is consummated and thereafter will be reviewed annually by the Board of Directors. [During the employment period, the salary will not be reduced.]
Bonus Program:	The Executive will be eligible for an annual bonus of up to 100% of Executive's base salary based on the objectives set by the Board.
Severance:	For termination without cause, salary continuation for the lesser of (1) twelve months or (2) the remaining term of the employment contract. For termination with cause (as defined in Section IV) or resignation, no salary continuation. For termination with performance cause (as defined in Section IV), salary continuation for three months.

	[Discuss termination for "Good Reason."]
Noncompete/Nonsolicit:	Executive will enter into a non-compete/nonsolicit agreement with the Company for the longer of (1) the remaining term of the contract and (2) two years from termination.

Appendix B: Letter of Intent with Seller

Investor
1515 Big Hitter Lane
Cash Flow, Wisconsin

CONFIDENTIAL

Techway
Street
City, State, Zip

Techway Parent CEO
Street
City, State, Zip

Dear Ladies & Gentlemen:

This letter agreement (the "Letter") sets forth the general terms pursuant to which Investor (the "Purchaser") is prepared to purchase all of the outstanding capital stock of Techway and any majority-owned subsidiaries of Techway (collectively, "Company") from the Techway Parent Co. ("Seller") (the "Transaction").

1. **Form of Transaction**. Subject to the terms of this Letter, Purchaser will purchase 100 percent of the Capital Stock of Company for the Purchase Price (as described in paragraph 2). As a result, Company will become a wholly owned subsidiary of Purchaser. For purposes of this Letter, "Capital Stock" includes all of the Company's common stock, preferred stock (if any), and any other securities (whether contingent or not) that are convertible into common stock or preferred stock. Purchaser will use its best efforts to structure the Transaction in the most tax-advantageous manner possible, which does not result in a tax or other economic detriment to Seller or Purchaser.

2. **Purchase Price**. The purchase price ("Purchase Price") shall be the sum of the following:

    (1) $95 million in cash.
    (2) $5 million in the form of performance-based promissory notes (the "Notes"). The Notes are described in detail in Section 3 of this Letter.

(3) Common stock in Purchaser equal to 9.2 percent of Purchaser's common stock that is currently outstanding (after giving effect to unexercised options in Purchaser)

Purchaser will work with Seller to provide at least 3 percent of the Purchase Price to the Company's key employees, as identified by Seller. (It is anticipated that the entire $95 million cash amount go to Seller, that the Notes be payable to the Company's key employees, and that the common stock in Purchaser be divided in the same 80/20 percent proportion among Seller and Company's key employees.)

3. **Notes.** The Notes shall have the following features:
   A. **Priority.** The Notes shall be:
      - Senior in liquidation only to the amounts that Purchaser owes to its parent company, Techway Parent Co. ("Parent") (except for indebtedness described below in this Section 3).
      - Junior to any acquisition debt that may be incurred in connection with the Transactions contemplated by this letter.
   B. **Performance Feature.** The Notes shall be payable in three equal installments: 12, 24, and 36 months after the closing of the Transactions contemplated by this Letter, provided, however, no amounts shall be due and payable under those Notes whose original holder is not employed by Company or one of its affiliates as of the scheduled payment date.

4. **Sources and Uses.** In summary, cash sources and cash uses of funds are as follows:

Cash Uses (millions)		Cash Sources (millions)	
Purchase Price		Senior Bank Debt	50.000
Cash	95.000	Performance Equity	3.000
Note	5.000	Cash Equity	50.000
Transaction Exp's	3.000		
	103.000		103.000

5. **Purchaser's Due Diligence Review.**
   (a) Purchaser's due diligence review ("Purchaser's Due Dili-

gence Review'') will consist of a general review of the business and prospects of the Company, including an investigation of Company's historical financial statements, its products, and competitive position, and the sustainability of its originations, revenue and cash flow, as well as customary legal, regulatory, tax, accounting, and investment structure due diligence. As part of Purchaser's Due Diligence Review, Purchaser will evaluate Company's future business prospects, will review its direct marketing and advertising processes, will assess the Company's ability to securitize its products, and will review loan files and underwriting procedures. Concurrent with Purchaser's Due Diligence Review, parties providing financing and their respective agents and representatives may also conduct due diligence reviews. Purchaser's Due Diligence Review will begin on the date upon which Purchaser and its agents, representatives, and financing sources are granted access to the Company's books, records, facilities, key personnel, officers, directors, independent accountants, and legal counsel in accordance with Section 9 below. The Seller agrees that such access will be granted promptly to the Purchaser, its agents, representatives, and financing sources following execution of this Letter. The Purchaser will complete due diligence within thirty days thereafter.

(b) Seller's due diligence review (''Seller's Due Diligence Review'') will consist of a general review of the business and prospects of the Purchaser, including an investigation of Purchaser's historical financial statements, its products, and competitive position. Seller's Due Diligence Review will begin on the date upon which Seller and its agents, and representatives are granted access to the Purchaser's key personnel, key officers, directors, independent accountants, and legal counsel. The Purchaser agrees that such access will be granted promptly to the Seller, its agents and representatives, following execution of this Letter. The Seller will complete due diligence on the earlier of (1) the date on which Purchaser completes its diligence, or (2) 30 days after execution of this Letter.

6. **Definitive Purchase Agreement.** The Purchaser will prepare and deliver to the Seller within ten days of the conclusion of

Purchaser's Due Diligence Review a definitive Purchase Agreement (the "Purchase Agreement"). The Purchase Agreement will contain terms and conditions customary in transactions of this type (including standard representations, warranties, covenants, and indemnifications), or which are reasonably necessary as a result of the Due Diligence Review. Representations regarding the Company will, for most items, survive closing for three years, and for other items, including without limitation environmental, taxes, ERISA, and title, the survival shall be for longer periods (and in some cases indefinite).

   7. **Closing Conditions.** Purchaser's obligation to consummate the Transactions contemplated by this Letter is subject to, among other things, the following conditions:

    i.   Completion of, and Purchaser's satisfaction, in its sole discretion, with the results of Purchaser's Due Diligence Review;

    ii. Negotiation and execution of a Purchase Agreement and all other necessary Transaction-related documentation mutually satisfactory to the parties thereto;

    iii. Receipt of third-party financing on terms and conditions satisfactory to the Purchaser;

    iv. Negotiation and execution of employment agreements with the CEO and other selected executives of the Company, identified by Purchaser during its due diligence, which agreements will contain noncompete/nonsolicit/confidentiality provisions. A draft employment agreement for the top five executives is to be provided as an attachment;

    v. Absence of a material adverse change in the financial condition, results of operations, business, assets, properties or prospects of Company since June 30, 2000;

    vi. Compliance of the Transactions contemplated hereby with all laws and regulations applicable thereto, including (a) obtaining all necessary governmental and third-party approvals and consents (including consent by all applicable state licensing authorities) and making all necessary filings with regulatory authorities (including Hart-Scott-Rodino filings and approvals), and (b) the expiration of all waiting periods during which objections to the Transaction contemplated hereby can be raised; and

vii. Compliance by the Seller with its obligations hereunder. The obligation of Seller to consummate the Transactions contemplated hereunder is subject to, among other things, the following conditions:

i. Completion of, and Seller's reasonable satisfaction with the results of Seller's Due Diligence Review (provided, however, Seller shall only be able to terminate this Letter based on this paragraph if Seller's Due Diligence Review reveals items that would reasonably cause Seller to believe that the Purchaser will lack the financial resources to repay the Note);

ii. Negotiation and execution of a Purchase Agreement and all other necessary Transaction-related documentation mutually satisfactory to the parties thereto;

iii. Compliance of the Transactions contemplated hereby with all laws and regulations applicable thereto, including (a) obtaining all necessary governmental and third party approvals and consents (including consent by all applicable state licensing authorities) and making all necessary filings with regulatory authorities (including Hart-Scott-Rodino filings and approvals), and (b) the expiration of all waiting periods during which objections to the Transaction contemplated hereby can be raised; and

iv. Compliance by the Purchaser with its obligations hereunder.

8. **Schedule**. Purchaser, Seller, and Company agree to use their reasonable efforts to adhere to the following schedule of events leading up to the closing (assuming acceptance of this Letter by September 5, 2000):

September 15, 2000:   Hart-Scott-Rodino filing will be prepared and filed, if necessary.

October 6, 2000:   Purchaser's Due Diligence Review will be completed.

October 16, 2000:   Purchaser will deliver a first draft of
                         the Purchase Agreement to Seller.

October 29, 2000:   Purchase Agreement will be exe-
                         cuted, and closing will occur as soon
                         as practicable thereafter.

9. **Cooperation.** Upon the Seller's acknowledgement of and agreement with the terms and conditions set forth in this Letter, the Seller will permit the Purchaser and its agents, representatives, and financing sources (including attorneys, accountants, and any financing sources, and their agents and representatives) access to the Company's books, records, portfolio tapes, facilities, key personnel, officers, directors, independent accountants, and legal counsel in connection with Purchaser's Due Diligence Review.

10. **Exclusivity.**

   A. **Cessation of Other Acquirer Activity.** Company and Seller agree that from the date of their acknowledgement of and agreement with the terms and conditions set forth in this Letter through the closing of the Transactions contemplated by this Letter, or the earlier termination of this Letter, neither Company nor any of its record and beneficial shareholders, officers, directors, affiliates, agents, or representatives will, directly or indirectly:

   i. Submit, solicit, initiate, encourage, or discuss with third parties any proposal or offer from any person relating to any (a) reorganization, dissolution or recapitalization of Company, (b) merger or consolidation involving Company, (c) sale of the stock of Company, (d) sale of any assets of Company outside the ordinary course of business or in connection with whole loan sales or securitizations unless consented to in advance by Purchaser, or (e) similar transaction or business combinations involving Company or its business or assets including without limitation any debt or equity financing thereof, or

   ii. Furnish any information with respect to, assist or participate in or facilitate in any other manner any effort or attempt by any person to do or seek the foregoing.

B. **Notification.** Company and Seller will, and will cause Company's officers, directors, affiliates, agents, and representatives, to terminate all discussions with any third-party regarding the foregoing and will notify Purchaser of the fact of receipt of any proposals or offers.

C. **Representation and Indemnification.** Company's and Seller's acknowledgement of and agreement with the terms and conditions set forth in this Letter also constitutes a representation and warranty that neither Company, Seller, nor any of Company's record and beneficial shareholders, officers, directors, affiliates, agents, or representatives have entered into any executory agreements or accepted any commitments concerning any of the foregoing transactions. Company and Seller hereby agree to indemnify and hold harmless Purchaser and each director, officer, investor, employee, and agent thereof (each, an "indemnified person") from and against any and all losses, claims, damages, liabilities (or actions or proceedings commenced or threatened in respect thereof), and expenses that arise out of, result from, or in any way relate to the breach of the foregoing representation and warranty. The obligations of Company and Seller under this paragraph will survive any termination of this Letter and will be effective regardless of whether a definitive agreement is executed.

11. **Conduct of the Business.** Upon acceptance of this Letter and until the earlier of closing the Transactions contemplated by this Letter or the termination of this Letter, Company agrees to preserve substantially intact its business operations and assets and to conduct its operations in the ordinary course of business consistent with past operations. Without limiting the generality of the foregoing, Company shall not, without the prior written consent of Purchaser, (i) make any material capital expenditures, (ii) make or pay any dividends or distributions of any kind, (iii) enter into any material contracts, commitments, or arrangements (except in the ordi-

nary course of business), (iv) change any compensation plans or pay any bonuses, (v) change any underwriting guidelines, or (vi) launch materially new products.

12. **Management.** It is anticipated that Company will be a stand-alone subsidiary of a holding company to be formed by our counsel for the purposes of consummating this acquisition. The CEO (named) will remain President and CEO of the Company for three years, pursuant to an employment agreement, a draft of which is attached to this Letter.

13. **Reimbursement of Fees and Expenses.** If the Transaction is not consummated by reason of a breach by the Seller or Company of any obligations under this Letter, the Seller and the Company hereby agree that Seller and the Company will jointly and severally reimburse the Purchaser and its affiliates for their out-of-pocket costs and expenses, including legal and other professional fees and expenses, incurred in connection with Purchaser's Due Diligence Review, the preparation, review, negotiation, execution, and delivery of this Letter, the definitive agreements and other documents relating to the Transaction, and the financing of the Transaction. If the Transaction is consummated, Seller and Purchaser will each bear their own expenses (and Seller will bear Company's expenses). No party to this Transaction has any liability to brokers in connection with this Transaction, or to which any other party to this Letter could become obligated. No employees of the Company will receive any payment, bonus, or other extraordinary compensation as a result of this Transaction.

14. **Termination.** Purchaser's offer hereunder will expire at 12:00 noon, Wisconsin Time, on September 5, 2000 ("Expiration"), unless the Seller and Company agree to the terms and conditions of this Letter by signing and returning to the Purchaser the enclosed counterpart of this Letter and the Purchaser receives such signed counterpart prior to that time. The Purchaser may terminate this Letter at any time if: (i) any information is disclosed to or discovered by the Purchaser or its representatives, after the conclusion of the Purchaser's Due Diligence Review, which the Purchaser believes in good faith may be materially adverse to the Transaction or to the financial condition, results of operations, business, assets, properties, or prospects of the Company, or (ii) the Purchaser believes in

good faith that one or more of the conditions to closing set forth herein will not be fulfilled. The Seller shall be permitted to terminate this Letter at any time after sixty days from the date hereof in the event that the Purchase Agreement is not executed on or before that time. Notwithstanding the foregoing, (i) this Letter shall not be terminated if the closing is delayed solely due to delays in obtaining regulatory approval, (ii) the Reimbursement of Fees and Expenses section shall not terminate even if this Letter is terminated, and (iii) the obligations under subparagraph "C" of the Exclusivity section of this Letter shall not terminate even if this Letter is terminated.

15. **Binding Effect.** Subject to the conditions set forth herein, the obligations of each of the parties under this letter shall be binding at the time this letter is executed; provided, however, that the parties acknowledge that not all terms to be reflected in the Purchase Agreement and related documents have been discussed and agree to negotiate in good faith to finalize these agreements setting forth such additional terms.

16. **Announcements.** All press releases and other announcements relating to the Transaction shall be subject to prior approval by Purchaser, Company, and Seller.

17. **Governing Law.** The Transaction shall be governed by the laws (which shall mean all laws other than conflict of laws) of the State of Delaware.

Please sign and date this Letter no later than the time of Expiration (as set forth in the "Termination" Section, above) in the spaces provided below to confirm our mutual understandings and agreements as set forth in this Letter and return a signed copy to the undersigned. By signing this Letter, you are representing that you have authority to consummate this Transaction and that you are the sole shareholder of the Company (and that no other shareholders exist whose approval could be necessary to consummate this Transaction).

PURCHASER

By: _____
Investor and Management

ACKNOWLEDGED AND AGREED TO

AS OF SEPTEMBER _____, 20_____

_____

Selling CEO *(or person with authority to sign for the corporation)*

Appendix C: Bank Commitment Letter

Date: _____

Investor
Address
City, State, Zip

Dear Investor:

The Bank Group is pleased to advise you of its commitment to provide a five (5) year revolving credit facility in the aggregate maximum principal amount of $50,000,000 (the "Credit Facility"), upon and subject to the terms and conditions set forth in this Commitment Letter and the attached Summary of Terms and Conditions (the "Term Sheet").

Based on our conversations with you and general information you have provided, the Credit Facility will be used to finance, in part, the planned recapitalization (the "Recapitalization") of Techway by Investor. Following consummation of the Recapitalization, the Credit Facility will be used to (i) meet future capital expenditure requirements of Techway, (ii) finance future acquisitions, and (iii) finance the ongoing working capital requirements of the Borrower.

As outlined in the Term Sheet, the Credit Facility will be secured by a first priority security interest in all of the Borrower's assets, including a pledge of the stock of Techway and all direct and indirect subsidiaries of Techway. Based on our discussions, we believe that the Credit Facility outlined in the Term Sheet will provide the Borrower with operating flexibility, allow sufficient room for anticipated growth, and is attractive from a pricing perspective.

As more fully set forth in the attached Term Sheet, the closing of the Credit Facility is subject to certain conditions precedent, including, without limitation, completion to the satisfaction of The Bank Group, of The Bank Group's legal review of the Borrower, Techway, and the structure and terms of the proposed recapitalization of Techway.

The commitments of The Bank Group (The "Lender") hereunder are based upon the financial and other information regarding Techway and its subsidiaries and affiliates (if any) previously provided to The Lender. Accordingly, the commitments hereunder are

subject to the conditions, among others, that (i) there shall not
have occurred after the date of such financial and other information
any material adverse change in the business, assets, liabilities (actual or contingent), operations, condition (financial or otherwise),
or prospects of Techway or its subsidiaries and affiliates (if any);
(ii) The Lender continues to be satisfied with the condition, assets,
properties, business, operations, and prospects of Techway and its
subsidiaries and affiliates (if any), shall not differ in any material
respect from the information previously provided to The Lender by
you that could have a material adverse effect on Techway or its
subsidiaries and affiliates (if any); and (iii) there shall be no compet-
ing issuance of debt, securities, or commercial bank facilities of
Techway and/or its subsidiaries and affiliates (if any) being offered,
placed, or arranged, except with the prior written consent of The
Lender. The commitment of The Lender hereunder is subject to
the agreements in this paragraph (as well as the other terms and
conditions of this letter, including the Term Sheet).

You agree that the Borrower may be required from time to
time during the term of the Credit Facility to enter into interest rate
protection agreements, currency swaps, and other hedging transactions as may be required by the Agent and/or The Lender. You
hereby represent and covenant that to the best of your knowledge
(i) all information, other than Projections (as defined below), which
has been or is hereafter made available to The Lender by you or any
of your representatives in connection with the transactions contemplated hereby ("Information"), is and will be complete and correct
in all material respects and does not and will not contain any untrue
statement of a material fact or omit to state a material fact necessary
to make the statements contained therein not misleading; and (ii)
all financial projections concerning Techway and its subsidiaries and
affiliates (if any), that have been or are hereafter made available to
The Lender by you (the "Projections"), have been or will be prepared in good faith based upon reasonable assumptions. You agree
to supplement the Information and the Projections from time to
time until the closing date so that the representation and warranty
in the preceding sentence is correct on the closing date. In issuing
this Commitment Letter and closing the Credit Facility, The Lender
will be using and relying on the Information and the Projections.

By executing this Commitment Letter, you agree to reimburse

The Lender from time to time on demand for all reasonable out-of-pocket fees and other expenses (including, but not limited to, the reasonable fees, disbursements, and other charges or professional fees) incurred in connection with the Credit Facility, including the preparation of definitive documentation for the Credit Facility, and the other transactions contemplated hereby.

By executing this Commitment Letter, you further agree to indemnify and hold harmless The Bank Group, each other Lender and each director, officer, shareholder, employee, representative, agent, attorney, and affiliate of The Bank Group and each other Lender and each of their directors, officers, shareholders, partners, employees, representatives, agents, attorneys, successors, and assigns (each such person or entity is referred to in this paragraph as an "Indemnified Person") from and against any losses, claims, costs, damages, demands, obligations, liabilities, or expenses, including, without limitation, reasonable attorneys' fees, or actions, suits, or proceedings (including, without limitation, any inquiry or investigation with respect thereto) which any Indemnified Person may sustain or incur or to which any Indemnified Person may become subject, insofar as such losses, claims, costs, damages, demands, obligations, liabilities, or expenses, or actions, suits, or proceedings, arise out of, in any way relate to, or result from, this letter, the Credit Facility or any of the other transactions contemplated hereby, and to reimburse upon demand each Indemnified Person for any and all legal and other expenses incurred in connection with investigating, preparing to defend or defending any such loss, claim, cost, damage, demand, obligation, liability, or expense, or action, suit, or proceeding (including any inquiry or investigation with respect thereto); *provided*, however, that you shall have no obligation under this indemnity provision for liabilities resulting from the gross negligence or willful misconduct of any Indemnified Person. The provisions of this paragraph shall be in addition to any right that an Indemnified Person shall have at common law or otherwise. No Indemnified Person shall be responsible or liable for consequential damages that may be alleged as a result of this letter.

The provisions of the immediately preceding two paragraphs shall remain in full force and effect regardless of whether definitive financing documentation shall be executed and delivered and notwithstanding the termination of the Commitment Letter of the commitment of The Lender hereunder.

You acknowledge and agree that the services of The Bank Group, as Arranger, will be on an exclusive basis during the term of this letter and that, during such term, no other bank or financial institution will be engaged or otherwise consulted or contacted by you regarding any other proposed senior bank facility for Techway and its subsidiaries and affiliates (if any).

Except as may be required by applicable law, this Commitment Letter, including the Term Sheet, and the contents hereof and thereof, shall not be disclosed by you to any third party without the prior written consent of The Bank Group, other than to your Board of Directors, the attorneys, financial advisers, equity underwriters, accountants, and other professional consultants representing the Borrower or Techway, in each case to the extent necessary in your reasonable judgment. You acknowledge and agree that The Bank Group may share with any of its respective affiliates any information relating to the Credit Facility, the Borrower, and its subsidiaries and affiliates. You further acknowledge and agree to the disclosure by The Bank Group of information relating to the Credit Facility to *Gold Sheets* and other similar bank trade publications, with such information to consist of deal terms and other information customarily found in such publications.

This Commitment Letter may be executed in counterparts which, taken together, shall constitute an original. This Commitment Letter, together with the Term Sheet, embodies the entire agreement and understanding between The Bank Group and you with respect to the specific matters set forth herein and therein, and supersedes all prior agreements and understandings relating to the subject matter hereof and thereof. No party has been authorized by The Bank Group to make any oral or written statements inconsistent with this letter.

THIS LETTER SHALL BE GOVERNED BY AND CONSTRUED IN ACCORDANCE WITH THE LAWS OF THE STATE OF NORTH CAROLINA, WITHOUT REGARD TO THE PRINCIPLES OF CONFLICTS OF LAW.

This letter may not be assigned by you or any Borrower without the prior written consent of The Bank Group.

If you are in agreement with the foregoing, please execute and return the enclosed copy of this Commitment Letter and Term Sheet, no later than the close of business on *(date to be defined)*. This Commitment Letter shall terminate if not so accepted by you prior to that time. This Commitment Letter shall become effective upon your delivery to us of executed counterparts of this Commitment Letter, together with (a) the Term Sheet and (b) payment of the Commitment Fee (as defined in the Term Sheet) in the aggregate amount of $500,000; provided, however, that in the event that you disclose the existence of this Commitment Letter to any third party, with or without the consent of The Bank Group, other than as expressly permitted herein or as may be required by applicable law, you shall be deemed to have accepted this Commitment Letter. Following acceptance by you, this Commitment Letter shall terminate on _____, unless the Credit Facility is closed by such time.

We are excited about the overall business prospects for the Borrower, and look forward to supporting the Borrower's financial needs as they grow and evolve. If you should have any questions regarding our proposal or our discussions, please do not hesitate to call me at _____.

Very truly yours,
The Bank Group

_____

Accepted on this _____ day of _____.

Investor

By: _____

Name: _____

Title: _____

Techway, Inc.
Summary of Terms and Conditions
The terms and conditions in this Term Sheet as not intended to be all inclusive, but rather set forth a framework from which a mutually satisfactory transaction may be structured.

Borrower:	Techway, Inc. ("Techway") and all subsidiaries on a joint and several basis (collectively, the "Borrower" or "Borrowers"). The Borrower may alternatively be a newly created entity (and its subsidiaries, if any) with an ownership and capitalization structure acceptable to the Lenders in all respects.
Arranger, Lender:	The Bank Group
Administrative Agent:	A bank to be named will be selected to "administer" the loan.
Lenders:	The Bank Group (The "Lender")
Facility:	$50,000,000 Revolving Credit Facility (the "Facility")
Swingline Loans:	A portion of the Facility not in excess of $5,000,000 shall be available for swingline loans to the Borrower (the "Swingline Loans") from The Bank Group on same day notice. Any such Swingline Loans shall reduce the available commitment under the Facility. Each of the Lenders shall acquire, under certain circumstances, an irrevocable and unconditional *pro rata* participation in each such Swingline Loan.
Repayment:	Amounts outstanding from time to time under the Facility shall be repaid in regularly scheduled installments of interest only (whether at LIBOR maturities or otherwise) until the Maturity Date (hereinafter defined), at which time all principal, interest, and all other amounts payable in connection with the Facility shall become due and payable in full.
Letters of Credit:	A $5,000,000 sublimit for Letters of Credit will be available under the Facility, subject to the payment of Letter of Credit Fee (based on the hereinafter defined Leverage Ratio and in the applicable amount set forth in *Exhibit A* [Pricing Grid] hereto) and administration charges.

Closing Date:	The date of the initial borrowing under the Facility (the "Closing Date").
Maturity:	The Facility shall mature (the "Maturity Date") and become due and payable in full on the fifth (5th) anniversary of the Closing Date.
Purpose:	To finance, in part, (i) the recapitalization (the "Recapitalization") of Techway, (ii) the Borrower's general working capital purposes, (iii) capital expenditures, and (iv) permitted acquisitions; it being understood and agreed that the aggregate outstanding amount of Facility proceeds used for general working capital purposes will not, at any time, exceed $10,000,000 in aggregate. Definitive terms and conditions of permitted acquisitions will be set forth in the loan documents.
Security:	The Facility shall be secured by the grant of a first priority lien in favor of the Agent, for the ratable benefit of itself and the Lenders, on all tangible and intangible assets of the Borrower, including, but not limited to, all equipment, all inventory, all general intangibles, and all contract rights, all stock or other ownership interests held or owned by the Borrower, and all real property.
Interest Rate:	At the Borrower's election, Base Rate and LIBOR options will be available as follows: **Base Rate Option:** Interest will accrue at the Agent's Base Rate, plus the applicable Additional Base Rate Interest Margin, and will be calculated on the basis of the actual number of days elapsed in a year of 365 days. The Base Rate will be the higher of the (i) Federal Funds Rate, as published by the Federal Reserve Bank, plus one-half of one percent, or (ii) the Prime commercial lending rate of the Agent as announced from time to time by the Agent at its headquarters (the "Prime Rate"). The Prime Rate is an index or base rate and shall not necessarily be its lowest or best rate charged to its customers or other banks. Advances and paydowns shall be made on a same-day basis if requested prior to 12:00 P.M. EST, and shall be

in minimum and incremental amounts of $100,000 Dollars.

Swingline Loans shall be maintained solely at the Base Rate, without the addition of any Additional Base Rate Interest Margin or Additional LIBOR Interest Rate Margin.

LIBOR Option:

Interest shall be determined for periods ("Interest Periods") of 30, 60, 90, or 180 days (as selected by the Borrower), and shall accrue at an annual rate equal to the London Interbank Offered Rate ("LIBOR") for corresponding deposits of U.S. dollars (adjusted for reserve requirements, if any), plus the applicable Additional LIBOR Interest Rate Margin. LIBOR shall mean reserve adjusted LIBOR as set forth on Telerate Page 3750 or as determined by the Agent if such information is not available. Interest will be paid at the end of each Interest Period or quarterly, whichever is earlier, and will be calculated on the basis of the actual number of days elapsed in a year of 360 days. LIBOR drawings shall not be permitted at any time there is a default under the Facility, shall require three (3) business days advance notice, and shall be in minimum and incremental amounts of Five Hundred Thousand Dollars ($500,000) and One Hundred Thousand Dollars ($100,000), respectively.

Interest Margins:

The applicable Additional Base Rate Interest Margin and the applicable Additional LIBOR Interest Rate Margin for the Facility shall correspond to the rates shown on the Pricing Grid attached to this Term Sheet as *Exhibit A* (the "Pricing Grid"), and shall be determined on the basis of the Borrower's ratio (the "Leverage Ratio") of Total Debt to trailing four (4) quarterly earnings before interest, taxes, depreciation, and amortization ("EBITDA"). The Leverage Ratio shall be calculated on a trailing four (4) quarter basis, and interest rate adjustments shall be applicable to the Facility on a prospective basis.

Default Rate: Upon the occurrence and during the continuance of an Event of Default that has continued unremedied beyond any applicable notice and/or grace period (i) the Borrower shall no longer have the option to request LIBOR Rate Loans or Swingline Loans, (ii) all amounts due and payable with respect to LIBOR Rate Loans and Swingline Loans shall bear interest at a rate per annum two percent (2%) in excess of the rate then applicable to Base Rate Loans, and (iii) all amounts due and payable with respect to Base Rate Loans shall bear interest at a rate per annum equal to two percent (2%) in excess of the rate then applicable to Base Rate Loans.

Unused and Other Fees:
Unused Fee: An unused fee will be payable by the Borrower on a quarterly basis, shall be based on the Pricing Grid, and shall be determined on the basis of the Leverage Ratio, as of the date of any determination.

Arrangement Fee: An Arrangement Fee, in the amount of Three Hundred Thousand and No/100 Dollars ($300,000.00), will be payable by the Borrower on the Closing Date. The Arrangement Fee will be split equally between the Arranger and Co-Lead Arranger.

Commitment Fee: A Commitment Fee, in the amount of Four Hundred Thousand and No/100 Dollars ($400,000.00), will be payable by the Borrower upon the Borrower's acceptance of the Lender's commitment. The Commitment Fee will be split evenly between the Lenders.

Voluntary Prepayments:
Prepayments shall be permitted in whole or in part without premium or penalty, provided, however, that (i) minimum and incremental prepayment amounts of One Hundred Thousand Dollars ($100,000) shall be required; (ii) two (2) business days prior notice shall be required for prepayments of LIBOR loans; and (iii) LIBOR loans may only be prepaid on the last day of the applicable Interest Period, unless breakage costs (if any) as determined by the Agent, are paid by the Borrower.

Mandatory Prepayments:
Mandatory prepayments shall be required in the amount of 100 percent of the net proceeds arising from any of the following events: (i) any sale or dis-

position of any of the assets of any Borrower which is (a) not in the ordinary course of business or (b) prohibited by the terms of this Agreement; (ii) the receipt by or on behalf of any Borrower of insurance proceeds (other than recoveries due to damage to tangible property, which recoveries are promptly applied toward repair or replacement of the damaged property); (iii) the reversion of any pension plan assets; (iv) the issuance by any Borrower of subordinated debt securities or other debt obligations (other than in connection with debt expressly permitted by the Lenders); and/or (v) the issuance by any Borrower of any equity interests in such Borrower. Any mandatory payment shall also reduce the Commitment amount of the Facility by the amount equal to such mandatory payment.

Conditions Precedent:

Customary for facilities of this nature, including, but not limited to, the Lenders' review and approval of all final documents, instruments, and agreements executed in connection with the Recapitalization (the "Recapitalization Documents"); the Recapitalization shall be consummated contemporaneously with the initial funding on the Closing Date and in accordance with the Recapitalization Documents and the Sources and Uses Table annexed hereto as *Exhibit C;* the corporate and capital structure of the Borrower before and on a *pro forma* basis after the Recapitalization shall be satisfactory to the Agent; all financial statements (including without limitation *pro forma* balance sheets) and projections requested by the Agent shall have been delivered and be in form and substance satisfactory thereto; lien searches and all filings and other recordings necessary to perfect the first priority liens of the Agent shall have been completed; delivery of landlord agreements and other closing documents requested by the Agent with respect to the real property collateral, in each such case in form and substance satisfactory to the Agent; payment of all fees and expenses due and payable on the Closing Date; credit documentation satisfactory to the Agent and Lenders; all governmental, shareholder, corporate, and third-party consents shall

have been obtained; no material adverse change including no material pending or threatened litigation,
bankruptcy, or other proceeding; satisfactory review
of all corporate documentation and other legal due
diligence; payment of all fees and expenses due to
the Agent, Lender, and the Lender's counsel; delivery
of opinion of Borrower's counsel in form and substance satisfactory to the Agent, satisfactory resolu-
tion of any potential solvency and/or contribution
issues; the Agent shall have received such other items
as reasonably requested by it; and any other conditions precedent reasonably deemed appropriate by
the Agent in the context of the proposed transaction.

Representations and Warranties: Customary for facilities of this nature, including, but
not limited to, corporate existence; corporate and
governmental authorization; enforceability; financial
information; no material adverse changes; compliance with laws and agreements (including environmental laws); compliance with ERISA; no material
litigation; payment of taxes; financial condition; and
full disclosure.

Affirmative Covenants: Customary for facilities of this nature, including, but
not limited to, receipt of financial information; noti-
fication of litigation, investigations and other adverse
changes; payment and performance of obligations,
conduct of business, maintenance of existence;
maintenance of management; maintenance of property and insurance (including hazard and business interruption coverage); maintenance of records and
accounts; inspection of property and books and
records (including field audits from time to time);
maintenance of primary accounts with the Agent or
Lender; compliance with laws (including environmental laws); payment of taxes; year 2000 compliance and ERISA.

Financial Covenants: The definitive loan documentation will include the
financial covenants set forth in *Exhibit B* hereto.

Negative Covenants: Customary for facilities of this nature, including, but
not limited to, restrictions and limitations on: indebt-
edness; liens; guaranty obligations; changes in business; sales of assets; mergers and acquisitions (i.e.,

acquisitions and/or mergers involving total indebtedness in excess of $5,000,000 will require, among other things, the consent of both The Bank Group and The Lender); loans, payments, and investments; transactions with affiliates; sale and leaseback transactions; optional prepayments of and material amendments to indebtedness; restrictive agreements; and changes in fiscal year or accounting method.

Events of
Default:

Customary for facilities of this nature, including, but not limited to: failure to pay any interest, principal, or fees under the Facility when due; failure to perform any covenant or agreement; inaccurate or false representations or warranties; cross-defaults (including cross-defaults to defaults under "material" contracts); insolvency or bankruptcy; ERISA; judgment defaults; change in control; and any other events of default deemed reasonably necessary by the Agent and/or Lender in the context of the proposed transaction.

Participations/
Assignments:

The Lender shall be permitted to sell participations or assignments of the interest(s) in the Facility, subject to criteria to be determined.

Increased Costs/
Change in
Circumstances:

Provisions customary in facilities of this type protecting the Lender in the event of unavailability of funding, illegality, capital adequacy requirements, increased costs, withholding taxes, and funding losses.

Required
Lenders:

On any date of determination, (a) if only two (2) Lenders shall be parties to the credit agreement, then both Lenders; or (b) if more than (2) Lenders shall be parties to the credit agreement, then those Lenders who collectively hold at least 66-2/3 percent of outstandings, or if no outstandings, those Lenders who collectively hold at least 66-2/3 percent of the aggregate commitment of the Lenders.

Governing Law:

[Applicable State] law (without reference to choice of law provisions) will govern.

Counsel to
Arranger and
Agent:
Expenses:

The Borrower shall be responsible for all reasonable legal and other out-of-pocket fees, costs, and expenses incurred by the Agent and Lender related to due diligence performed by or on behalf of the Agent and/or Lender in connection with the transaction, the execution of the loan documentation, and future administration of the definitive credit documentation.

Miscellaneous: This summary of terms and conditions does not purport to summarize all the conditions, covenants, representations, warranties, and other provisions which would be contained in definitive credit documentation for the Facility contemplated hereby.

Exhibit A: Pricing Grid

If the Total Debt to EBITDA Ratio is:	Less than 1.5 to 1.0	Equal to or greater than 1.5 to 1.0, but less than 2.0 to 1.0	Equal to or greater than 2.0 to 1.0
then the Additional LIBOR Interest Rate Margin for the Facility shall be:	1.50%	2.00%	2.50%
then the Additional Base Rate Interest Rate Margin for the Facility shall be:	0.00%	0.00%	0.50%
then the Unused Fee shall be:	0.30%	0.375%	0.50%
then the Letter of Credit Fee shall be:	1.50%	2.00%	2.50%

Exhibit B: Financial Covenants

1. *Minimum Adjusted EBITDA.* The Borrower will at all times maintain, on a consolidated basis, Adjusted EBITDA of not less than (1) $4,250,000 during fiscal year 1999; (ii) $5,000,000 during fiscal year 2000; (iii) $5,250,000 during fiscal year 2001; and (iv) $6,000,000 during fiscal year 2002 and during each fiscal year thereafter. Minimum Adjusted EBITDA shall be measured on the last

day of each fiscal quarter, and at the end of each of the Borrower's fiscal years, throughout the term of the Loan on a four (4) quarter trailing basis.

2. *Fixed Charge Coverage Ratio.* The Borrower will at all times maintain, on a consolidated basis, a Fixed Charge Coverage Ratio of not less than 2.00 to 1.00. For purposes of the foregoing, "Fixed Charge Coverage Ratio" shall mean the Borrower's EBITDA, minus capital expenditures, divided by the sum of Interest Expense, plus cash taxes paid, plus principal payments on the Facilities and payments for current capital lease obligations. The Fixed Charge Coverage Ratio shall be measured on the last day of each fiscal quarter, and at the end of each of the Borrower's fiscal years, throughout the term of the Loan on a four (4) quarter trailing basis.

3. *Total Debt to EBITDA Ratio.* The Borrower will at all times maintain, on a consolidated basis, a Total Debt to EBITDA Ratio of not more than 2.75 to 1.00. For purposes hereof, the "Total Debt to EBITDA Ratio" shall mean the ratio of Total Debt to Adjusted EBITDA (a) calculated and tested using (i) the Borrower's twelve (12) month trailing Adjusted EBITDA results and (ii) Total Debt as of the date of calculation, and (b) measured on the last day of each fiscal quarter, throughout the term of the Loan.

4. *Total Debt to Capitalization.* The Borrower will at all times maintain, on a consolidated basis, a Total Debt to Capitalization Ratio of not more than 0.50 to 1.00. For purposes hereof, the "Total Debt to Capitalization Ratio" shall mean Total Debt, divided by the sum of Total Debt, plus cash equity contributed. The Total Debt to Capitalization Ratio shall be measured on the last day of each fiscal quarter, and at the end of each of the Borrower's fiscal years, throughout the term of the Loan on a four (4) quarter trailing basis.

Exhibit C: Sources and Uses Table

Sources of Funds		Uses of Funds	
Revolver	$ 13,300,000	Purchase Price for	
Investor	$ 46,000,000	Techway	$ 95,000,000
Seller Equity		Fees and Expenses	$ 3,300,000
Contribution	$ 400,000	Equity Ownership	$ 5,000,000
New Senior Term	$ 40,000,000	Other	$ 0
New Common			$103,300,000
Stock	$ 3,600,000		
	$103,300,000		

Appendix D: Confidentiality Agreement

[Date]
[Name/address]

Dear   :

As an inducement to [Company Name] (the "Company") to furnish us with information regarding the Company and its business in order to enable us to evaluate our interest in acquiring the stock assets of the Company (the "Evaluation") and in consideration of the Company's disclosure thereof to us, we enter into this confidentiality agreement (this "Agreement") and hereby agree as follows:

As used herein, "Confidential Information" means all data, reports, interpretations, forecasts, and records, to the extent they contain information concerning the Company, that is not available to the general public and which the Company will provide to us in the course of our discussions with the Company. However, the term "Confidential Information" does not include information which (i) is or becomes available to the public other than as a result of a disclosure by us or our representative, (ii) was available to us prior to its disclosure to us by the Company or its representatives, (iii) becomes available to us from a source other than the Company or its representatives, provided that such source is not known by us either to be bound by a confidentiality agreement with the Company or its representatives or to otherwise be prohibited from transmitting the information to us by a contractual, legal, or fiduciary obligation, or (iv) is independently developed by us.

All Confidential Information will be held and treated by us and our Representatives (as defined below) in confidence and will not be disclosed by us or our Representatives except (i) in connection with the Evaluation, (ii) as may be required by law or deemed advisable by our attorneys in connection with any legal or governmental proceeding, or (iii) with the prior consent of the Company. Our "Representatives" means any of our agents, directors, officers, representatives, advisers (including, without limitation, our attorneys, accountants, bankers, and consultants), affiliates, and employees that actually receive written Confidential Information from us.

We undertake not to use any of the Confidential Information delivered to us for any purpose other than the Evaluation.

Except with the other party's written consent or if required by law, neither we nor you nor our respective representatives will disclose (i) that the Evaluation has occurred or is occurring, (ii) that we are negotiating for the acquisition of the stock or assets of the Company, or (iii) any of the potential terms or conditions of such acquisition. [**Add for a public company**: The Company acknowledges and agrees that we may be compelled by securities laws requirements to disclose the information referred to in the preceding sentence and, in such case, the Company agrees that such disclosure may be made and will not constitute a breach of this Agreement.]

This Agreement shall be governed by and construed in accordance with the laws of the State of _____ without regard to the conflicts of law provisions thereof. No amendment to this Agreement shall be binding upon any party hereto unless in writing and signed by both parties hereto. Any provision of this Agreement which is illegal, invalid, prohibited, or unenforceable shall be ineffective to the extent of such illegality, invalidity, prohibition, or unenforceability without invalidating or impairing the remaining provisions hereof.

This agreement does not bind the parties to enter into any other contract or agreement. This Agreement represents the entire understanding between the parties with respect to the subject matter hereof and supercedes all prior oral and written communications, agreements, and understandings relating thereto. This Agreement may be executed in counterparts and copies of original signatures sent by facsimile shall be binding evidence of this Agreement's execution.

The undersigned's obligations and the obligations of our Representatives under this Agreement shall terminate upon the earlier to occur of (i) Investor's consummation of an acquisition of, or other business transaction relating to, all or part of the Company's assets or stock or (ii) one year from the date hereof.

To the extent that the Investor or its affiliates provide to the Company any information regarding the Investor that is not available to the general public, the Company agrees that it (and its respective agents, directors, officers, representatives, advisers, affiliates, and employees) will treat all such confidential information with the same level of confidentiality afforded the Company hereunder and will not use such confidential information for any purpose other than in connection with the Evaluation.

[**Add where feasible**: The Company and its shareholders agree that from the date hereof until the first to occur of (i) the termination by the Investor of its due diligence regarding the Company without a decision to proceed to negotiate a definitive purchase agreement, or (ii) the sixtieth day following the completion by the Company of its responses to the Investor's requests for due diligence information, neither the Company nor its shareholders shall entertain, initiate, or continue discussion of any offer to sell, or solicit or continue to solicit any proposals regarding the sale of, all or any part of the stock or assets of the Company with any party other than the Investor; provided, however, that this period shall be extended for so long as the parties hereto are continuing to negotiate in good faith.]

If the foregoing reflects our agreement, kindly sign and return a copy of this Agreement to us.

Very truly yours,

Investor

By: Its General Partner

By: _____

[Name]

_____

[Title]

Agreed to as of the
date set forth above:
[Name of Company]

By: _____ [Note: Add signature for each shareholder if
agreement includes the exclusivity clause.]

An Authorized Officer

Appendix E: Executive Reference Check Form

1. Integrity of Executive
2. Is he or she deal savvy? Disciplined in pricing? Does he or she have due diligence discipline/experience?
3. Describe his or her financing knowledge; ability to handle lenders.
4. Vision
   a. Does this choice make sense/hold water; synergies realistic; revenue growth realistic?
   b. Has he or she done such work before; is he or she a strong leader?
5. Operating Skills
   a. Does he or she understand how to keep and motivate people? Is the executive detail oriented?
   b. Is he or she focused on expense/margins? Financial savvy?
   c. What level of salesmanship, charisma, and intelligence does he or she have?
   d. Does the executive have the ability to manage budget/expenses?
   e. What about the quality of the team; have managers followed him or her in the past?
   f. Does he or she keep promises? How often have results varied from operating plans?
6. Investor Relations
   a. Does the executive have the ability to work with venture capitalists? Is he or she open to input?
   b. Does he or she understand and report to Board?
   c. Would the executive be good in front of public analysts?
7. Strengths and Weaknesses
8. Would you put money behind the executive and this effort? What would you worry about as an investor?
9. What is his or her profile in the industry and credibility?
10. What are his or her industry contacts and relationships with potential targets (if doing a roll-up)?
11. Who else would be good to talk to about this executive?

Appendix F: Working Group List

WORKING GROUP LIST		
COMPANY/CONTACT	OFFICE	HOME/OTHER
MANAGEMENT TEAM Company Address	Phone: (123) 456-7890 Fax: (123) 456-7890 Email@mail.com	Home Address Phone: (123) 456-7890 Fax: (123) 456-7890 Pager: (800) 888-8888
CEO	Phone: (123) 456-7890 Fax: (123) 456-7890 Email@mail.com	Home Address Phone: (123) 456-7890 Fax: (123) 456-7890 Pager: (800) 888-8888
Chairman	Phone: (123) 456-7890 Fax: (123) 456-7890 Email@mail.com	Home Address Phone: (123) 456-7890 Fax: (123) 456-7890 Pager: (800) 888-8888
President	Phone: (123) 456-7890 Fax: (123) 456-7890 Email@mail.com	Home Address Phone: (123) 456-7890 Fax: (123) 456-7890 Pager: (800) 888-8888
CFO	Phone: (123) 456-7890 Fax: (123) 456-7890 Email@mail.com	Home Address Phone: (123) 456-7890 Fax: (123) 456-7890 Pager: (800) 888-8888
BUYER'S LAW FIRM		
Address		
Partner	Phone: (123) 456-7890 Fax: (123) 456-7890 Email@mail.com	Home Address Phone: (123) 456-7890 Fax: (123) 456-7890 Pager: (800) 888-8888
Associate	Phone: (123) 456-7890 Fax: (123) 456-7890 Email@mail.com	Home Address Phone: (123) 456-7890 Fax: (123) 456-7890 Pager: (800) 888-8888

(continued)

BUYER'S ACCOUNTING FIRM

Address

Partner	Phone: (123) 456-7890	Home Address
	Fax: (123) 456-7890	Phone: (123) 456-7890
	Email@mail.com	Fax: (123) 456-7890
		Pager: (800) 888-8888
Associate	Phone: (123) 456-7890	Home Address
	Fax: (123) 456-7890	Phone: (123) 456-7890
	Email@mail.com	Fax: (123) 456-7890
		Pager: (800) 888-8888

BUYOUT FIRM

Address

Partner	Phone: (123) 456-7890	Home Address
	Fax: (123) 456-7890	Phone: (123) 456-7890
	Email@mail.com	Fax: (123) 456-7890
		Pager: (800) 888-8888
Associate	Phone: (123) 456-7890	Home Address
	Fax: (123) 456-7890	Phone: (123) 456-7890
	Email@mail.com	Fax: (123) 456-7890
		Pager: (800) 888-8888
Associate	Phone: (123) 456-7890	Home Address
	Fax: (123) 456-7890	Phone: (123) 456-7890
	Email@mail.com	Fax: (123) 456-7890
		Pager: (800) 888-8888

SELLER'S LAW FIRM

Address

Partner	Phone: (123) 456-7890	Home Address
	Fax: (123) 456-7890	Phone: (123) 456-7890
	Email@mail.com	Fax: (123) 456-7890
		Pager: (800) 888-8888
Associate	Phone: (123) 456-7890	Home Address
	Fax: (123) 456-7890	Phone: (123) 456-7890
	Email@mail.com	Fax: (123) 456-7890
		Pager: (800) 888-8888

(continued)

SELLER'S ACCOUNTING FIRM		
Address		
Partner	Phone: (123) 456-7890 Fax: (123) 456-7890 Email@mail.com	Home Address Phone: (123) 456-7890 Fax: (123) 456-7890 Pager: (800) 888-8888
Associate	Phone: (123) 456-7890 Fax: (123) 456-7890 Email@mail.com	Home Address Phone: (123) 456-7890 Fax: (123) 456-7890 Pager: (800) 888-8888
BANK 1		
Address		
Managing Director	Phone: (123) 456-7890 Fax: (123) 456-7890 Email@mail.com	Home Address Phone: (123) 456-7890 Fax: (123) 456-7890 Pager: (800) 888-8888
Associate	Phone: (123) 456-7890 Fax: (123) 456-7890 Email@mail.com	Home Address Phone: (123) 456-7890 Fax: (123) 456-7890 Pager: (800) 888-8888
BANK 2		
Managing Director	Phone: (123) 456-7890 Fax: (123) 456-7890 Email@mail.com	Home Address Phone: (123) 456-7890 Fax: (123) 456-7890 Pager: (800) 888-8888
Associate	Phone: (123) 456-7890 Fax: (123) 456-7890 Email@mail.com	Home Address Phone: (123) 456-7890 Fax: (123) 456-7890 Pager: (800) 888-8888
INVESTMENT BANK		
Managing Director	Phone: (123) 456-7890 Fax: (123) 456-7890 Email@mail.com	Home Address Phone: (123) 456-7890 Fax: (123) 456-7890 Pager: (800) 888-8888 (continued)

INVESTMENT BANK (continued)

| Principal | Phone: (123) 456-7890
Fax: (123) 456-7890
Email@mail.com | Home Address
Phone: (123) 456-7890
Fax: (123) 456-7890
Pager: (800) 888-8888 |
| Associate | Phone: (123) 456-7890
Fax: (123) 456-7890
Email@mail.com | Home Address
Phone: (123) 456-7890
Fax: (123) 456-7890
Pager: (800) 888-8888 |

Appendix G: Time and Responsibility Schedule

Code	Responsibility	Responsible Party	Complete Y/N	Status
F	Detailed Financial Statements by Month (FY '98 & '99 YTD)	TECHWAY, IG		Rec'd '98 and '99 Jan–Jun
F	Management Letters (or any qualitative text)	TECHWAY, IG		No formal mgmt. letters; requested description of adjustments from IG
F	Depreciation Schedules and Spending (FY '96, '97, '98, & '99 YTD)	TECHWAY, IG		IG is working on
F	Audited Financial Statements (FY '97, '98, & '99 six months), when available	TECHWAY, IG		Rec'd '98, '97 in DR (MS requesting copy of '97)
F	1999–2001 projections	TECHWAY, IG		Rec'd projections (work in progress)
F	Tax Returns (FY '96, '97, & '98)	TECHWAY, IG		Rec'd '95, '96, '97 (MS requesting 98)
F	Analysis of Accounts Receivable and other balance sheet items	TECHWAY, IG		1/99–5/99 balance sheets in DR, comparative A/R agings 6/98–6/99 in DR, many more schedules arrived this week, IG is working on
F	Schedule of bill rates by branch, business line, and/ or region	TECHWAY, IG		IG is working on
D	Customer Contracts (current and historical contracts); please include amendments, if any	TECHWAY		Rec'd some contracts for Staffing Solutions and Pro-Drivers. Need to request representative contracts; need to have discussion w/SP about contracts/ agreements in general.
D	Other Material Contracts (including license & employment agreements)	TECHWAY		Requesting Outstanding Warrant, Separation Agreement, Promissory Note
D	Insurance Policies	ABC		Information will be in DR on Thursday 9/16

Code	Responsibility	Responsible Party	Complete Y/N	Status
D	Lease Summaries, please note capital or operating	TECHWAY		Denver lease in DR. Request leases for NYC, Knoxville, & Dallas.
D	Patents, Trademarks, Service Marks, Copyrights, or Intellectual Property	TECHWAY		Rec'd documentation (I.5)
D	Description of any current or less than 3-year-old suits/disputes	TECHWAY		Rec'd legal update (I.2) and letter from T&K (I.2), KH reviewed: many outstanding legal items (mostly employee-related issues)—is this typical for a company of this size?
D	Description of any Pending or Threatened Litigation	TECHWAY		Rec'd legal update (I.2) and letter from T&K (I.2), KH reviewed (see above)
D	Any Agreements with Bankers, Brokers, Finders, or Consultants	TECHWAY		Rec'd BT engagement letter (I.6), KH reviewed; Niven, Farrington & Kiley agreements in DR (requesting)
D	Fully Diluted Share Ownership Table	TECHWAY		Rec'd summary options (G.14) and shareholder list as of 7/31/99 (A.5)
G	Board of Directors packages and minutes, last 24 months	TECHWAY		MS requesting from SP (not on our original request list)
G	Customer Comments/Audit/Quality Feedback	TECHWAY, ISP		IGS conducting blind sponsor interviews
G	Publicity/Articles	TECHWAY		In progress
G	Detailed Systems Description & Review	TECHWAY		Overview given during mgmt. presentation, more info at Dallas presentation
G	Interviews with staffing industry research analysts	TECHWAY		MS to do
G	Interviews with eSolutions industry research analysts	TECHWAY		KH to do
HR	Employee Handbook	TECHWAY		As of 1/98 in DR
HR	Policies & Procedures Manual	TECHWAY		Internal Operating Systems Procedures in DR

Code	Responsibility	Responsible Party	Complete Y/N	Status
HR	Newsletters, etc.	TECHWAY		Covered in Dallas
HR	Payroll, please indicate title and department or other headcount proxy (by business line, function, region)	TECHWAY, Shelly		IG is working on
HR	Stock Option Plan, if any	TECHWAY, Shelly		Rec'd various option plans (G.14), Shelly reviewing
HR	Pension Plan/Deferred Comp Plan, if any	TECHWAY, Shelly		Rec'd deferred comp plan (G.12), Shelly reviewing
HR	Detailed Organizational Charts	TECHWAY		Rec'd current legal entity structure (I.2)
HR	Results of Recent Inspections (OSHA, EEOC, etc.)	TECHWAY, Shelly		Insurance DD
HR	Workers' Compensation Ratings	TECHWAY, Shelly		W. Peterson Workers' Comp Presentation in DR
HR	Hiring & Employment & Turnover by division, "level," team etc. ('96, '97, '98, '99 YTD)	TECHWAY		*Discuss*
HR	Detail of current benefit plans and costs per employee (include wage and benefit rates)	TECHWAY		401(k) plans in DR; schedule of benefit plans in DR; staff training & development plan in DR
HR	Recruiting process and employee retention	TECHWAY		Site visit
M	Schedule of management carry distribution, planned executive compensation packages, planned employee stock option plan, existing employment agreements	TECHWAY		Requested info from AR
M	Legal structure of business	TECHWAY		Requested info from AR
M	Business descriptions of XYZ acquisitions with status of transaction	TECHWAY		Requested info from AR; rec'd strategic info
M	LOIs for XYZ acquisitions, transaction structure detail	TECHWAY		Requested info from AR

Code	Responsibility	Responsible Party	Complete Y/N	Status
M	Financial statements and projections for XYZ acquisitions	TECHWAY		Rec'd updated spreadsheet from Andrew on 9/7

Codes:
F: Financial Information
D: Documents
G: General
R: References
I: Interviews
V: Visits
HR: Human Resources/Organization
M: Management
IG: Investor Group

Appendix H: Due Diligence Checklist

Table of Contents

Industry and Company Overview

Industry Classification
1. Client definition/Form 10-K
2. Business section of prospectuses

3. Trade association publications/data
4. Manufacturing process or principal areas of value added
5. Production—sales cycle
6. Customer profile
7. SIC code
8. Security analysts' reports

Growth Trends and Prospects; Size and Profitability of Other Firms in Each Industry Segment

1. Industry's performance and trends
   a. Industry's historical performance
      i.   Rate of increase in sales and earnings
      ii. Market share growth, primary and secondary demand
      iii. Consistency among companies
      iv. Comparison of the industry's performance with that of other industries
      v.   Comparison of the company's performance with that of its industry
      vi. Determination of the cause of any company variations
      vii. Financial market acceptance, including credit ratings
   b. Stability of companies within industry
      i.   Turnover of competitors
      ii. Volatility of earnings and access to financial markets
      iii. Credit ratings changes
      iv. Mergers, acquisitions, and consolidations
      v.   Bankruptcies and reorganizations
   c. Trends within industry and potential impact upon the company's future operations. Examples of such trends include:
      i.   Scarcity of raw materials
      ii. New regulations
      iii. Shift in product mix or demand
      iv. Increase or erosion in profit margins
      v.   Increased competition or demand from abroad
2. Structure of competition in the industry
   a. Industry structure
   b. Identity of principal competitors and share of market
      i.   The company's market share and position within the industry
      ii. Elements of competition
         (a) Price

        (b) Quality and features
        (c) Delivery or service
        (d) Engineering
        (e) Advertising
    iii. Shifts of competitive structure within the industry
        (a) Market share changes
        (b) Price reductions
        (c) Extended credit terms
        (d) Producing and holding merchandise
  c. Susceptibility to changes in economic environment
    i. Product substitution or alternatives potential
    ii. Cost/price relationships
    iii. Predominant suppliers
    iv. Likelihood of forward or backward integration
3. Industry Business Characteristics
  a. Research and development
    i. Dependence on R&D and technology
    ii. Product or process successes by others
    iii. The company's success compared with competitors'
    iv. Importance of patents and cases of infringement
    v. Rate of R&D expenditures compared with norm
    vi. Potential obsolescence due to:
        (a) New equipment or processes
        (b) Technology
        (c) Products
  b. Marketing and distribution
    i. Method of distribution and control of these channels
    ii. Advertising or promotional expenditures
    iii. Margin structure throughout the distribution chain
  c. Manufacturing process
  d. Labor relations
    i. Organization status
    ii. Strike history
    iii. Wage and benefit trends
    iv. Availability and skill level
  e. Seasonality or cyclicality of industry

Company's Relative Position in the Industry
1. Relative sales and earnings levels and growth rates

2. Market shares and positions
3. Company strengths and weaknesses vis-à-vis relevant competitive factors in the industry
4. Company's geographic coverage and customer type
   a. Analyze stability
   b. Demographic trends
5. Reputation and product recognition

Products

Major Individual Products and Product Lines
1. Sales—unit and dollar volume
   a. Five-year historical and current interim figures
   b. Projections
      i. Management
      ii. Independent industry analysts
   c. Product catalog and price list
2. Quality and feature comparisons
3. Pricing
   a. Seasonality or cyclicality
   b. History of discounting and price reductions
   c. Ability to pass along cost increases
   d. Preferred customer discounts
4. Product life cycle
   a. Pending obsolescence due to:
      i.   New equipment or processes
      ii. New products
      iii. Underlying demand or demographic shift
5. Seasonality or cyclicality of product demand
6. Substitutes and complementary products

Product Development
1. Resources and requirements as compared to the industry
2. Historical and projected R&D expenditures
3. Feasible studies on marketing and production (i.e., is the technology marketable?)
4. Patents
   a. Licensing agreements
   b. Actual or potential cases of infringement

Earnings
1. Profit contribution by product line
   a. Five-year historical and current interim figures
   b. Projections
      i. Management
      ii. Independent industry analysts
2. Stability and consistency of earnings
3. Earnings growth
   a. Acquisitions
   b. Internal growth

Demand and Customer Analysis

List of Major Customers
1. Industry position of customers
2. Dollar size of sales
3. Customer turnover and loyalty
4. Domestic vs. international breakdown

Purchase Decision
1. Price
2. Quality/features
3. Engineering
4. Customer decision process
5. Brand and trademarks (i.e., are the company's name and trade-mark well known?)

Marketing

Marketing Focus (e.g., advertising, packaging, delivery)
1. Advertising
   a. Expenditure relative to industry
   b. Importance to marketing strategy
2. Design and packaging
3. Discounting
4. Trade shows
5. Customer contact method
6. Marketing expense

Marketing Staff
1. List and evaluate
2. Structure of incentive system
3. Branch offices, warehouses, service facilities

Distribution

Channels
1. In-house capability
   a. Transportation
   b. Order processing
2. Retail operations
   a. Layout
   b. Number of locations and their geographic distribution
3. Dependence on outside channels
   a. Flexibility of distribution channel
   b. Margins along distribution chain

Production

Description of Processes
1. Nature of manufacturing processes
   a. Batch or line process
   b. Labor or capital intensive
   c. Wage structure and demands
      i. Unionization and history of labor relations
      ii. Recent or pending strike activity
   d. Abundance, age, and educational level of workforce
   e. Licenses or patents
2. Inventory control
   a. Breakdown by finished goods, work in process, and raw materials
   b. Warehousing
3. Flow of materials and plant efficiency (and compared to industry)
4. Quality control
5. Maintenance procedure and expense
6. Hazards and insurance
7. Internal vs. outside services for various production stages

Raw Materials and Other Inputs
1. Cost
   a. Trends and variability
      i. Extent of substitutability
      ii. Ability to pass-through cost increases
2. Competition for and control of supply
   a. Same industry vs. outside
   b. Major suppliers
      i. Contracts
      ii. Financial condition of suppliers (particularly foreign)
      iii. Dependability
   c. Purchasing arrangements
3. Subcontractors for parts or subassemblies

Facilities and Equipment
1. Condition and age
   a. Planned capital expenditures
   b. Capacity utilization
      i. Historical
      ii. Planned
   c. Facilities
      i. Owned vs. leased facilities
      ii. General-use or specialized capacity
      iii. Factors preventing capacity expansion
         (a) Zoning
         (b) Production process
         (c) Access
2. Maintenance expense
   a. Expected replacement near term
   b. Expected replacement long term
3. Power, water, and waste disposal
   a. Availability
   b. Adequacy

Litigation

Material and Pending Litigation
1. Potential exposure
   a. Consequences to operations

b. Consequences to financial condition
2. Insurance

Accounting Responsibility and Function

Quality and Size of Financial, Accounting, and Internal Audit Staff—Reporting System
1. Size of internal financial staff
2. Do they have/require internal auditors?
3. Review internal audit reports

Existence of Ongoing Records
1. Description
2. Equipment used to keep records
3. Accuracy of interim financials

Differences between Book and Tax Records

Budgeting System
1. Integration of costing and financial records
2. Analysis of costing system
3. Replacement cost accounting

Frequency and Adequacy of Physical Counts
1. Review with external auditors

Variations in Company's Accounting Policies from Industry Norms
1. Revenue recognition
2. Inventory
3. Replacement cost accounting
4. Depreciation
5. Treatment of foreign exchange gains or losses

Credit Control Procedures
1. Any recent changes in customer credit procedures?
2. Review credit manuals

Accountants
1. Status of audits
2. Accountants' management letter

a. Suggested improvements
b. Formal reviews and changes during last five years

SEC or FASB Opinions or Payments
1. Pooling issues
2. Revenue recognition

Insurance
1. Review pertinent policies

Profitability

Cost Accounting
1. Major elements
2. Overhead history
3. Allocation

Sales
1. Returns and allowances
2. Recognition of income—sale or delivery
   a. Installment sales
   b. Affiliates
3. Intercompany sales and profits
4. Consolidation policies

Profitability Forecast
1. Factors most likely to affect estimates
2. Change in financing structure and effect on profits
3. Overhead or corporate expense

Other Sources of Income
1. Royalties
2. Rents

Treatment of Minority Interest

Asset Management

Inventory
1. Inventory valuation and reserve structure
2. Breakdown work-in-progress, raw materials, and finished goods

Receivables
1. Aging schedule
2. Bad debt allowance

Prepaids
1. Identification
2. Valuation

Other Assets
1. Notes receivable
2. Intangible assets
   a. Identification
   b. Amortization

Fixed Assets
1. Book value
2. Replacement cost
3. Original cost and/or adjustments for purchase accounting
4. Potential write-offs
5. Depreciation
   a. Average life
   b. Type of depreciation
      i. Book vs. tax
   c. Accelerated to account for obsolescence
6. List of properties

Current Liabilities
1. Credit by major vendors
2. Discounts received or lost
3. Provisions for outstanding liabilities and contingencies

Other Liabilities
1. Penalties
2. Litigation
3. Additional taxes
4. Contingent
5. Pension-funding items

Capital Structure

Long-Term Debt
1. Amount outstanding
2. Rates
3. Maturity—prepayment provisions and penalties
4. Debt ratings
5. Covenants
   a. Coverage—interest, fixed charges, assets
   b. Principle repayments
   c. Ratio requirements
6. Convertibility
7. Events of default

Short-Term Debt—Lines of Credit
1. Interest expenses during start-up
2. Availability and draw-down
   a. Current
   b. Historical
   c. Cost

Lease Obligations
1. Capital leases
2. Operating leases

Preferred or Hybrid Securities
1. Review documents
2. Redemption features
3. Change of control provisions

Shareowners' Equity
1. Paid-in
2. Retained earnings
3. Treasury stock

Cash Flow

Working Capital Requirement
1. Relationship among inventories, receivables, and payables

2. Minimum cash required to run business
3. Ability to convert nonproductive assets into cash for working capital

Capital Expenditures
1. Desired
2. Required

Depreciation and Amortization
1. Adequacy of estimated useful life of equipment being written off
2. Goodwill

Taxes
1. Deferred taxes: revenue recognition, depreciation
2. Reserves for prior year's taxes
3. States in which returns are filed
4. Treatment and availability of investment tax credit
5. Availability of Net Operating Losses (NOL)
6. Allocation
7. Foreign vs. domestic
8. Puerto Rico

Dividend Policy and Restrictions
1. Dividend policy
2. Dividend restrictions

Management

List Key Personnel—Salaries and Titles
1. Turnover and experience
2. Depth of management
3. Recruiting and training
4. Affiliations

Compensation
1. Wage scale, promotion, and review
2. Employee contracts and service agreements
3. Incentive awards (e.g., stock options plans, earn-outs)

4. Insurance (life and medical), autos, personal loans, and vacations
5. Deferred

Board of Directors
1. Age and service
2. Other directorships and affiliations
3. Meetings—review frequency and substance
4. List of committees and assignments
5. Insider or related-party transactions

Shareholders

Security Issues
1. Rights of each class
2. Stock options
3. Stockholder agreements

Shareholders
1. Principal holders of various classes
2. Geographic distribution
3. Institutions
4. Unidentified

Securities Convertible into Common and Major Holders Thereof

Industrial Relations

Employees
1. Number of employees
2. Source of labor
3. Skilled vs. unskilled

Competition for Labor
1. Turnover
2. Ability to vary workforce

Unions
1. History of strikes
2. Next scheduled bargaining

Work Conditions
1. Accident frequency
2. Last OSHA review
3. Morale—grievances and suits
4. Wage scale and promotion review and policies

Compensation and Benefits
1. Compensation structure
   a. Frequency
   b. Overtime
   c. Profit sharing
   d. Vacations and holidays
   e. Guarantees and indemnities
2. Pension plan
   a. Level of benefits
   b. Extent of funding of accrued pension benefits
      i. Unfunded past service liability
      ii. History of expenditures
   c. Last revision
   d. Transferability
   e. Effect on profitability
3. Life insurance and medical benefits

Document Checklist

I.   List of Participants (business and home address, phone number, facsimile number)
     A. Client team
     B. Investor team
     C. Attorneys
     D. Accountants
     E. Lenders
     F. Other involved parties
II. Financials
     A. 10K—audited last five years

B. 10Q—unaudited stub period
C. Annual reports
D. Registration statements (filed or pending?)
E. 8K reports on recent unscheduled material events or corporate changes
F. Five-year plan with assumptions
G. Historical budgets
H. Policy manual
I. Proxies
J. Accountant letters
K. Pension plans including latest actuarial evaluation
L. Filings unique to industry (e.g., bank call reports, insurance convention blanks)

III. Product Lines
A. Sales and earnings reports
B. Price lists
C. Market size and share estimates

IV. Industry Publications

V. Legal Documents
A. Articles of incorporation and bylaws
B. Domicile of major operations (name and address of subsidiaries)
C. Indenture agreements
D. Corporate history
   1. Name changes
   2. Ownership structure
   3. Acquisitions
E. Patents, trademarks, and copyrights
F. Licensing agreements
   1. Distribution
   2. Technology
   3. Franchises
   4. Royalty agreements—basis, expiration, renewal, and cancellation
G. Government contracts
H. Noncompete restrictions
I. Warranty and service agreements
J. Assets pledged or notes cosigned
K. Litigation or suits in progress or pending

L. Relationship with financial and business community
    1. Institutional lenders
    2. Investment bankers
    3. Analysts and broker presentations
M. Union contracts

Appendix I: Directory of Private Equity Investment Firms

It's important to identify a private equity investment firm whose interests match your transaction. Some firms only work on very large deals, and many venture capital firms only invest in technology companies and do not back management buyouts. Fortunately, the Internet has made searching for firms much easier, and with this list I've tried to provide you with the Web addresses of the various firms. Review those Web sites carefully before you send out any material. For each firm listed I have included the amount of capital and made some annotations about its focus, which can help you initially identify a firm that may best match your needs.

This list of firms is not by any means a complete list. There are hundreds of firms, and if I tried to list them all, the list would comprise the whole book. While a majority of the firms listed have multiple office locations, for the most part, I have included only their primary office location, so check their Web site to see if they have an office close to you. You'll be able to get detailed personal contact information from most sites as well.

If you are an investor and I left your firm off this list, or an investor who would have preferred to have been left off the list, I apologize.

This list, and additional updates and links, can also be found online at www.buyoutbook.com.

ABS Capital Partners
1 South Street
Baltimore, MD 21202
Phone: 410-895-4400
Fax: 410-895-4380
www.abscapital.com
Capital: More than $900 million
Contact: Don Hebb, Tim Weglicki

> Affiliated with Alex Brown (a unit of Deutsch Bank); technology and health care focus.

Acacia Venture Partners
101 California Street
Suite 3160
San Francisco, CA 94111

Phone: 415-433-4200
Fax: 415-433-4250
www.acaciavp.com
Capital: More than $200 million
Contacts: Harold Friedman, Sage Givens

Accel Partners
428 University Avenue
Palo Alto, CA 94301
Phone: 650-614-4800
Fax: 650-614-4880
www.accel.com
Capital: More than $2 billion
Contact: Jim Breyer

> Leading technology investment firm with focus on telecom. Transformation fund in partnership with KKR (Accel-KKR).

Advanced Technology Ventures
281 Winter Street, Suite 350
Waltham, MA 02451
Phone: 781-290-0707
Fax: 781-684-0045
www.atvcapital.com
Capital: More than $300 million

Advantage Capital Partners
909 Poydras Street, Suite 2230
New Orleans, LA 70112
Phone: 504-522-4850
Fax: 504-522-4950
www.advantagecap.com
Capital: Approximately $200 million

Advent International
75 State Street
Boston, MA 02109
Phone: 617-951-9400
Fax: 617-951-0566
www.adventinternational.com
Capital: More than $3.5 billion

> Leading global investment firm with large domestic and European capabilities.

Agio Capital Partners I, L.P.
US Bank Place, Suite 4600

601 Second Avenue South
Minneapolis, MN 55402
Phone: 612-339-8408
Fax: 612-349-4232
www.agiocap@aol.com
Capital: Approximately $42 million

Allied Capital Corporation
1919 Pennsylvania Avenue, 3rd Floor
Washington, DC 20006-3434
Phone: 202-331-1112
Fax: 202-659-2053
www.alliedcapital.com
Capital: Approximately $800 million
Contacts: Cabell Williams, Gary Truscott, Tom Westbrook

Large mezzanine debt investor with equity capabilities.

Alta Communications
One Post Office Square, Suite 3800
Boston, MA 02109
Phone: 617-482-8020
Fax: 617-482-1944
Capital: More than $400 million

ARCH Venture Partners
8725 West Higgins Road, Suite 290
Chicago, IL 60631
Phone: 773-380-6600
Fax: 773-380-6606
www.archventure.com
Capital: More than $300 million

Primarily early stage venture firm.

Argentum Group
The Chrysler Building
405 Lexington Avenue
New York, NY 10174
Phone: 212-949-6262
Fax: 212-949-8294
Capital: Approximately $20 million

Arlington Partners
600 New Hampshire Avenue
6th Floor

Washington, DC 20037
Phone: 202-337-7500
Fax: 202-337-7525
Capital: More than $450 million
Contact: Paul Stern, Jeffrey Freed

Austin Ventures
114 W. 7th Street, Suite 1300
Austin, TX 78701
Phone: 512-485-1900
Fax: 512-476-3952
www.austinventures.com
Capital: More than $1 billion
      Large Internet and telecom investment firm.

Bain Capital, Inc.
Two Copley Plaza
Boston, MA 02116
Phone: 617-572-3000
Fax: 617-572-3274
www.baincap.com
Capital: More than $2 billion

Baker Capital Corp.
540 Madison Avenue, 29th Floor
New York, NY 10022
Phone: 212-848-2000
Fax: 212-486-0660
www.bakercapital.com
Capital: More than $400 million

BancBoston Capital/BancBoston Ventures
175 Federal Street, 10th Floor
Boston, MA 02110
Phone: 617-434-2509
Fax: 617-434-1153
www.BKB.com
Capital: More than $2 billion
      Large equity investor affiliated with the commercial bank in Boston.
      Many of the large banks such as Chase Manhattan, First Union, and
      BankAmerica have equity groups.

Banc of America Capital Corporation
100 North Tryon Street, 10th Floor
Charlotte, NC 28255
Phone: 704-386-8063

Fax: 704-386-6432
Capital: More than $250 million

BankAmerica Ventures
950 Tower Lane, Suite 700
Foster City, CA 94404
Phone: 650-378-6000
Fax: 650-378-6040
www.bankamerica.com
Capital: More than $400 million

Bankers Trust Capital Corporation
130 Liberty Street, 25th Floor
New York, NY 10006
Phone: 212-250-5563
Fax: 212-669-1749
www.bankerstrust.com
Capital: More than $200 million

Battery Ventures
20 William Street, Suite 200
Wellesley, MA 02481
Phone: 781-577-1000
Fax: 781-577-1001
www.battery.com
Capital: More than $800 million

Large communications and Internet venture investor.

Behrman Capital, Inc.
126 East 56th Street
New York, NY 10022
Phone: 212-980-6500
Fax: 212-980-7024
Capital: More than $1.5 billion
Contact: Grant Behrman, Bill Matthes

Benchmark Capital
2480 Sandhill Road, Suite 200
Menlo Park, CA 94025
Phone: 650-854-8180
Fax: 650-854-8183
www.benchmark.com
Capital: More than $1.5 billion

Leading venture firm famous for some huge Internet hits such as eBay.

Berkshire Partners LLC
One Boston Place
Boston, MA 02108
Phone: 617-227-0050
Fax: 617-227-6105
www.berkshirepartners.com
Capital: Approximately $1.6 billion

Bessemer Venture Partners
83 Walnut Street
Wellesley Hills, MA 02481
Phone: 781-237-6050
Fax: 781-235-7068
www.bessemervp.com
Capital: More than $300 million

Blue Chip Venture Company
1100 Chiquita Center
250 East Fifth Street
Cincinnati, OH 45202
Phone: 513-723-2300
Fax: 513-723-2306
www.bcvc.com
Capital: More than $150 million

Blue Water Capital, LLC
8300 Greensboro Drive, Suite 440
McLean, VA 22101
Phone: 703-448-8821
Fax: 703-448-1849
www.bluewatercapital.com
Capital: More than $75 million
Contact: Reid Miles

Boston Capital Ventures
Old City Hall
45 School Street
Boston, MA 02108
Phone: 617-227-6550
Fax: 617-227-3847
www.bcv.com
Capital: More than $100 million

Boston Ventures Management, Inc.
One Federal Street, 10th Floor

Boston, MA 02110
Phone: 617-350-1500
Fax: 617-350-1572
Capital: More than $500 million

Bradford Ventures Ltd.
1 Rockefeller Plaza, Suite 1722
New York, NY 10020
Phone: 212-218-6900
Fax: 212-218-6901
Capital: Approximately $100 million

Brantley Partners
20600 Chagrin Boulevard, Suite 1150
Cleveland, OH 44122
Phone: 216-283-4800
Fax: 216-283-5324
Capital: More than $150 million

Brentwood Associates
11150 Santa Monica Boulevard, Suite 1200
Los Angeles, CA 90025
Phone: 310-477-6611
www.brentwoodvc.com
Capital: More than $800 million
Contacts: Bill Barnum, David Wong

   Longstanding Los Angeles–based buyout and growth equity investor.

Brinson Partners, Inc.
209 S. LaSalle Street
Chicago, IL 60604-1295
Phone: 312-220-7100
Fax: 312-220-7110
www.brinsonpartners.com
Capital: Approximately $7.6 billion

   Large fund adviser and equity investment firm.

Brockway Moran & Partners
225 NE Mizer Boulevard
Boca Raton, FL 33432
Phone: 561-750-2000
Fax: 561-750-2001
Capital: More than $300 million

Brown, McMillan & Co., LLC
930 Montgomery Street, Suite 301
San Francisco, CA 94133
Phone: 415-273-7160
Fax: 415-273-7171
www.brownmcmillan.com
Capital: More than $40 million
Contact: Cabot Brown

The Cambria Group
1600 El Camino Real, Suite 155
Menlo Park, CA 94025
Phone: 650-329-8600
Fax: 650-329-8601
www.cambriagroup.com
Capital: More than $10 million
Contact: Lew Davies

Canaan Partners
105 Rowayton Avenue
Rowayton, CT 06853
Phone: 203-855-0400
Fax: 203-854-9117
www.canaan.com
Capital: Approximately $600 million

Capital Resource Partners
85 Merrimac Street, Suite 200
Boston, MA 02114
Phone: 617-723-9000
Fax: 617-723-9819
www.crp.com
Capital: More than $800 million

Capital Southwest Corporation
12900 Preston Road, Suite 700
Dallas, TX 75230
Phone: 972-233-8242
Fax: 972-233-7362
www.capitalsouthwest.com
Capital: More than $20 million

Cardinal Health Partners, L.P.
221 Nassau Street
Princeton, NJ 08542

Phone: 609-924-6452
Fax: 609-683-0174
www.cardinalhealthpartners.com
Capital: More than $50 million

Health care industry focus.

The Carlyle Group
1001 Pennsylvania Avenue N.W.
Washington, DC
Capital: More than $10 billion
Contact: David Rubenstein, Ed Mathias

The Centennial Funds
1428 15th Street
Denver, CO 80202-1318
Phone: 303-405-7500
Fax: 303-405-7575
www.centennial.com
Capital: More than $700 million

CenterPoint Venture Partners
Two Galleria Tower
13455 Noel Road, Suite 1670
Dallas, TX 75240
Phone: 972-702-1101
Fax: 972-702-1103
www.cpventures.com
Capital: More than $150 million

Charles River Ventures
1000 Winter Street, Suite 3300
Waltham, MA 02451
Phone: 781-487-7060
Fax: 781-487-7065
www.crv.com
Capital: More than $500 million

Chase Capital Partners
380 Madison Avenue, 12th Floor
New York, NY 10017-2070
Phone: 212-622-3100
Fax: 212-622-3101
www.chasecapital.com
Capital: Approximately $10 billion

Contact: Jeff Walker
> The most prominent of the in-bank equity investors.

Chisholm Private Capital Partners, L.P.
10830 E. 45th Street, Suite 307
Tulsa, OK 74146
Phone: 918-663-3500
Fax: 918-663-1140
www.chisholmvc.com
Capital: More than $10 million

Code Hennessy & Simmons LLC
10 South Wacker Drive, Suite 3175
Chicago, IL 60606
Phone: 312-876-1840
Fax: 312-876-3854
www.chsonline.com
Capital: Approximately $1.3 billion

Colorado Venture Management
4845 Pearl East Circle, Suite 300
Boulder, CO 80303
Phone: 303-440-4055
Fax: 303-440-4636
Capital: Approximately $15 million

Columbia Capital
201 N. Union Street, #300
Alexandria, VA 22314
Phone: 703-519-2000
Fax: 703-519-3904
www.colcap.com
Contact: Jim Fleming, Harry Hopper
Capital: More than $1 billion

Commerce Capital, L.P.
611 Commerce Street, Suite 2602
Nashville, TN 37203
Phone: 615-244-1432
Fax: 615-242-1407
www.commercecap.com
Capital: More than $10 million

Cornerstone Equity Investors, LLC
717 Fifth Avenue, 11th Floor

New York, NY 10022
Phone: 212-753-0901
Fax: 212-826-6798
www.cornerstone-equity.com
Capital: Approximately $1 billion

Cravey, Green & Wahlen Inc.
12 Piedmont Center, Suite 210
Atlanta, GA 30305
Phone: 404-816-3255
Fax: 404-816-3258
Capital: More than $250 million

Crescendo Venture Management, LLC
800 LaSalle Avenue, Suite 2250
Minneapolis, MN 55402
Phone: 612-607-2800
Fax: 612-607-2801
www.crescendoventures.com
Capital: More than $400 million

Crosspoint Venture Partners
2925 Woodside Road
Woodside, CA 94062
Phone: 650-851-7600
Fax: 650-851-7661
www.cpvp.com
Capital: More than $500 million

The Crossroads Group
1717 Main Street, Suite 2500
Dallas, TX 75201
Phone: 214-698-2777
Fax: 214-698-2778
www.crossroadsgroup.com
Capital: More than $1.5 billion

Darby Overseas Investments Ltd.
1133 Connecticut Avenue, N.W.
Suite 200
Washington, DC 20036
Phone: 202-872-0500
Fax: 202-872-1816
Capital: Approximately $150 million

Delphi Ventures
3000 Sand Hill Road
Building 1, Suite 135
Menlo Park, CA 94025
Phone: 650-854-9650
Fax: 650-854-2961
www.delphiventures.com
Capital: More than $300 million

Desai Capital Management, Inc.
540 Madison Avenue, 36th Floor
New York, NY 10022
Phone: 212-838-9191
Fax: 212-838-9807
www.desaicapital.com

DLJ Merchant Banking Partners
277 Park Avenue, 19th Floor
New York, NY 10172
Phone: 212-892-3000
Fax: 212-892-7552
www.dlj.com
Capital: Approximately $4 billion equity; $2 billion mezzanine

Draper International
50 California Street, Suite 2925
San Francisco, CA 94111
Phone: 415-616-4050
Fax: 415-616-4060
www.draperintl.com
Capital: More than $50 million

E. M. Warburg, Pincus & Co., LLC
466 Lexington Avenue
New York, NY 10017-3146
Phone: 212-878-9358
Fax: 212-878-6167
www.warburgpincus.com
One of the largest and most long-standing equity firms.
Capital: More than $10 billion

Edison Venture Fund
1009 Lenox Drive #4
Lawrenceville, NJ 08648
Phone: 609-896-1900

Fax: 609-896-0066
www.edisonventure.com
Capital: More than $200 million

Enterprise Partners
7979 Ivanhoe Avenue, Suite 550
La Jolla, CA 92037
858-454-8833
Fax: 858-454-2489
www.ent.com
Capital: More than $400 million

Equus Capital Corporation
2929 Allen Parkway, 25th Floor
Houston, TX 77019
Phone: 713-529-0900
Fax: 713-529-9545
Capital: More than $100 million

Evercore Partners Inc.
65 East 55th Street
New York, NY 10022
Phone: 212-857-3100
Fax: 212-857-3101
Capital: More than $500 million

FBR Technology Venture Partners, L. P.
1001 19th Street North
Arlington, VA 22209
Phone: 703-312-9500
Fax: 703-469-1002
www.fbr.com
Capital: More than $600 million
Contacts: Hooks Johnston, Gene Riechers

Fenway Partners Inc.
152 West 57th Street, 59th Floor
New York, NY 10019
Phone: 212-698-4000
Fax: 212-581-1205
Capital: More than $200 million

First Analysis Corporation
233 S. Wacker Drive, Suite 9500
Chicago, IL 60606

Phone: 312-258-1400
Fax: 312-258-0334
www.firstanalysisvc.com
Capital: More than $300 million

First Union Capital Partners
One First Union Center, 5th Floor
Charlotte, NC 28288-0732
Phone: 704-374-4806
Fax: 704-374-6711
Capital: More than $1 billion
Contact: Jim Cook, Bob Calton

Flatiron Partners
257 Park Avenue, 12th Floor
New York, NY 10010
Phone: 212-228-3800
Fax: 212-228-0552
www.flatironpartners.com
Capital: More than $500 million

Fleet Equity Partners
50 Kennedy Plaza
Providence, RI 02903
Phone: 401-278-6770
Fax: 401-278-6387
www.fleetequitypartners.com
Capital: More than $1 billion

Florida Capital Ventures, Ltd.
880 Riverside Plaza
100 West Kennedy Boulevard
Tampa, FL 33602
Phone: 813-229-2294
Fax: 813-229-2028
Capital: More than $300 million

Francisco Partners
One Maritime Plaza #2500
San Francisco, CA 94111
Phone: 415-277-2900
Fax: 415-986-1320
www.franciscopartners.com
Capital: Approximately $1.8 billion
Contact: Dave Stanton, Neil Garfinkel

Friedman, Fleischer & Lowe, LLC
One Maritime Plaza, Suite 1000
San Francisco, CA 94111
Phone: 415-445-9850
Fax: 415-445-9851
www.fflpventures.com
Capital: More than $350 million
Contact: Spencer Fleischer

Frontenac Company
135 S. LaSalle Street, Suite 3800
Chicago, IL 60603
Phone: 312-368-0044
Fax: 312-368-9520
www.frontenac.com
Capital: More than $300 million

GE Capital Equity Group
120 Long Ridge Road
Stamford, CT 06927
Phone: 203-357-3100
      800-976-0675
Fax: 203-357-3945
Capital: More than $250 million

Greenwich Street Capital Partners, Inc.
388 Greenwich Street, 36th Floor
New York, NY 10013
Phone: 212-816-8600
Fax: 212-816-0166
Capital: More than $1 billion

Greylock Management Corporation
One Federal Street, 26th Floor
Boston, MA 02110-2065
Phone: 617-423-5525
Fax: 617-482-0059
www.greylock.com
Capital: More than $500 million

    One of the most successful and enduring venture firms.

GTCR Golder Rauner, LLC
6100 Sears Tower
Chicago, IL 60606-6402

Phone: 312-382-2200
Fax: 312-382-2201
www.gtcr.com
Capital: More than $2.5 billion
    Long-standing Chicago-based buildup equity firm.

Halifax Group, LLC
702 Oberlin Road, Suite 150
Raleigh, NC 27529
Phone: 919-743-2525
        888-749-3067
Fax: 919-743-2526
Capital: Approximately $250 million
Contact: David Dupree

Hambrecht & Quist Technology Partners, L.P.
1 Bush Street, Suite 1200
San Francisco, CA 94104
Phone: 415-439-3000
Fax: 415-439-3818
www.hamquist.com
Capital: More than $600 million

Hancock Park Associates
1925 Century Park East, #810
Los Angeles, CA 90067
Phone: 310-553-5550
Capital: More than $20 million
Contact: Mike Fourticq

Harbourvest Partners, LLC
One Financial Center, 44th Floor
Boston, MA 02111
Phone: 617-348-3707
Fax: 617-350-0305
www.hvpllc.com
Capital: Approximately $5.3 billion

Harvest Partners, Inc.
230 Park Avenue, 33rd Floor
New York, NY 10017-1216
Phone: 212-838-7776
Fax: 212-593-0734
Capital: Approximately $600 million

HealthCare Ventures, LLC
44 Nassau Street
Princeton, NJ 08542
Phone: 609-430-3900
Fax: 609-430-9525
www.hcven.com
Capital: Approximately $475 million

Hellman and Friedman
One Maritime Plaza, 12th Floor
San Francisco, CA 94111
Phone: 415-788-5111
Fax: 415-788-0176
www.HF.com
Capital: More than $12 billion

Hicks, Muse, Tate & Furst, Inc.
200 Crescent Court, Suite 1600
Dallas, TX 75201
Phone: 214-740-7300
Fax: 214-720-7888
www.hmtf.com
Capital: More than $5 billion

Highland Capital Partners
Two International Place
Boston, MA 02110
Phone: 617-531-1500
Fax: 617-531-1550
www.hcp.com
Capital: Approximately $500 million

Houston Partners
P.O. Box 2023
401 Louisiana, 8th Floor
Houston, TX 77252-2023
Phone: 713-222-8600
Fax: 713-222-8932
Capital: More than $20 million

Intersouth Partners
P.O. Box 13546
Research Triangle Park, NC 27709
Phone: 919-481-6889
Fax: 919-481-0225

www.intersouth.com
Capital: More than $60 million

InterWest Partners
3000 Sand Hill Road
Building 3, Suite 225
Menlo Park, CA 94025-7112
Phone: 650-854-8585
Fax: 650-854-4706
www.interwest.com
Capital: More than $800 million

IVP—Institutional Venture Partners
3000 Sand Hill Road
Building 2, Suite 290
Menlo Park, CA 94025
Phone: 650-854-0132
Fax: 650-854-5762
www.ivp.com
Capital: More than $1 billion

J. H. Whitney & Company
177 Broad Street, 15th Floor
Stamford, CT 06901
Phone: 203-973-1400
Fax: 203-973-1422
www.jhwhitney.com
Capital: More than $2 billion
Contacts: Peter Castleman and Bill Laverack

Kansas City Equity Partners
233 West 47th Street
Kansas City, MO 64112
Phone: 816-960-1771
Fax: 816-960-1777
www.kcep.com
Capital: More than $75 million

Kelso & Company
320 Park Avenue, 24th Floor
New York, NY 10022
Phone: 212-751-3939
Fax: 212-223-2379
Capital: More than $2 million

Key Equity Capital Corporation
127 Public Square, 6th Floor
Cleveland, OH 44114
Phone: 216-689-5776
Fax: 216-689-3204
Capital: Approximately $125 million

Kinetic Ventures, LLC
Two Wisconsin Circle, Suite 620
Chevy Chase, MD 20815
Phone: 301-652-8066
Fax: 301-652-8310
Capital: More than $150 million
Contact: Jake Tarr

Kleiner Perkins Caufield & Byers
2750 Sand Hill Road
Menlo Park, CA 94025
Phone: 650-233-2750
Fax: 650-233-3300
www.kpcb.com
Capital: More than $1.2 billion

> The biggest name in the venture capital world.

Kohlberg Kravis Roberts & Company
9 West 57th Street, Suite 4200
New York, NY 10019
Phone: 212-750-8300
Fax: 212-750-0003
www.kkr.com
Capital: More than $10 billion

> The granddaddy of the big leveraged buyout.

Landmark Partners Inc.
760 Hopmeadow Street
Simsbury, CT 06070
Phone: 860-651-9760
Fax: 860-651-8890
www.landmarkpartners.com
Capital: More than $300 million

Leonard Green & Partners, LP
11111 Santa Monica Boulevard, Suite 2000
Los Angeles, CA 90025

Phone: 310-954-0444
Fax: 310-954-0404
Capital: Approximately $1 billion

Littlejohn & Levy, Inc.
450 Lexington Avenue, Suite 3350
New York, NY 10017
Phone: 212-286-8600
Fax: 212-286-8626
Capital: More than $1 billion

Lucent Venture Partners
600 Mountain Avenue
Room 6A-406
Murray Hill, NJ 07974
Phone: 908-582-8538
Fax: 908-582-6747
www.lucent.com
Capital: More than $100 million

> Many corporations such as Lucent, Boeing, Dow Chemical, and others have private investment arms.

Madison Dearborn Partners
Three First National Place, Suite 3800
Chicago, IL 60602
Phone: 312-895-1000
Fax: 312-895-1001
www.mdcp.com
Capital: More than $1 billion
Contact: John Canning

> One of Chicago's most successful investment firms.

Marquette Venture Partners
520 Lake Cook Road, Suite 450
Deerfield, IL 60015
Phone: 847-940-1700
Fax: 847-940-1724
Capital: More than $150 million

Maveron, LLC
800 Fifth Avenue, Suite 4100
Seattle, WA 98104
Phone: 206-447-1300
Fax: 206-470-1150

www.maveron.com
Capital: More than $100 million

Mayfield Fund
2800 Sand Hill Road, Suite 250
Menlo Park, CA 94025
Phone: 650-854-5560
Fax: 650-854-5712
www.mayfield.com
Capital: More than $1 billion

McCown DeLeeuw & Co.
3000 Sand Hill Road
Building 3, Suite 290
Menlo Park, CA 94025-7111
Phone: 650-854-6000
Fax: 650-854-0853
www.mdcpartners.com
Capital: More than $1.2 billion
Contact: Bob Hellman

Menlo Ventures
3000 Sand Hill Road
Building 4, Suite 100
Menlo Park, CA 94025
Phone: 650-854-8540
Fax: 650-854-7059
www.menloventures.com
Capital: More than $1 billion

Morganthaler Ventures
Terminal Towerity Bank Building
50 Public Square, Suite 2700
Cleveland, OH 44113
Phone: 216-416-7500
Fax: 216-416-7501
www.morganthaler.com
Capital: Approximately $600 million
Contact: Peter Taft

Nassau Capital, Inc.
22 Chambers Street, 2nd Floor
Princeton, NJ 08542
Phone: 609-924-3555

Fax: 609-924-8887
www.nassau.com
> Firm affiliated with Princeton University. Several of the larger universities, such as Princeton, Harvard, and Yale, have investment firms associated with their endowments.

New Enterprise Associates
1119 St. Paul Street
Baltimore, MD 21202
Phone: 410-244-0115
Fax: 410-752-7721
www.nea.com
Capital: More than $3 billion

Noro-Moseley Partners
9 North Parkway Square
4200 Northside Parkway Northwest
Atlanta, GA 30327
Phone: 404-233-1966
Fax: 404-239-9280
Capital: Approximately $100 million

The North Carolina Enterprise Fund, L.P.
3600 Glenwood Avenue, Suite 107
Raleigh, NC 27612
Phone: 919-781-2691
Fax: 919-783-9195
www.ncef.com
Capital: More than $20 million

Norwest Venture Partners
245 Lytton Avenue, Suite 250
Palo Alto, CA 94301
Phone: 650-321-8000
Fax: 650-321-8010
www.norwestvp.com
Capital: More than $800 million

Oak Investment Partners
One Gorham Island
Westport, CT 06880
Phone: 203-226-8346
Fax: 203-227-0372
www.oakinv.com
Capital: More than $1.6 billion

Oaktree Capital Management, LLC
550 South Hope Street, 22nd Floor
Los Angeles, CA 90071
Phone: 213-694-1501
Fax: 213-694-1594
Capital: Approximately $8.5 billion

Patricof & Co. Ventures, Inc.
445 Park Avenue
New York, NY 10022
Phone: 212-753-6300
Fax: 212-319-6155
www.patricof.com
Capital: More than $1 billion
Contact: George Jenkins

Polaris Venture Partners
Bay Colony Corporate Center
1000 Winter Street, Suite 3350
Waltham, MA 02451
Phone: 781-290-0770
Fax: 781-290-0880
www.polarisventures.com
Capital: More than $800 million
Contact: Alan Spoon

Providence Equity Partners, Inc.
50 Kennedy Plaza, 9th Floor
Providence, RI 02903
Phone: 401-751-1700
Fax: 401-751-1790
Capital: More than $1.5 billion
Contact: Paul Salem

Questor
9 W. 57th Street, 34th Floor
New York, NY 10019
Phone: 212-297-1599
Fax: 212-297-1588
Capital: More than $1 billion
Contact: Henry Drucker
Firm targets turnaround situations.

Redpoint Ventures
3000 Sand Hill Road, Suite 290

Menlo Park, CA 94025
Phone: 650-926-5600
Fax: 650-854-5762
www.redpointventures.com
Capital: More than $800 million
Contact: John Walecka

Riggs Capital Partners
800 17th Street N.W.
Washington, DC 20006
Phone: 202-835-5075
Fax: 202-835-5506
www.riggsbank.com
Capital: More than $100 million
Contact: Carter Beese

Riordan, Lewis and Haden
300 South Grand Avenue, 29th Floor
Los Angeles, CA 90071
Phone: 213-229-8500
Fax: 213-229-8597
Capital: Approximately $150 million

RRE Investors
126 East 56th Street
New York, NY 10022
Phone: 212-418-5110
www.rre.com
Capital: More than $250 million

Saugatuck Capital Company
One Canterbury Green
Stamford, CT 06901
Phone: 203-348-6669
Fax: 203-324-6995
www.saugatuckcapital.com
Capital: More than $90 million

Saunders Karp & Meguire
667 Madison Avenue
New York, NY 10021
Phone: 212-303-6600
Fax: 212-755-1624
www.skmequity.com
Capital: Approximately $500 million

Schroder Ventures
787 Seventh Avenue
New York, NY 10019
Phone: 212-735-0700
Fax: 212-735-0711
Capital: Approximately $1.7 billion

Sevin Rosen Funds
Two Galleria Tower
13455 Noel Road, Suite 1670, LB 24
Dallas, TX 75240
Phone: 972-702-1100
Fax: 972-702-1103
www.srfunds.com
Capital: More than $500 million

Sierra Ventures
3000 Sand Hill Road
Building 4, #210
Menlo Park, CA 94025
Phone: 650-854-1000
Fax: 650-854-5593
www.sierraven.com
Capital: More than $600 million

SOFTBANK Technology Ventures
333 W. San Carlos Street, Suite 1225
San Jose, CA 95110
Phone: 408-271-2265
Fax: 408-271-2270
www.sbvc.com
Capital: More than $500 million

South Atlantic Venture Funds
614 West Bay Street
Tampa, FL 33606-2704
Phone: 813-253-2500
Fax: 813-253-2360
www.southatlantic.com
Capital: More than $70 million

Sprout Group
277 Park Avenue, 21st Floor
New York, NY 10172
Phone: 212-892-3600

Fax: 212-892-3444
www.sproutgroup.com
Capital: More than $2 billion

> Venture firm affiliated with the investment bank Donaldson, Lufkin & Jenrette.

Sterling Venture Partners
111 S. Calvert Street, Suite 2810
Baltimore, MD 21202
Phone: 410-347-2905
Fax: 410-347-3140
www.sterlingcap.com
Capital: More than $50 million

Stonington Partners, Inc.
767 Fifth Avenue, 48th Floor
New York, NY 10153
Phone: 212-339-8500
Fax: 212-339-8585
www.stongington.com
Capital: Approximately $20 billion

St. Paul Venture Capital
10400 Viking Drive, Suite 550
Eden Prairie, MN 55344
Phone: 612-995-7474
Fax: 612-995-7475
www.stpaulvc.com
Capital: More than $800 million

Summit Partners
600 Atlantic Avenue, 28th Floor
Boston, MA 02210
Phone: 617-824-1000
Fax: 617-824-1100
www.summitpartners.com
Capital: More than $4 billion
Contact: Marty Mannion

Sutter Hill Ventures
755 Page Mill Road, Suite A-200
Palo Alto, CA 94304
Phone: 650-493-5600
Fax: 650-858-1854

www.shv.com
Capital: More than $400 million

TA Associates, Inc.
High Street Tower, Suite 2500
125 High Street
Boston, MA 02110
Phone: 617-574-6700
Fax: 617-574-6728
www.ta.com
Capital: More than $2.5 billion

TCW/Crescent Mezzanine, LLC
11100 Santa Monica Boulevard, Suite 2000
Los Angeles, CA 90025
Phone: 310-235-5900
Fax: 310-235-5967

Texas-Pacific Group
201 Main Street, Suite 2420
Fort Worth, TX 76102
Phone: 817-871-4000
Fax: 817-871-4010
www.texpac.com
Capital: More than $7 billion
Contact: David Benderman, Jim Coulter, Kelvin Davis

> Rapidly growing technology and contrarian strategy investment firms.

Thayer Capital Partners
1455 Pennsylvania Avenue N.W.
Suite 350
Washington, DC 20004
Phone: 202-371-0150
Fax: 202-371-0391
www.thayercapital.com
Capital: More than $1.2 billion
Contact: Barry Johnson, Rick Rickertsen

> Firm targets MBOs and growth equity in IT services, electronics manufacturing, and business services.

Thoma Cressey Equity Partners
233 South Wacker Drive, Suite 4460
Chicago, IL 60606

Phone: 312-777-4444
Fax: 312-777-4445
www.tc.nu
Capital: More than $450 million

Three Cities Research, Inc.
650 Madison Avenue, 24th Floor
New York, NY 10022
Phone: 212-838-9660
Fax: 212-980-1142
www.tcr-ny.com
Capital: More than $440 million

Trident Capital
2480 Sand Hill Road, Suite 100
Menlo Park, CA 94025
Phone: 650-233-4300
Fax: 650-233-4333
www.tridentcap.com
Capital: More than $400 million
Contact: Don Dixon

U.S. Venture Partners
2180 Sand Hill Road, Suite 300
Menlo Park, CA 94025
Phone: 650-854-9080
Fax: 650-854-3018
www.usvp.com
Capital: More than $700 million

Venrock Associates
30 Rockefeller Plaza, Room 5508
New York, NY 10112
Phone: 212-649-5600
Fax: 212-649-5788
www.venrock.com
Capital: More than $500 million

Vestar Capital Partners
245 Park Avenue, 41st Floor
New York, NY 10067-4098
Phone: 212-351-1600
Fax: 212-808-4922
www.vestarcap.com
Capital: More than $1 billion

Wakefield Group
1110 East Morehead Street
P.O. Box 36329
Charlotte, NC 28236
Phone: 704-372-0355
Fax: 704-372-8216
www.wakefieldgroup.com

Weiss, Peck & Greer Venture Partners
555 California Street, Suite 3130
San Francisco, CA 94104
Phone: 415-622-6864
Fax: 415-989-5108
WPGVP.com
Capital: More than $700 million

Welsh, Carson, Anderson & Stowe
320 Park Avenue, 25th Floor
New York, NY 10022
Phone: 212-893-9500
Fax: 212-893-9575
www.welshcarson.com
Capital: More than $7 billion
Contact: Russ Carson

    Long-standing information technology and health care investor.

Wellspring Associates, LLC
620 Fifth Avenue, Suite 216
New York, NY 10020-1579
Phone: 212-332-7555
Fax: 212-332-7575

Weston Presidio Capital
One Federal Street, 21st Floor
Boston, MA 02110
Phone: 617-988-2500
Fax: 617-988-2515
www.westonpresidio.com
Capital: More than $900 million

Willis Stein & Partners, LLC
227 West Monroe Street, Suite 4300
Chicago, IL 60606
Phone: 312-422-2400

Fax: 312-422-2418
Capital: More than $1 billion

Private Equity Funds: Europe

Abingworth Management Limited
Princess House
38 Jermyn Street
London SW1Y 6DN
United Kingdom
Phone: 44-020-7534-1500
Fax: 44-020-7287-0480
www.abingworth.com
Capital: Approximately £100 million

ABN AMRO Corporate Investments
Foppingadreef 22 (AA 3240)
P.O. Box 283
1000 EA Amsterdam
Netherlands
Phone: 31-20-628-0732
Fax: 31-20-628-7822
www.abnamro.nl
Capital: More than $1 billion

Abtrust Fund Managers Limited
One Albyn Place
Aberdeen AB10 1YG
United Kingdom
Phone: 44-1224-631999
Fax: 44-1224-647010
Capital: Approximately £60 million

A.C.T. Venture Capital Limited
The Merrion Business Centre
58 Howard Street
Belfast BT1 6PJ
United Kingdom
Phone: 44-1232-247266
Fax: 44-1232-247372
Capital: Approximately £75 million

Advent Venture Partners
25 Buckingham Gate

London SW1E 6LD
United Kingdom
Phone: 44-171-630-9811
Fax: 44-171-828-1474
E-mail: info@advent.ventures.com
Capital: Approximately $250 million

Allianz Capital Partners GmbH
Theresienstraße 1-5
80333 Munich
Germany
Phone: 49-89-3800-7582
Fax: 49-89-3800-7586
E-mail: margit.kaserer@allianz.de
Capital: More than $1 billion

Alpha Group
89 rue Taitbout
75009 Paris
France
Phone: 33-1-5321-8888
Fax: 33-1-4016-4323
Capital: More than Euro 550 million

Alpinvest Holding NV
3 Postbus 5073
1410 AB Naarden
Netherlands
Phone: 31-35-695-2600
Fax: 31-35-694-7525
www.alpinvest.com
Capital: More than Euro 750 million

Apax Partners and Co. Ventures Ltd.
15 Portland Place
London W1N 3AA
United Kingdom
Phone: 44-171-872-6300
Fax: 44-171-636-6475
www.apax.com
Capital: More than $300 million

Apax Partners et Cie.
45 Avenue Kléber
75784 Paris Cedex 16

France
Phone: 33-1-6365-0100
Fax: 33-1-5365-0101/06
www.apax.com

AXA Asset Management Gestion
58 Avenue de La Gramdearmee
75017 Paris
France
Phone: 33-1-5537-5000
Fax: 33-1-5537-5501
Capital: More than Ffr500 million

Banexi Ventures Partners
12 rue Chauchat
75009 Paris
France
Phone: 33-1-4014-2663
Fax: 33-1-4014-3896
www.banexiventurej.com
Capital: More than Ffr400 million

Barclays Acquisition Finance
Barclays Bank plc
54 Lombard Street
London EC3P 3AH
United Kingdom
Phone: 44-171-699-3186
Fax: 44-171-699-2770

Baring Venture Partners Ltd.
33 Cavendish Square
London W1M 0BQ
United Kingdom
Phone: 44-171-290-5000
Fax: 44-171-290-5020
www.bpep.com
Capital: More than £285 million

BC Partners
185 Piccadilly
London W1V 9FN
United Kingdom
Phone: 44-171-408-1282
Fax: 44-171-493-1368

www.bcpartners.com
Capital: More than $1 billion

BNP Private Equity
12 rue Chauchat
75009 Paris
France
Phone: 33-1-6016-8600
Fax: 33-1-6016-6960
E-mail: bnppeinfo@bnpgroup.com
Capital: More than Ffr4 billion

Candover
20 Old Bailey
London EC4M 7LN
United Kingdom
Phone: 44-20-7489-9848
Fax: 44-20-7248-5483
www.candover.com
Capital: Approximately £850 million

Capital for Companies
Quayside House
Canal Wharf
Leeds LS11 5PU
United Kingdom
Phone: 44-113-243-8043
Fax: 44-113-245-1777
www.cfc.vct.co.uk
Capital: Approximately £22 million

Cinven Limited
Pinners Hall
105-108 Old Broad Street
London EC2N 1EH
United Kingdom
Phone: 44-171-661-3333
Fax: 44-171-256-2225
www.cinven.com
Capital: More than $2.5 billion

Commerz Beteiligungsgesellschaft mbH
Kaiserstrasse 16
D-60311 Frankfurt am Main
Germany

Phone: 49-69-136-2 96 82
Fax: 49-69-136-2 98 76
www.obg.commerzbank.de

Copernicus Capital Management
u. Krak. Przedmiescie 79, 2nd Floor
00079 Warsaw
Poland
Phone: 48-22-268580
Fax: 48-22-254462
E-mail: 100710.1515@compuserve
Capital: Approximately $25 million

Credit Agricole Indosuez
122 Leadenhall Street
London EC3V 4QH
United Kingdom
Phone: 44-171-971-4454/4405
Fax: 44-171-628-4362
E-mail: mary.clippingdale@indosuez.co.uk
Capital: Approximately £30 million

CVC Capital Partners Ltd.
Huson House
8-10 Tavistock Street
London WC2E 7PP
United Kingdom
Phone: 44-020-7420-4200
Fax: 44-020-7420-4231
www.cvceurope.com
Capital: Approximately $2.5 billion

DLJ Phoenix Private Equity Limited
99 Bishopsgate
London EC2M 34F
United Kingdom
Phone: 44-207-655-7600
Fax: 44-207-655-7683
E-mail: dljppe@dlj.com
Capital: Approximately £350 million

Elderstreet Investments Ltd.
32 Bedford Row
London EC1N 4HE
United Kingdom

Phone: 44-171-831-5088
Fax: 44-171-831-5099
www.elderstreet.com
Capital: £40 million

Euroventures France
27 rue de la Ville lEvque
75008 Paris
France
Phone: 33-1-4007-0518
Fax: 33-1-4924-9972
Capital: Approximately Ffr240 million

Excel Partners
Claudio Coelle 78
28001 Madrid
Spain
Phone: 34-1-578-3676
Fax: 34-1-431-9303
www.excelpartners.com
Capital: Approximately $100 million

Four Seasons Venture Capital AB
Sveavagen 17
P.O. Box 1415
11184 Stockholm
Sweden
Phone: 46-8-15420
Fax: 46-8-216995
www.fourseasons.se
Capital: Approximately Sek 475 million

Gemini Capital Fund Management Ltd.
Maskit Street
P.O. Box 12548
Industrial Zone
Herzliya 46733
Israel
Phone: 972-9-958-3596
Fax: 972-9-958-4842
Capital: Approximately $25 million

Glaxo Wellcome plc.
Glaxo Wellcome House
Berkeley Avenue

Greenford
Middlesex WB6 0NN
United Kingdom
Phone: 44-0207-493-4060
Fax: 44-0208-966-8330
www.glaxowellcome.co.uk
Capital: Approximately $1.4 billion

Goldman Sachs International
Peterborough Court
133 Fleet Street
London EC4A 2BB
United Kingdom
Phone: 44-171-774-1000
Fax: 44-171-774-4123
www.gs.com
Capital: Approximately £1 billion

H.S.B.C. Ventures UK Limited
H.S.B.C. Bank plc, 2nd Floor
27-32 Poultry
London EC2P 2BX
United Kingdom
Phone: 44-171-260-7935
Fax: 44-171-260-6767
Capital: Approximately £25 million

Hannover Finanz GmbH
Gunther Wagner Allee 13
30177 Hanover
Germany
Phone: 49-511-280-070
Fax: 49-511-280-0737
www.hannoverfinanz.de
Capital: Approximately DM 730 million

HSBC Private Equity
Vintner's Place
68 Upper Thames Street
London EC4V 3BJ
United Kingdom
Phone: 44-171-336-9955
Fax: 44-171-336-9961
Capital: Approximately £1.1 billion

Innoventure Equity Partners AG
Gerbergasse 5
8023 Zurich
Switzerland
Phone: 41-1-211-4171
Fax: 41-1-211-4230
www.innoventure.ch

Kleinwort Benson Development Capital Limited
P.O. Box 18075
Riverbank House
2 Swan Lane
London EC4R 3UX
United Kingdom
Phone: 44-020-7623-8000
Fax: 44-020-7626-8616
www.drkbpe.com
Capital: Approximately Euro180 million

Kreditanstalt Für Wiederaufbau (KFW)
Palmengartenstrasse 5-9
60325 Frankfurt am Main
Germany
Phone: 49-69-71310
Fax: 49-69-7431-2944
Capital: Approximately DM 1.13 billion

LBO France
1 rue François 1 er
75008 Paris
France
Phone: 33-1-4235-0021
Fax: 33-1-4561-0064

Mercury Private Equity
33 King William Street
London EC4R 9AS
United Kingdom
Phone: 44-171-280-2800
Fax: 44-171-203-5833
Capital: Approximately £600 million

Murray Johnstone Private Equity Limited
7 West Nile Street
Glasgow G1 2PX

United Kingdom
Phone: 44-141-226-3131
Fax: 44-141-248-5636
www.murrayj.com
Capital: Approximately £300 million

Nash, Sells and Partners Limited
25 Buckingham Gate
London SW1E 6LD
United Kingdom
Phone: 44-171-828-6944
Fax: 44-171-828-9958
www.nashsells.co.uk
Capital: Approximately £100 million

Natwest Acquisition Finance
38 Bishopsgate
London EC2N 4DP
United Kingdom
Phone: 44-020-7665-6000
Fax: 44-020-7665-6101
www.nwacqfin.com
Capital: Approximately £2 billion

Nordic Capital
Stureplan 4 A
SE-11435 Stockholm
Sweden
Phone: 46-8-440-5050
Fax: 46-8-611-7998
www.nordiccapital.se
Capital: Approximately Skr 3.2 billion

Northern Venture Managers Limited
Northumberland House
Princess Square
Newcastle Upon Tyne NE1 8ER
United Kingdom
Phone: 44-191-232-7068
Fax: 44-191-232-4070
Capital: Approximately £35 million

NSM Finances SA
3 avenue Hoche
75008 Paris

France
Phone: 33-1-4766-6609
Fax: 33-1-4888-5348
Capital: Approximately Ffr550 million

Pantheon Ventures Limited
43-44 Albermarle Street
London W1X 3FE
United Kingdom
Phone: 44-171-493-5685
Fax: 44-171-629-0844
Capital: Approximately £500 million

Proven Private Equity
42 Craven Street
London WC2N 5NG
United Kingdom
Phone: 44-171-451-6500
Fax: 44-171-839-8349
E-mail: info@proven.co.uk
Capital: Approximately £70 million

Royal Bank of Scotland Leveraged Finance
138-142 Holburn
London EC1N 2TH
United Kingdom
Phone: 44-171-427-8304
Fax: 44-171-427-8473

Siparex Group
139 rue Vendme
69477 Lyon Cedex 06
France
Phone: 33-04-7283-2323
Fax: 33-04-7283-2300
www.siparex.com
Capital: Approximately Euro 453 million (capital under management)

Skandia Investment
Box 5295
10246 Stockholm
Sweden
Phone: 46-8-788-1030
Fax: 46-8-203566
www.skandia.se/ski

Capital: Approximately Skr 1.600 million

Sofinnova Partners SA
17 rue de Surène
75008 Paris
France
Phone: 33-1-53-054100
Fax: 33-1-53-064129
www.sofinnova.fr
Capital: Approximately $250 million

Swedfund International A
P.O. Box 3286
SE-10365 Stockholm
Sweden
Phone: 46-8-725-9400
Fax: 46-8-203093
www.swedfund.se
Capital: Approximately Skr 600 million

3i Group plc
91 Waterloo Road
London SE18XP
United Kingdom
Phone: 44-171-928-3131
Fax: 44-171-928-0058
Capital: More than $3 billion

Appendix J: Directory of Debt-Financing Sources

Commercial Banks and Senior Lenders

The banks below are only a small fraction of the lenders out there who back management buyouts. Contact your largest local banks first to see if they back such transactions. When pursuing your deal, you will probably want to identify an equity partner first, but it's fine to approach banks and equity partners simultaneously. As I've mentioned, in many cases the larger banks have equity groups that work with the debt side, so you may be able to find all of the capital for your deal in one place.

ABN AMRO Bank N.V.
135 South LaSalle Street, Suite 725
Chicago, IL 60674-9135
Phone: 312-904-2051
Fax: 312-904-4456

American Capital Strategies, Ltd.
Three Bethesda Metro Center, Suite 860
Bethesda, MD 20814
Phone: 301-951-6122
Fax: 301-654-6714
www.american-capital.com

Antares Capital Corporation
311 South Wacker Drive, Suite 275
Chicago, IL 60606
Phone: 312-697-3999
Fax: 312-697-3998
E-mail: antareslev@msc.com

AT&T Capital Corporation
44 Whippany Road
Morristown, NJ 07962
Phone: 973-397-4304
Fax: 973-397-4368

BancBoston Securities, Inc.
Corporate Finance Department
Mail Stop 01-09-03
100 Federal Street
Boston, MA 02110
Phone: 617-434-2200

Banc One Capital Markets
120 South LaSalle Street
Chicago, IL 60603
Phone: 312-661-5211
Fax: 312-661-7352

Bankamerica Business Credit, Inc.
231 South LaSalle Street, 16th Floor
Chicago, IL 60697
Phone: 312-974-2400
Fax: 312-974-8744

Bank of America
555 South Flower Street
Department 3283, 11th Floor
Los Angeles, CA 90071
Phone: 213-228-2694
Fax: 213-228-2641

Banque Paribas Merchant Banking Group
787 Seventh Avenue
New York, NY 10019-6016
Phone: 212-841-2115
Fax: 212-841-2363

Business Capital Group, Inc.
3503 N.W. 63rd Street, Suite 600
Oklahoma City, OK 73116
Phone: 405-842-1010
Fax: 405-842-9981

CIGNA Investments, Inc.
Leveraged Investments
S-307
900 Cottage Grove Road
Hartford, CT 06152-2307
Phone: 860-726-4077
Fax: 860-726-7203

The CIT Group/Business Credit, Inc.
1211 Avenue of the Americas
New York, NY 10036
Phone: 212-536-1296
Fax: 212-536-1293
www.citgroup.com

CITICORP Securities, Inc.
399 Park Avenue, 6th Floor, Zone 4
New York, NY 10022
Phone: 212-559-3540
Fax: 212-793-1290

Citizens Business Credit Corporation
Citizens Bank Building
28 State Street
Boston, MA 02109
Phone: 617-725-5830
Fax: 617-725-5827

Congress Financial Corporation
1133 Avenue of the Americas
New York, NY 10036
Phone: 212-840-2000
Fax: 212-545-4555

Credit Lyonnais Leveraged and Financial Sponsor Group
1301 Avenue of the Americas
New York, NY 10019
Phone: 212-261-7871
Fax: 212-459-3176

Deutsche Banc Alex. Brown, Inc.
130 Liberty Street, 30th Floor
New York, NY 10006
Phone: 212-250-7179
Fax: 212-250-7200

Fleet Capital Corporation
200 Glastonbury Boulevard
Glastonbury, CT 06033
Phone: 860-659-3200
Fax: 860-657-7768
www.fleetcapital.com

Foothill Capital Corporation
11111 Santa Monica Boulevard, Suite 1500
Los Angeles, CA 90025-3333
Phone: 310-996-7000
Fax: 310-478-4860

Fremont Financial Corporation
2020 Santa Monica Boulevard, Suite 600

Santa Monica, CA 90404-2023
Phone: 310-315-5550
Fax: 310-315-5561

The Fuji Bank, Limited
2 World Trade Center
New York, NY 10088
Phone: 212-898-2051

GE Capital Commercial Finance
201 High Ridge Road
Stamford, CT 06927-5100
Phone: 203-316-7500
Fax: 203-316-7815
www.gecommercialfinance.com

Heller Financial Inc., Corporate Finance Group
500 West Monroe Street
Chicago, IL 60661
Phone: 312-441-6878
Fax: 312-441-7367
www.hellerfin.com

HSBC Securities, Inc.
140 Broadway, 5th Floor
New York, NY 10005-1185
Phone: 212-658-2751
Fax: 212-658-2587

Indosuez Capital
1211 Avenue of the Americas, 7th Floor
New York, NY 10036
Phone: 212-278-2222
Fax: 212-278-2203

LaSalle Business Credit, Inc.
135 South LaSalle Street, Suite 400
Chicago, IL 60603
Phone: 312-904-7410
Fax: 312-904-7425

Legg Mason Wood Walker, Inc.
100 Light Street
Baltimore, MD 21202
Phone: 410-539-0000
Fax: 410-539-4508

Massachusetts Mutual Life Insurance Company
1295 State Street
Springfield, MA 01111
Phone: 413-744-6089
Fax: 413-744-6127

Mellon Business Credit
Mellon Bank Center
1735 Market Street, 6th Floor
Philadelphia, PA 19103
Phone: 215-553-2162
Fax: 215-553-0201

Mercantile Business Credit, Inc.
100 South Brentwood Boulevard, Suite 500
St. Louis, MO 63105
Phone: 314-579-8500
Fax: 314-579-8501

Nationsbanc Montgomery Securities, Inc.
600 Montgomery Street
San Francisco, CA 94111
Phone: 415-627-2000
Fax: 415-913-5704

Nations Bank Capital Markets, Inc.
Leveraged Finance Group
800 Market Street
St. Louis, MO 63101
Phone: 314-466-6000
Fax: 314-466-6645

Newcourt Capital
2 Gatehall Drive
Parsippany, NJ 07054
Phone: 973-355-7625

New York Life Insurance Company
51 Madison Avenue, Room 203
New York, NY 10010
Phone: 212-576-6525

PNC Business Credit
70 East 52nd Street, 25th Floor
New York, NY 10022

Phone: 212-223-3626
Fax: 212-223-6780

Sanwa Business Credit Corporation
500 Glenpointe Centre West, 4th Floor
Teaneck, NJ 07666-6802
Phone: 201-836-4006
Fax: 201-836-4744

Société Générale
1221 Avenue of the Americas, 8th Floor
New York, NY 10020
Phone: 212-278-6000
Fax: 212-278-6178

State Street Bank & Trust Company
3414 Peachtree Road, N.E., Suite 1010
Atlanta, GA 30326
Phone: 404-364-9500
Fax: 404-261-4469

Summit Private Capital Group
11 Minuteman Court
Basking Ridge, NJ 07920
Phone: 908-781-2545
Fax: 908-781-2646
E-mail: spcg1@aol.com

SunAmerica Corporate Finance
One SunAmerica Center, 38th Floor
Los Angeles, CA 90067
Phone: 310-772-6300
Fax: 310-772-6078

Transamerica Business Credit Corporation
9399 West Higgins Road, Suite 600
Rosemont, IL 60018
Phone: 847-685-1102
Fax: 847-685-1143

Travelers Insurance Company
One Tower Square
Hartford, CT 06183-2030
Phone: 860-277-3992
Fax: 860-954-3730

Union Bank of California, N.A.
70 South Lake Avenue, Suite 900
Pasadena, CA 91101
Phone: 626-304-1855
Fax: 626-304-1845

Appendix K: The Financial Model—
A More Detailed Look

This section takes a more detailed look at the drivers of the financial model discussed in Chapter 8 (see Figure 8-1). Each of these underlying sheets creates outputs that are then used to determine rates of return for each investor, performance characteristics, cash flow, financing ratios, and other key statistics in the summary sheet. You'll find them interesting to review. What's critical for you, however, is to have a model that reflects the nuances of *your* business. Every company is different and has different drivers. Your model should reflect the drivers important to you.

Working with the model is very straightforward after you have entered in the primary data. The model is driven by basic entries such as the purchase price, the financing sources, and the basic income statement and balance sheet parameters for the company. A multipage spreadsheet for our example company, Techway, is presented here in Appendix K.

The summary rolls up all of the key metrics and gives a snapshot of the whole deal. It tells you whether or not it works.

The Return Analysis is a more detailed analysis of the rates of return on equity, testing the sensitivity of the returns to exits in years three, four, and five.

The Summary Income Statements provide projections of income for ten years. The key income statement assumptions actually drive the numbers in the Summary Operating Assumptions, which shows all of the key margins and allows you to test results with different margin levels.

The Balance Sheets and Balance Sheet Assumptions also work together, providing the detailed balance sheet and the assumptions driving the balance sheet, respectively. These balance sheet assumptions are extremely important and are often overlooked or underweighted in a deal analysis. But it is important to consider that as a company grows, so does its balance sheet (e.g., receivables and inventory) and this growth *uses cash*.

This cash flow use is real and takes cash away from paying down debt. As we've emphasized, when you're looking to buy a company, look carefully at the balance sheet and at trends over several years, because often sellers will bleed as much cash off the balance sheet as they can just before a sale, leaving the buyer with an underfunded balance sheet. To avoid this, you must delineate in your deal with the sellers that they must manage the balance sheet in the common course before selling the company. Also, on some occasions there are large opportunities for the buyer in managing the balance sheet assets more efficiently, such as through controlling inventories or managing receivables or payables more tightly. This can generate lots of cash to pay down debt and improve returns.

The Balance Sheet Assumptions analysis has several other important elements, such as your leverage coverage ratios and, very importantly, your annual capital expenditures. Capital expenditures are required to maintain equipment and to grow a business. It is critical to carefully review capital expenditures when you are looking at any deal. Investment bankers like buyers to focus only on EBITDA (earnings before interest, taxes, depreciation, and amortization) as the purchase metric, but EBITDA does not tell you the full picture because it does not include capital expenditures. In addition to EBITDA you should look carefully at EBITDA minus capital expenditures, which is true cash flow, to see what multiples you are paying for the true cash flow generated by the company. Again, beware because sellers of companies defer many required capital expenditures in advance of selling a company because they know they will be selling it and don't want to spend the money. As such, when you buy a company, count on having a capital expenditure deficit that you will have to make up after closing.

The next section, Cash Flow Statements, is important because cash is king in any deal, and this page lays out the cash flows based on all of the previous assumptions and shows you how much cash you will have to pay down debt over the years. Finally, the last section, Financing Assumptions, looks in detail at each of your debt facilities, and on this page you factor in required amortization payments on the debt to be sure you can handle the required payments.

The model, as you can see, is a critical tool in managing the review of the deal dynamics. Versions of this model are available from several companies. By updating key parameters as the deal progresses, you can continue to monitor your potential returns, identify trouble spots, and know your limits in negotiations.

Techway base case summary.

A: Sources and Uses of Funds

Sources of Funds	Amount ($)	Interest Rate
Cash From Balance Sheet	0	
New Revolver	13.25	0.09
New Senior Term A	40	0.09
New Senior Term B	0	0
New Senior Term C	0	0
New Sub Debt	0	0.12
Note to Sellers	0	0.12
New Preferred Equity (PIK)	46	0.15
Rollover of Equity--Seller's (a)	0.4	0
New Common Stock	3.6	
	$ 103.3	

Uses of Funds	Amount ($)
Cash to Owners	95
Equity Ownership	5
Note to Owners	0
Excess Cash	0
Value to Owners	100
Repay Debt	0
New Cash Infusion	0
Buyer Expenses	3.25
	$103.3

(a) Some portion rollover equity rolled into preferred.

B: Pro Forma Capital Structure

PF Capital Structure	Based on Market Value		Cal 1998 xEBITDA	Fisc 1999 xEBITDA
Revolver	13.25	12.8%	0.8	0.8
New Senior Term A	40	38.7%	2.3	2.3
New Senior Term B	0	0.0%	0.0	0.0
New Senior Term C	0	0.0%	0.0	0.0
New Sub Debt	0	0.0%	0.0	0.0
Total Debt	53.25	51.0%	3.1	3.1
Note to Sellers	0	0.0%	0.0	0.0
PIK Preferred	46	44.6%	2.7	2.7
Rollover Equity	0.4	0.4%	0.0	0.0
Common Stock	3.6	3.5%	0.2	0.2
Total Equity	50	48.4%	2.9	2.9
Total Cap (incl. Cash)	103.25	100.0%	6.1	6.0

C: Equity Ownership

Equity Ownership	Equity Common	Equity Preferred	Total	% of Investment Common	% of Investment Preferred	Ownership Common	Warrants	PreOption Ownership	Perform Options	Fully Dil. Ownership
Rollover Equity--Parent	0.4	4.6	5	8.5%	10.0%	8.5%	0.0%	8.5%	0.0%	8.5%
Equity Investor	3.6	41.4	45	76.5%	90.0%	76.5%	0.0%	76.5%	0.0%	76.5%
Management Ownership*	0.7	0	0.7	15.0%	0.0%	15.0%	0.0%	15.0%	0.0%	15.0%
Sub Debt	0	0	0	0.0%	0.0%	0.0%	0.0%	0.0%	0.0%	0.0%
PIK Warrants	0	0	0	0.0%	0.0%	0.0%	0.0%	0.0%	0.0%	0.0%
Total Ownership	$4.7	$46.0	$50.7	100.0%	100.0%	100.0%	0.0%	100.0%	0.0%	100.0%

(continued)

D: Internal Rate of Return

Internal Rate of Return

Multiple of EBITDA	Total Investor Return			Investor Investment Gain			Management Coinvest Equity Value		
	Year 3	Year 4	Year 5	Year 3	Year 4	Year 5	Year 3	Year 4	Year 5
6.00	36.9%	31.3%	28.4%	$70.5	$88.8	$111.9	$10.3	$12.0	$14.4
7.00	45.2%	36.7%	32.3%	$92.7	$112.3	$137.3	$14.7	$16.7	$19.4
8.00	52.6%	41.6%	35.8%	$115.0	$135.9	$162.7	$19.0	$21.3	$24.4

E: Income Statement Projections

	Fiscal Year Ending December,				Calendar		Projected twelve months ended December,					
	1996	1997	1998	1999	2000	2001	2002	2003	2004	2005	2006	2007
Net Revenues	$270.5	$256.5	$278.0	$300.0	$325.0	$350.0	$374.5	$400.7	$428.8	$458.8	$490.9	$525.3
% Growth		-5.2%	8.4%	7.9%	8.3%	7.7%	7.0%	7.0%	7.0%	7.0%	7.0%	7.0%
EBITDA (before management fee)	3.1	0.0	17.1	17.5	24.0	29.3	31.0	33.4	36.1	39.2	43.1	45.6
% of Net Revenue	1.1%	0.0%	6.1%	5.8%	7.4%	8.4%	8.3%	8.3%	8.4%	8.5%	8.6%	8.7%
EBITA (before management fee)	0.5	-2.8	14.8	14.3	20.6	25.7	27.5	29.4	31.5	33.7	36.0	38.6
% of Net Revenue	0.2%	-1.1%	5.3%	4.8%	6.3%	7.3%	7.3%	7.3%	7.3%	7.3%	7.3%	7.3%
Capital Expenditures	0.0	1.6	2.3	4.5	4.5	2.2	2.3	2.5	2.6	2.8	3.0	3.2
Net Debt			53.3	50.8	46.3	36.0	24.2	10.6	-5.0	-22.8	-43.5	-65.6
Total Debt Outstanding			53.3	50.8	46.3	36.0	24.2	10.6	0.0	0.0	0.0	0.0
EBITDA/Total Interest			3.6	3.6	5.2	7.0	9.5	15.3	37.8			
EBITDA--Capex/Total Interest			3.1	2.7	4.2	6.5	8.8	14.1	35.0			
Total Debt/EBITDA			3.1	2.9	1.9	1.2	0.8	0.3	0.0	0.0	0.0	0.0

*Management equity to be funded in some combination of cash from management and loans from the company. For simplicity, not included in sources of funds.

The Techway Base Case—Return Analysis

IRR - Year 3

Multiple	EBITDA	Enterprise Value	Equity Value		1999	2000	2001	IRR	Return Multiple	Investment Gain
				Investor Equity						
0.37 x	$29.1	$174.6	$68.6	($3.6)	$0.0	$0.0	$52.5	144.3%	14.6 x	$48.9
0.45 x	$29.1	$203.6	$97.7	($3.6)	$0.0	$0.0	$74.7	174.9%	20.8 x	$71.1
0.53 x	$29.1	$232.7	$126.8	($3.6)	$0.0	$0.0	$97.0	199.8%	26.9 x	$93.4
				Preferred Stock						
				($41.4)	$0.0	$0.0	$63.0	15.0%	1.5 x	$21.6
				($41.4)	$0.0	$0.0	$63.0	15.0%	1.5 x	$21.6
				($41.4)	$0.0	$0.0	$63.0	15.0%	1.5 x	$21.6
				Total Investor Return						
				($45.0)	$0.0	$0.0	$115.5	36.9%	2.6 x	$70.5
				($45.0)	$0.0	$0.0	$137.7	45.2%	3.1 x	$92.7
				($45.0)	$0.0	$0.0	$160.0	52.6%	3.6 x	$115.0

IRR - Year 4

Multiple	EBITDA	Enterprise Value	Equity Value		1999	2000	2001	2002	IRR	Return Multiple	Investment Gain
				Investor Equity							
0.37 x	$30.8	$184.8	$80.2	($3.6)	$0.0	$0.0	$0.0	$61.3	103.2%	17.0 x	$57.7
0.45 x	$30.8	$215.6	$111.0	($3.6)	$0.0	$0.0	$0.0	$84.9	120.4%	23.6 x	$81.3
0.53 x	$30.8	$246.4	$141.8	($3.6)	$0.0	$0.0	$0.0	$108.5	134.3%	30.1 x	$104.9
				Preferred Stock							
				($41.4)	$0.0	$0.0	$0.0	$72.4	15.0%	1.7 x	$31.0
				($41.4)	$0.0	$0.0	$0.0	$72.4	15.0%	1.7 x	$31.0
				($41.4)	$0.0	$0.0	$0.0	$72.4	15.0%	1.7 x	$31.0
				Total Investor Return							
				($45.0)	$0.0	$0.0	$0.0	$133.8	31.3%	3.0 x	$88.8
				($45.0)	$0.0	$0.0	$0.0	$157.3	36.7%	3.5 x	$112.3
				($45.0)	$0.0	$0.0	$0.0	$180.9	41.6%	4.0 x	$135.9

IRR - Year 5

Multiple	EBITDA	Enterprise Value	Equity Value	Investor Equity	1999	2000	2001	2002	2003	IRR	Return Multiple	Investment Gain
0.37 x	$33.2	$199.3	$96.3	($3.6)	$0.0	$0.0	$0.0	$0.0	$73.6	82.9%	20.5 x	$70.0
0.45 x	$33.2	$232.6	$129.5	($3.6)	$0.0	$0.0	$0.0	$0.0	$99.1	94.0%	27.5 x	$95.5
0.53 x	$33.2	$265.8	$162.7	($3.6)	$0.0	$0.0	$0.0	$0.0	$124.5	103.1%	34.6 x	$120.9
				Preferred Stock								
				($41.4)	$0.0	$0.0	$0.0	$0.0	$83.3	15.0%	2.0 x	$41.9
				($41.4)	$0.0	$0.0	$0.0	$0.0	$83.3	15.0%	2.0 x	$41.9
				($41.4)	$0.0	$0.0	$0.0	$0.0	$83.3	15.0%	2.0 x	$41.9
				Total Investor Return								
				($45.0)	$0.0	$0.0	$0.0	$0.0	$156.9	28.4%	3.5 x	$111.9
				($45.0)	$0.0	$0.0	$0.0	$0.0	$182.3	32.3%	4.1 x	$137.3
				($45.0)	$0.0	$0.0	$0.0	$0.0	$207.7	35.8%	4.6 x	$162.7

(continued)

The Techway Base Case—Summary Income Statements

	Fiscal Year Ending December,			Calendar			Projected Twelve Months Ended December,						
	1996	1997	1998	1998	1999	2000	2001	2002	2003	2004	2005	2006	2007
Net Sales	$270.5	$256.5	$278.0	$278.0	$300.0	$325.0	$350.0	$374.5	$400.7	$428.8	$458.8	$490.9	$525.3
Cost of Sales	247.6	243.4	244.0	244.0	267.0	287.2	308.6	330.3	353.4	378.1	404.6	432.9	463.2
Gross Profit	23.0	13.1	34.0	34.0	33.0	37.8	41.4	44.2	47.3	50.7	54.2	58.0	62.1
Selling Expenses	10.6	5.4	9.9	9.9	9.6	9.0	8.4	9.0	9.6	10.3	11.0	11.8	12.6
Unallocated Use & Corporate Overhead	2.5	2.0	2.7	2.7	2.7	2.9	3.2	3.4	3.7	3.9	4.2	4.5	4.8
G & A Expenses	8.7	7.3	5.5	5.5	7.3	6.5	5.5	5.9	6.3	6.8	7.3	7.8	8.3
Other, Net	0.8	1.1	1.0	1.0	(0.8)	(1.1)	(1.5)	(1.6)	(1.7)	(1.8)	(2.0)	(2.1)	(2.2)
Management Fee					0.2	0.2	0.2	0.2	0.2	0.2	0.2	0.2	0.2
EBITA	0.5	(2.8)	14.8	14.8	14.1	20.4	25.5	27.3	29.2	31.3	33.5	35.8	38.4
Depreciation on Existing Basis	2.7	2.8	2.2	2.2	3.2	3.4	3.6	1.5	1.5	1.5	1.5	1.5	1.5
Depreciation on Post Acq Capex								2.0	2.5	3.1	4.0	5.5	5.5
EBITDA	3.1	0.0	17.1	17.1	17.3	23.8	29.1	30.8	33.2	35.9	39.0	42.9	45.4
Depreciation (from above)	2.7	2.8	2.2	2.2	3.2	3.4	3.6	3.5	4.0	4.7	5.5	7.1	7.1
Acquisition Goodwill					0.0	0.0	0.0	0.0	0.0	0.0	0.0	0.0	0.0
Existing Goodwill					0.0	0.0	0.0	0.0	0.0	0.0	0.0	0.0	0.0
Amortization of Financing Fees					0.7	0.7	0.7	0.7	0.7	0.0	0.0	0.0	0.0
Total Depreciation & Amortization	2.7	2.8	2.2	2.2	3.9	4.1	4.3	4.2	4.7	4.7	5.5	7.1	7.1

EBIT	0.5	(2.8)	14.8	14.8	13.5	19.7	24.8	26.6	28.6	31.3	33.5	35.8	38.4
(Interest Income)				0.0	0.0	0.0	0.0	0.0	0.0	0.0	(0.2)	(0.9)	(1.7)
New Revolver Interest Expense				0.0	1.2	1.0	0.6	0.0	0.0	0.0	0.0	0.0	0.0
Senior Cash Interest Expense				2.2	3.6	3.6	3.6	3.2	2.2	1.0	0.0	0.0	0.0
Sub Debt/Note to Owners Cash Interest				0.0	0.0	0.0	0.0	0.0	0.0	0.0	0.0	0.0	0.0
Total Interest Expense				2.2	4.8	4.6	4.2	3.2	2.2	1.0	(0.2)	(0.9)	(1.7)
Pre-Tax Income	0.5	(2.8)	14.8	12.6	8.7	15.1	20.7	23.4	26.4	30.3	33.7	36.7	40.1
Current Income Taxes at (40.0%)	0.0	0.0	0.5	2.2	3.5	6.1	8.3	9.4	10.6	12.1	13.5	14.7	16.0
Deferred Income Taxes at (40.0%)	0.0	0.0	0.0	0.0	0.0	0.0	0.0	0.0	0.0	0.0	0.0	0.0	0.0
Net Income	$0.5	($2.8)	$14.3	$10.5	$5.2	$9.1	$12.4	$14.0	$15.8	$18.2	$20.2	$22.0	$24.1
PIK Preferred Dividend	0.0	0.0	0.0	6.9	6.9	7.9	9.1	10.5	12.1	13.9	16.0	18.4	21.1
Net Income to Common	$0.5	($2.8)	$14.3	$3.6	($1.7)	$1.2	$3.3	$3.5	$3.8	$4.3	$4.2	$3.7	$3.0

(continued)

Techway Base Case—Summary Operating Assumptions

	Fiscal Year Ending December,			Calendar			Projected Twelve Months Ended December,						
	1996	1997	1998	1998	1999	2000	2001	2002	2003	2004	2005	2006	2007
Income Statement Assumptions													
Sales Growth		-5.2%	8.4%		7.9%	8.3%	7.7%	7.0%	7.0%	7.0%	7.0%	7.0%	7.0%
Sales CAGR					7.9%	8.1%	8.0%	7.7%	7.6%	7.5%	7.4%	7.4%	7.3%
Cost of Sales as a % of Sales	91.5%	94.9%	87.8%	87.8%	89.0%	88.4%	88.2%	88.2%	88.2%	88.2%	88.2%	88.2%	88.2%
Gross Profit	8.5%	5.1%	12.2%	12.2%	11.0%	11.6%	11.8%	11.8%	11.8%	11.8%	11.8%	11.8%	11.8%
Selling Expenses as a % of Sales	3.9%	2.1%	3.6%	3.6%	3.2%	2.8%	2.4%	2.4%	2.4%	2.4%	2.4%	2.4%	2.4%
Unallocated & Corp. Expenses as % of Sales	0.9%	0.8%	1.0%	1.0%	0.9%	0.9%	0.9%	0.9%	0.9%	0.9%	0.9%	0.9%	0.9%
G & A Expenses as % Sales	3.2%	2.9%	2.0%	2.0%	2.4%	2.0%	1.6%	1.6%	1.6%	1.6%	1.6%	1.6%	1.6%
Other Expenses as a % of Sales	0.3%	0.4%	0.4%	0.4%	-0.3%	-0.3%	-0.4%	-0.4%	-0.4%	-0.4%	-0.4%	-0.4%	-0.4%
TOTAL EXPENSES	8.3%	6.2%	6.9%	6.9%	6.2%	5.3%	4.5%	4.5%	4.5%	4.5%	4.5%	4.5%	4.5%

EBITDA Margin	1.1%	0.0%	6.1%	6.1%	5.8%	7.3%	8.3%	8.2%	8.3%	8.4%	8.5%	8.7%	8.6%
EBITDA Growth					1.5%	37.3%	22.4%	5.9%	7.8%	8.2%	8.6%	9.9%	5.9%
EBITDA CAGR					1.5%	18.1%	19.5%	15.9%	14.3%	13.2%	12.6%	12.2%	11.5%
Depreciation	1.0%	1.1%	0.8%		1.1%	1.0%	1.3%	0.4%	0.4%	0.4%	0.3%	0.3%	0.3%
EBIT Margin	0.2%	-1.1%	5.3%		4.7%	6.3%	7.3%	7.3%	7.3%	7.3%	7.3%	7.3%	7.3%
Capex as a % of Sales	0.0%	0.6%	0.8%		1.5%	1.4%	0.6%	0.6%	0.6%	0.6%	0.6%	0.6%	0.6%
Working Capital as a % of Sales		17.4%	15.5%		15.4%	15.5%	15.6%	15.7%	15.8%	15.8%	15.9%	15.9%	16.0%
Effective Tax Rate	40.0%	40.0%	40.0%		40.0%	40.0%	40.0%	40.0%	40.0%	40.0%	40.0%	40.0%	40.0%

(continued)

Techway Base Case—Balance Sheets

	Dec-97	Dec-98	Adjust.	Closing 1998	1999	2000	2001	2002	2003	2004	2005	2006	2007
					Projected Twelve Months Ended December,								
Cash and Equivalents	$0.0	$0.0	$0.0	$0.0	$0.0	$0.0	$0.0	$0.0	$0.0	$5.0	$22.8	$43.5	$65.6
Accounts Receivable	76.7	74.7	0.0	74.7	80.6	87.4	94.1	100.7	107.7	115.3	123.3	132.0	141.2
Unbilled/Other	5.4	14.9	0.0	14.9	11.1	11.9	12.8	13.7	14.7	15.7	16.8	18.0	19.2
Prepaid Expenses	0.0	0.0	0.0	0.0	0.0	0.1	0.1	0.1	0.1	0.1	0.1	0.1	0.1
Total Current Assets	82.1	89.7	0.0	89.7	91.8	99.3	106.9	114.4	122.4	136.0	163.0	193.5	226.1
Gross Property, Plant & Equip.	53.9	52.4	0.0	52.4	56.9	61.4	63.6	65.9	68.4	71.0	73.8	76.8	80.1
Less Accumulated Depreciation	(36.7)	(37.1)	0.0	(37.1)	(40.3)	(43.7)	(47.3)	(50.9)	(54.9)	(59.5)	(65.1)	(72.1)	(79.2)
Net Property, Plant & Equip.	17.3	15.3	0.0	15.3	16.6	17.7	16.2	15.0	13.5	11.5	8.7	4.7	0.9
Acquisition Goodwill	0.0	0.0	0.0	0.0	0.0	0.0	0.0	0.0	0.0	0.0	0.0	0.0	0.0
Existing Goodwill	0.0	0.0	0.0	0.0	0.0	0.0	0.0	0.0	0.0	0.0	0.0	0.0	0.0
Transaction Fees & Expenses	0.0	0.0	3.3	3.3	2.6	2.0	1.3	0.7	0.0	0.0	0.0	0.0	0.0
Other Assets	0.0	0.0	0.0	0.0	0.0	0.0	0.0	0.0	0.0	0.0	0.0	0.0	0.0
TOTAL ASSETS	$99.4	$104.9	$3.3	$108.2	$111.0	$119.0	$124.5	$130.1	$135.9	$147.4	$171.8	$198.2	$227.0
Accounts Payable	$17.2	$16.2	$0.0	$16.2	$17.4	$18.9	$20.4	$21.8	$23.3	$24.9	$26.7	$28.5	$30.5
Accrued Liabilities	17.6	25.1	0.0	25.1	23.8	25.8	27.8	29.8	31.8	34.1	36.5	39.0	41.7
Overdraft	2.6	4.2	0.0	4.2	4.2	4.2	4.2	4.2	4.2	4.2	4.2	4.2	4.2
Total Current Liabilities	37.4	45.5		45.5	45.5	48.9	52.3	55.7	59.3	63.2	67.3	71.7	76.5

New Revolver			13.3	13.3	10.8	6.3	0.0	0.0	0.0	0.0	0.0	0.0	0.0
New Senior Term A			40.0	40.0	40.0	40.0	36.0	24.2	10.6	0.0	0.0	0.0	0.0
New Senior Term B			0.0	0.0	0.0	0.0	0.0	0.0	0.0	0.0	0.0	0.0	0.0
New Senior Term C			0.0	0.0	0.0	0.0	0.0	0.0	0.0	0.0	0.0	0.0	0.0
New Sub Debt			0.0	0.0	0.0	0.0	0.0	0.0	0.0	0.0	0.0	0.0	0.0
Seller's Note			0.0	0.0	0.0	0.0	0.0	0.0	0.0	0.0	0.0	0.0	0.0
Total Debt	0.0	0.0	53.3	53.3	50.8	46.3	36.0	24.2	10.6	0.0	0.0	0.0	0.0
Other LT Liabilities	0.0	0.0	0.0	0.0	0.0	0.0	0.0	0.0	0.0	0.0	0.0	0.0	0.0
Existing Debt	0.0	0.0	0.0	0.0	0.0	0.0	0.0	0.0	0.0	0.0	0.0	0.0	0.0
Total Liabilities	37.4	45.5	53.3	98.7	96.3	95.2	88.3	79.9	69.9	63.2	67.3	71.7	76.5
Preferred	0.0	0.0	46.0	46.0	52.9	60.8	70.0	80.5	92.5	106.4	122.4	140.7	161.8
Common Stock	0.0	0.0	4.7	4.7	4.7	4.7	4.7	4.7	4.7	4.7	4.7	4.7	4.7
Additional Paid in Capital	0.0	0.0	(100.7)	(100.7)	(100.7)	(100.7)	(100.7)	(100.7)	(100.7)	(100.7)	(100.7)	(100.7)	(100.7)
Retained Earnings	62.0	59.5	0.0	59.5	57.8	58.9	62.2	65.8	69.5	73.8	78.1	81.8	84.7
TOTAL LIABILITIES AND STOCKHOLDERS' EQUITY	$99.4	$104.9	$3.3	$108.2	$111.0	$119.0	$124.5	$130.1	$135.9	$147.4	$171.8	$198.2	$227.0

(continued)

Techway Base Case—Balance Sheet Assumptions

	1997	1998					Projected Twelve Months Ended December,				
			1999	2000	2001	2002	2003	2004	2005	2006	2007
Balance Sheet Assumptions											
Days Receivable	109.1	98.1	98.1	98.1	98.1	98.1	98.1	98.1	98.1	98.1	98.1
% of Sales	29.9%	26.9%	26.9%	26.9%	26.9%	26.9%	26.9%	26.9%	26.9%	26.9%	26.9%
Days Unbilled/Other	8.0	22.3	15.1	15.1	15.1	15.1	15.1	15.1	15.1	15.1	15.1
% of Sales	2.1%	5.4%	3.7%	3.7%	3.7%	3.7%	3.7%	3.7%	3.7%	3.7%	3.7%
Other Current Assets % of Sales	0.0%	0.0%	0.0%	0.0%	0.0%	0.0%	0.0%	0.0%	0.0%	0.0%	0.0%
Days Payables	25.7	24.2	23.9	24.0	24.1	24.1	24.1	24.1	24.1	24.1	24.1
% of Sales	6.7%	5.8%	5.8%	5.8%	5.8%	5.8%	5.8%	5.8%	5.8%	5.8%	5.8%
Accrued Expenses % of Sales	6.9%	9.0%	7.9%	7.9%	7.9%	7.9%	7.9%	7.9%	7.9%	7.9%	7.9%
Other Current Liabilities % of Sales	1.0%	1.5%	1.4%	1.3%	1.2%	1.1%	1.0%	1.0%	0.9%	0.8%	0.8%
Coverages											
EBITDA/Total Interest Expense		3.6 x	3.6 x	5.2 x	7.0 x	9.5 x	15.3 x	37.8 x			
Total Debt/EBITDA		3.1	2.9	1.9	1.2	0.8	0.3	0.0	0.0	0.0	0.0
Net Debt/EBITDA		3.1	2.9	1.9	1.2	0.8	0.3	NM	NM	NM	NM
Bank Debt/EBITDA		3.1	2.9	1.9	1.2	0.8	0.3	0.0	0.0	0.0	0.0
Senior Debt/EBITDA		3.1	2.9	1.9	1.2	0.8	0.3	0.0	0.0	0.0	0.0

Credit Statistics

(EBITDA-CAPEX)/Total Interest Expense	3.1 x	2.7 x	4.2 x	6.5 x	8.8 x	14.1 x	35.0 x	0.0	0.0	0.0
Total Debt/(EBITDA-CAPEX)	3.6	4.0	2.4	1.3	0.8	0.3	0.0	NM	NM	NM
Net Debt/(EBITDA-CAPEX)	3.6	4.0	2.4	1.3	0.8	0.3	NM	0.0	0.0	0.0
Bank Debt/(EBITDA-CAPEX)	3.6	4.0	2.4	1.3	0.8	0.3	0.0	0.0	0.0	0.0
Senior Debt/(EBITDA-CAPEX)	3.6	4.0	2.4	1.3	0.8	0.3	0.0	0.0	0.0	0.0
Total Debt / Total Capitalization	32.6%	30.6%	27.1%	20.8%	13.8%	6.0%	0.0%	0.0%	0.0%	0.0%
Net Debt / Net Capitalization	32.6%	30.6%	27.1%	20.8%	13.8%	6.0%	(2.8%)	(12.5%)	(23.7%)	(35.4%)

Cash Flow Statement Assumptions

Increase in Other Long-Term Assets			0	0	0	0	0	0	0	0
Increase in Other Long-Term Liabilities			0	0	0	0	0	0	0	0

	1997	1998									
Capital Expenditures	1.6	2.3	4.5	4.5	2.2	2.3	2.5	2.6	2.8	3.0	3.2

Other Financial Data

Acquisition Goodwill	20	Years
Existing Goodwill	20	Years
Capitalized Fees Amortized Over	5	Years

(continued)

Techway Base Case—Cash Flow Statements

	Projected Twelve Months Ended December,								
	1999	2000	2001	2002	2003	2004	2005	2006	2007
Net Income to Common	($1.7)	$1.2	$3.3	$3.5	$3.8	$4.3	$4.2	$3.7	$3.0
Depreciation on Existing Basis	3.2	3.4	3.6	1.5	1.5	1.5	1.5	1.5	1.5
Depreciation on Post Acq Capex	0.0	0.0	0.0	2.0	2.5	3.1	4.0	5.5	5.5
Acquisition Goodwill	0.0	0.0	0.0	0.0	0.0	0.0	0.0	0.0	0.0
Existing Goodwill	0.0	0.0	0.0	0.0	0.0	0.0	0.0	0.0	0.0
Amortization of Financing Fees	0.7	0.7	0.7	0.7	0.7	0.0	0.0	0.0	0.0
Deferred Taxes	0.0	0.0	0.0	0.0	0.0	0.0	0.0	0.0	0.0
Non-cash interest expense	0.0	0.0	0.0	0.0	0.0	0.0	0.0	0.0	0.0
PIK Preferred Dividend	6.9	7.9	9.1	10.5	12.1	13.9	16.0	18.4	21.1
Funds from Operations	9.1	13.1	16.7	18.2	20.5	22.9	25.8	29.1	31.1
Change in Accounts Receivable	(5.9)	(6.7)	(6.7)	(6.6)	(7.0)	(7.5)	(8.1)	(8.6)	(9.2)
Change in Inventory	3.8	(0.8)	(0.9)	(0.9)	(1.0)	(1.0)	(1.1)	(1.2)	(1.3)
Change in Other Assets	(0.0)	(0.0)	(0.0)	(0.0)	(0.0)	(0.0)	(0.0)	(0.0)	(0.0)
Change in Payables	1.3	1.5	1.5	1.4	1.5	1.6	1.7	1.9	2.0
Change in Accrued Liabilities	(1.3)	2.0	2.0	1.9	2.1	2.2	2.4	2.6	2.7
Change in Other Current Liabilities	0.0	0.0	0.0	0.0	0.0	0.0	0.0	0.0	0.0
Cash Flow from Operations	6.9	9.0	12.5	14.1	16.1	18.2	20.7	23.7	25.3

Capital Expenditures	(4.5)	(4.5)	(2.2)	(2.3)	(2.5)	(2.6)	(2.8)	(3.0)	(3.2)
Acquisition Financing	0.0								
Gain on Sale of Assets (a)	0.0								
Total Mandatory Debt Repayments	0.0	0.0	0.0	0.0	0.0	0.0	0.0	0.0	0.0
Free Cash Flow Available to Pay Down Debt	2.4	4.5	10.3	11.8	13.6	15.5	17.9	20.7	22.1
Debt Additions/(Repayments)	(2.4)	(4.5)	(10.3)	(11.8)	(13.6)	(10.6)	0.0	0.0	0.0
Debt Repayments	(2.4)	(4.5)	(10.3)	(11.8)	(13.6)	(10.6)	0.0	0.0	0.0
Change in Cash and Equivalents	0.0	0.0	0.0	0.0	0.0	5.0	17.9	20.7	22.1
Beginning Cash and Equivalents	0.0	0.0	0.0	0.0	0.0	0.0	5.0	22.8	43.5
Ending Cash and Equivalents	$0.0	$0.0	$0.0	$0.0	$0.0	$5.0	$22.8	$43.5	$65.6
Cumulative Cash	$2.4	$7.0	$17.3	$29.1	$42.7	$58.2	$76.1	$96.8	$118.9

(a) Assumes real estate sold for $75 million with a basis of $25 million and taxed at the 20% capital gains rate.

Techway Base Case—Financing Assumptions

Interest Rate on Excess Cash   4.0%

						Projected Twelve Months Ended December,				
	1998	1999	2000	2001	2002	2003	2004	2005	2006	2007
Interest Rates on Debt										
New Revolver	9.0%	9.0%	9.0%	9.0%	9.0%	9.0%	9.0%	9.0%	9.0%	9.0%
New Senior Term A	9.0%	9.0%	9.0%	9.0%	9.0%	9.0%	9.0%	9.0%	9.0%	9.0%
New Senior Term B	0.0%	0.0%	0.0%	0.0%	0.0%	0.0%	0.0%	0.0%	0.0%	0.0%
New Senior Term C	0.0%	0.0%	0.0%	0.0%	0.0%	0.0%	0.0%	0.0%	0.0%	0.0%
New Sub Debt	12.0%	12.0%	12.0%	12.0%	12.0%	12.0%	12.0%	12.0%	12.0%	12.0%
Seller's Note	12.0%	12.0%	12.0%	12.0%	12.0%	12.0%	12.0%	12.0%	12.0%	12.0%
New Preferred Equity (PIK)	15.0%	15.0%	15.0%	15.0%	15.0%	15.0%	15.0%	15.0%	15.0%	15.0%
Existing Straight Debt Interest Expense Schedule										
New Revolver	$0.0	$1.2	$1.0	$0.6	$0.0	$0.0	$0.0	$0.0	$0.0	$0.0
New Senior Term A	0.0	3.6	3.6	3.6	3.2	2.2	1.0	0.0	0.0	0.0
New Senior Term B	0.0	0.0	0.0	0.0	0.0	0.0	0.0	0.0	0.0	0.0
New Senior Term C	0.0	0.0	0.0	0.0	0.0	0.0	0.0	0.0	0.0	0.0
New Sub Debt	0.0	0.0	0.0	0.0	0.0	0.0	0.0	0.0	0.0	0.0
Seller's Note	0.0	0.0	0.0	0.0	0.0	0.0	0.0	0.0	0.0	0.0
Total Existing Straight Debt Interest Expense	$0.0	$4.8	$4.6	$4.2	$3.2	$2.2	$1.0	$0.0	$0.0	$0.0

Existing Straight Debt Mandatory Repayment

New Revolver	$0.0	$0.0	$0.0	$0.0	$0.0	$0.0	$0.0
New Senior Term A	0.0	0.0	0.0	0.0	0.0	0.0	0.0
New Senior Term B	0.0	0.0	0.0	0.0	0.0	0.0	0.0
New Senior Term C	0.0	0.0	0.0	0.0	0.0	0.0	0.0
New Sub Debt	0.0	0.0	0.0	0.0	0.0	0.0	0.0
Seller's Note	0.0	0.0	0.0	0.0	0.0	0.0	0.0
Total Existing Straight Debt Mandatory Repayment	$0.0	$0.0	$0.0	$0.0	$0.0	$0.0	$0.0

Existing Straight Debt Non Mandatory Repayment

New Revolver	$0.0	$2.4	$4.5	$6.3	$0.0	$0.0	$0.0	$0.0
New Senior Term A	0.0	0.0	0.0	4.0	11.8	13.6	10.6	0.0
New Senior Term B	0.0	0.0	0.0	0.0	0.0	0.0	0.0	0.0
New Senior Term C	0.0	0.0	0.0	0.0	0.0	0.0	0.0	0.0
New Sub Debt	0.0	0.0	0.0	0.0	0.0	0.0	0.0	0.0
Seller's Note	0.0	0.0	0.0	0.0	0.0	0.0	0.0	0.0
Total Existing Straight Debt Non Mandatory Repayment	$0.0	$2.4	$4.5	$10.3	$11.8	$13.6	$10.6	$0.0

Debt Outstanding After Transaction

	New Debt							
New Revolver	$13.3	$10.8	$6.3	$0.0	$0.0	$0.0	$0.0	$0.0
New Senior Term A	40.0	40.0	40.0	36.0	24.2	10.6	0.0	0.0
New Senior Term B	0.0	0.0	0.0	0.0	0.0	0.0	0.0	0.0
New Senior Term C	0.0	0.0	0.0	0.0	0.0	0.0	0.0	0.0
New Sub Debt	0.0	0.0	0.0	0.0	0.0	0.0	0.0	0.0
Seller's Note	0.0	0.0	0.0	0.0	0.0	0.0	0.0	0.0
Total Existing Straight Debt Outstanding	$53.3	$50.8	$46.3	$36.0	$24.2	$10.6	$0.0	$0.0

(continued)

Techway Base Case—Financing Assumptions (cont.)

Seller's Note	$0.0	$0.0	$0.0	$0.0	$0.0	$0.0	$0.0	$0.0	$0.0	$0.0
Repayment	$0.0	$0.0	$0.0	$0.0	$0.0	$0.0	$0.0	$0.0	$0.0	$0.0
Accrued Interest	0.0	0.0	0.0	0.0	0.0	0.0	0.0	0.0	0.0	0.0
Ending Seller's Note	$0.0	$0.0	$0.0	$0.0	$0.0	$0.0	$0.0	$0.0	$0.0	$0.0
New Preferred Equity (PIK)	$46.0	$46.0	$52.9	$60.8	$70.0	$80.5	$92.5	$106.4	$122.4	$140.7
New Preferred Equity Dividend		6.9	7.9	9.1	10.5	12.1	13.9	16.0	18.4	21.1
Ending New Preferred Equity	$46.0	$52.9	$60.8	$70.0	$80.5	$92.5	$106.4	$122.4	$140.7	$161.8

	Projected Twelve Months Ended December,				
CASE	1999	2000	2001	2002	2003
BASE CASE					
Sales Growth	7.9%	8.3%	7.7%	7.0%	7.0%
Gross Margin	11.0%	11.6%	11.8%	11.8%	11.8%
Selling Expenses as a % of Sales	3.2%	2.8%	2.4%	2.4%	2.4%
Unallocated & Corp. Expenses as % of Sales	0.9%	0.9%	0.9%	0.9%	0.9%
Administrative Expenses as % Sales	2.4%	2.0%	1.6%	1.6%	1.6%
Other Expenses as a % of Sales	-0.3%	-0.3%	-0.4%	-0.4%	-0.4%

Sales	$300.0	$325.0	$350.0
Gross Margin	33.0	37.8	41.4
Selling Expenses	9.6	9.0	8.4
Distribution Expenses	2.7	2.9	3.2
Administrative Expenses	7.3	6.5	5.5
Other, Net	(0.8)	(1.1)	(1.5)

INVESTOR UPSIDE CASE

Sales Growth	7.9%	8.3%	7.7%	7.0%	7.0%
Gross Margin	11.0%	12.8%	12.8%	12.8%	12.8%
Selling Expenses as a % of Sales	3.2%	2.8%	2.4%	2.4%	2.4%
Unallocated & Corp. Expenses as % of Sales	0.9%	0.9%	0.9%	0.9%	0.9%
Administrative Expenses as % of Sales	2.4%	2.0%	1.6%	1.6%	1.6%
Other Expenses as a % of Sales	-0.3%	-0.3%	-0.4%	-0.4%	-0.4%

INVESTOR DOWNSIDE CASE

Sales Growth	7.9%	8.3%	7.7%	7.0%	7.0%
Gross Margin	11.0%	11.6%	11.8%	11.8%	11.8%
Selling Expenses as a % of Sales	3.6%	3.6%	3.6%	3.6%	3.6%
Unallocated & Corp. Expenses as % of Sales	1.0%	1.0%	1.0%	1.0%	1.0%
Administrative Expenses as % of Sales	2.0%	2.0%	2.0%	2.0%	2.0%
Other Expenses as a % of Sales	0.4%	0.4%	0.4%	0.4%	0.4%

INDEX